Maximum Movies–Pulp Fictions

Also by Peter Stanfield

Hollywood, Westerns and the 1930s: The Lost Trail
Horse Opera: The Strange History of the 1930s Singing Cowboy
Body and Soul: Jazz and Blues in American Film, 1927–63

Edited Collections
Mob Culture: Hidden Histories of the American Gangster Film
"Un-American" Hollywood: Politics and Film in the Blacklist Era

Maximum Movies
Pulp Fictions

Film Culture and the Worlds of Samuel Fuller, Mickey Spillane, and Jim Thompson

PETER STANFIELD

RUTGERS UNIVERSITY PRESS

NEW BRUNSWICK, NEW JERSEY, AND LONDON

UNIVERSITY OF WINCHESTER

LIBRARY OF CONGRESS CATALOGING-IN-PUBLICATION DATA

Stanfield, Peter, 1958–
 Maximum movies—pulp fictions : film culture and the worlds of Samuel Fuller,
Mickey Spillane, and Jim Thompson / Peter Stanfield.
  p. cm.
 Includes bibliographical references and index.
 ISBN 978-0-8135-5061-9 (hardcover : alk. paper) — ISBN 978-0-8135-5062-6
(pbk. : alk. paper)
  1. Film noir—History and criticism. 2. Film criticism—United States—
History—20th century. 3. Film criticism—Great Britain—History—20th century.
4. Fuller, Samuel, 1912–1997—Criticism and interpretation. 5. Spillane, Mickey,
1918–2006—Criticism and interpretation. 6. Spillane, Mickey, 1918–2006—film
adaptations. 7. Thompson, Jim, 1906–1977—Criticism and interpretation.
8. Thompson, Jim, 1906–1977—Film adaptations. 9. Detective and mystery
stories—Film adaptations. 10. Detective and mystery stories, American—History
and criticism. I. Title.
 PN1995.9.F54S6855   2011
 791.43′655—dc22   2010041968

A British Cataloging-in-Publication record for this book is available
from the British Library.

Copyright © 2011 by Peter Stanfield

Foreword Copyright © by Richard Maltby

Visit our website: http://rutgerspress.rutgers.edu

Manufactured in the United States of America

For Damian, Andy, Kasia, and Mum

CONTENTS

FOREWORD

Maximum Movies—Pulp Fictions describes two improbably imbricated worlds and the piece of cultural history their intersections provoked.

One of those worlds was occupied by a clutch of noisy, garish pulp movies pumped out for the grind houses at the end of the urban exhibition chain by the studios' B-divisions and the fly-by-night independent production companies that replaced them—Globe Enterprises, Parklane Pictures, Pajemer Productions, Associates and Aldrich. These were the disposable products of a postwar mass culture that packaged sex, violence, and "True Action" to working-class American men in magazines like *Inside Detective, Crime Confessions, Wildcat Adventures*, and *Rage for Men* and in paperbacks with titles like *Homicide Johnny* and *The Wayward Ones* (with minor abridgments). Constructed from a toolbox of interchangeable generic parts, these expendable objects delivered their maximum impact when they were consumed in "a fit of excitement" and immediately discarded, to be replaced by a new sensation as soon as the program changed. They fed a sub-terranean male culture in inarticulate revolt against the enervating, feminized middlebrow world of conspicuous domestic suburban consumption. And despite their contradictory promise that their readers and viewers could escape consumer culture by consuming fantasy, some of these objects were occasion-ally salvaged from aesthetic contempt by critics on a parallel mission to find what Manny Farber called "a bit of male truth" in the activity of filmgoing. Like Otis Ferguson and Robert Warshow, Farber emphasized the immediacy of the movie experience, insisting that its ephemerality had nothing to do with the contemplative consumption of art. These critics found this experience at its most intense in the fast, functional, faceless action movies that played move-ment against space and shone in the vitality of their grace notes, their exact defining of male action, their "hard combat with low, common-place ideas." Of course Farber was slumming, but his dialogue with the class accents of pulp culture engaged both the kinetic energies and the unrefined complexities of serially produced industrial culture.

The other world of *Maximum Movies* is the Britain of the long 1960s, where for a moment a group of "unruly and truant" critics put pulp movies at the center of an emergent film culture. Lawrence Alloway, in particular, extended

Farber's critical insights by calling for a film criticism that acknowledged both the industrial processes of popular cinema's production in runs, sets, and cycles and the specific kind of communication—"high impact, strong participation, hard to remember"—it provided. For most of the twentieth century much of what appealed to European intellectuals about American popular culture was its machine aesthetic: Hollywood made movies and movie stars like Detroit made automobiles, with no deference to tradition or hierarchies of taste. Little of the American class conflicts coded in these products survived the Atlantic crossing, and at disembarkation they were uniformly reclassified and usually condemned as mass culture. This transplanted "American" pulp culture— George Orwell famously called it "ballast"—arrived on European docks decontextualized, apparently unencumbered by autonomous meaning, and thus available for critical invention and validation as unselfconscious, underdetermined, spontaneous, authentic, primitive.

While surrealists and pop artists celebrated mechanistic production processes and elevated individual objects to iconic status, a more earnest group of critics sought a methodology for evaluating and discriminating *within*, rather than *against*, commercial popular culture. Their method had to address the class politics not of the objects themselves but of their consumption. For the cinephiles of *New Left Review*, asking themselves how they could love Hollywood's products and hate the repressive capitalism that produced them, the mystery and fascination of American cinema lay as much in their own condition of "Americanitis" as it did in their self-appointed task of accounting for the popularity of mass culture among the working classes. Contradictory elements of their position played out in the adoption of auteurism as the dominant critical position taken by British cinephiles in the 1960s and early 1970s. Combining a Leavisite commitment to moral seriousness with an analysis of style and mise-en-scène derived from *Cahiers du cinéma*, early auteurism's ambition to validate the serious study of American film unselfconsciously celebrated a masculine cinema.

As both Pierre Bourdieu and Michael Denning have observed, the project of "elevating the junior branch" of cultural expression belongs to a bourgeois critical underclass seeking to overturn cultural hierarchies by legitimizing the aesthetically illegitimate and, in the process, achieving the best return on its speculative investment of cultural capital. Critical rebels against the class hierarchies of culture celebrated Hollywood mavericks as dime-store Dostoyevskys and American heretics in acts of critical discrimination that disregarded the surface politics and the crude sensationalism of their movies. The cinephiles' contradictory relations with Hollywood temporarily resolved themselves in an explication of the subversive subtexts of an antibourgeois *art brut* that offered a radical critique of capitalism, consumerism, and eventually even patriarchy. Great energies were poured into validating Sam Fuller's, Nicholas Ray's, and

Roger Corman's exploitation cinema as subversive instruments of an oppositional culture, and with varying degrees of success, these reinterpretations were
re-exported back to the colonizers as civilized explanations of what their savage
cultural products were really about. What was largely lost on this detour from
pulp through F. R. Leavis to structuralism were some of the most significant
critical insights that emerged from Alloway's extension of Farber, Ferguson,
et al.: the attempt to abandon an elitist contemplation of the individual movie
and focus on the complexities of Hollywood's serial production of industrial
goods.

Then, in the mid-1970s, this wave of critical engagement died almost as
suddenly as it had begun. The little books that had made an American cinema
of authors and genres legible just stopped, as if a girl in the audience had
suddenly shouted out that the emperor had no clothes. What had happened was
Theory: the appropriation of screen culture by literary dissidents in search of
greenfield intellectual real estate on which to develop their grand theories of
signification, ideology, and the subject. Theory turned movies into text and,
in the process, emasculated the action movies that had energized an earlier
agenda. This critical history can be traced in the booklets published as part of
the Edinburgh Film Festivals of the 1970s, as homage turned into suffocation
while a not-quite-yet academic criticism preoccupied itself with issues of
reading and representation and the authenticity of its own aesthetico-political
vanguardism. In a critical arena preoccupied with the politics of identity, angry
white men were yesterday's cultural capital. Reinscribed within an oppressive
ideological apparatus driven by a sexualized gaze, Hollywood resumed its
position as the enemy to be combated. It was, as I found out, a bad time to start
a PhD on the postwar American Cinema of Dissent.

In some respects the balance of our understanding of classical Hollywood
has not yet recovered from this disjuncture. The critical trajectory that elevated
a masculine cinema to cultural prominence also set it up for critique, particularly from an emergent feminism in search of a different form of subversion, one
that succeeded, ironically, in finding Brechtian rereadings of the dominant
middlebrow products of classical Hollywood's address to its middlebrow, female
consumers. The ironies of this critical history abound, but they are of little use
in helping us understand what Hollywood was or what its audiences did with its
products.

Writing about the cultural capital of Jim Thompson, Peter Stanfield traces
an arc from lowbrow entertainment to a highbrow's *objet trouvé* to the middlebrow art-house fare of the neo-noir revival, a three-phase process that James
Naremore has encapsulated as popularization, appropriation, and recycling.
Many of the subjects of *Maximum Movies* have traveled this journey from trash
to art to collectability, returning to consumer culture when the Criterion
Collection adds another of Hollywood's "most underrated film directors" to its

canon of American film. This book's achievement lies not just in its energetic description of this history but also in its exploration of the symbiotic relationship between the avant-garde and the industries of cultural production. Just as the avant-garde's transgressions operate as a form of research and development for commercial culture, *Maximum Movies* explores how pulp has refreshed and reinvigorated the avant-garde. At least as importantly, Stanfield's engagement with Farber's and Alloway's understanding of movies points us to still unexplored ways of examining the contradictions and aesthetic tensions of cinema as industrialized culture and new opportunities to consider the life of films in the social world.

Richard Maltby

ACKNOWLEDGMENTS

The "originator of jazz and stomps," Jelly Roll Morton, once sang "I'm the winin' boy, don't deny my name." Others whose names cannot be denied include Richard Maltby, Will Straw, and Frank Krutnik. A warm thank you to Richard for his foreword and for the support and guidance he has given to me across the years. Like Richard, Will has now read more than his fair share of my rough drafts, including the whole of this book in an embryonic stage. I am truly grateful to him. Frank has performed a similar task of reading my nascent efforts, and his help with the Thompson chapter is greatly appreciated. Finally, my thanks to Leslie Mitchner for giving *Maximum Movies—Pulp Fictions* a home, and a good one at that.

Some small parts of this book have been published previously. A sketchy version of the Thompson chapter appeared as "'Film Noir Like You've Never Seen': Jim Thompson Adaptations and Cycles of Neo-noir," in *Genre and Contemporary Hollywood*, ed. Steve Neale (London: British Film Institute, 2002). I have recycled a few sections of "Maximum Movies: Lawrence Alloway's Pop Art Film Criticism," *Screen* 49, no. 2 (summer 2008): 179–93. Similarly, a few paragraphs have also been lifted from "Going Underground with Manny Farber & Jonas Mekas," in *Explorations in New Cinema History: Approaches and Case Studies*, ed. Daniel Biltereyst, Richard Maltby, and Philippe Meers (Chichester, UK: Wiley-Blackwell, forthcoming [2011]). Unless otherwise noted, all illustrations are from the collection of the author and are in the public domain or available for reproduction under fair usage.

Peter Stanfield

Maximum Movies—Pulp Fictions

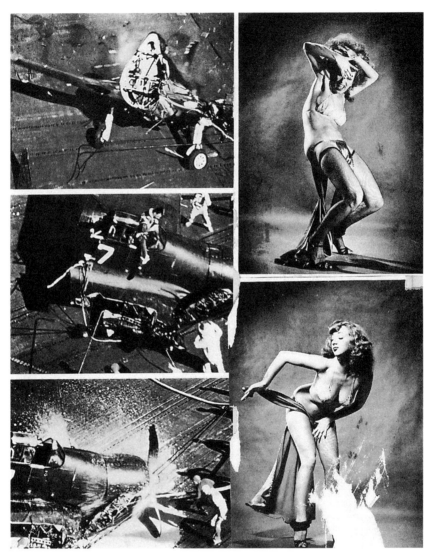

1. Eduardo Paolozzi, *Yours till the Boys Come Home.*
Courtesy of Tate Images.

Introduction

Yours till the Boys Come Home

In a collage by Eduardo Paolozzi, titled *Yours till the Boys Come Home*, three photographs of U.S. Navy fighter aircraft are pasted alongside two photographs of a burlesque dancer. The aircraft have crash-landed on a carrier. In the top left-hand panel the nose of the aircraft has been obliterated, and debris fills the air. In the top-right adjoining panel, the dancer pulls herself into the shape of a letter *S*, her arms wrapped around her head as if she were cowering from the impact. In the lower right-hand panel the dancer leans forward, breasts exposed toward the viewer. With knees bent, her backside is cocked toward the lower left-hand panel, which depicts a plane being sprayed with white foam by two firefighters. A splash of white paint obscures part of her leg, visually echoing the foam spray and the flying debris. In the left-hand middle image, which links to both photographs of the dancer, a pilot is climbing out of the cockpit of his wrecked aircraft as two men rush to his aid.

Made in the early 1950s, the collage is part of a series by the British artist that filled his sketchbooks. Gleeful, exuberant, and sexually playful, the collages are pointed commentaries on the abundance of commercial goods as portrayed in the period's slick magazines—the promised world of tomorrow available, "to you," today. As Greil Marcus has written, Paolozzi was "someone who liked to argue with what wasn't yet called pop culture—the cheap, the fast sounds and images that in the years immediately after the Second World War seemed to be coming together everywhere, the sounds and images connecting to each other in ways that seemed at once natural and inexplicable, the artefacts of this emerging folk culture of the modern market speaking in code, speaking a secret language. Cutting and pasting, Paolozzi is someone who is trying to learn that language and speak it himself."[1] *Yours till The Boys Come Home* suggests, however, that Paolozzi was already fluent in the language of commodity culture, particularly the man-machine-sex contraction that underpinned the rhetorical devices

3

used by Madison Avenue to address male consumers. Exemplified by the Harley Earl aesthetic of matching jet-plane design to domestic and office goods and to the tail fins and chrome extremities on automobiles, the accelerated culture of the 1950s was Paolozzi's subject and object of study.

Along with his colleagues who congregated at the Institute of Contemporary Arts in London, among them Richard Hamilton and Lawrence Alloway, Paolozzi was an avid consumer of the movies. In the period's pulp films—science fiction, war movies, westerns, and gangster pictures—they found a kinetic immediacy that spoke eloquently to the concerns of the day. Fleet of foot and unencumbered by tradition, noisy and garish, lacking in refinement if not complexity, the movies existed only in the present even as they looked to the future. Consumed in a fit of excitement, the movie was worn out and forgotten before the audience had even left the cinema. If films were easily forgettable, like the lunch Paolozzi had the day before, or the newspaper he read that morning, it did not matter because there was always a new sensation on offer elsewhere, nor did it matter that the program changed the day after. Regulated production with built-in obsolescence, streamlined by convention with interchangeable parts, ensured this fact of his maximum moviegoing experience, an experience that promised maximum impact, with a surfeit of attractions to maintain maximum interest, maximum excitement today, along with the promise of more of the same tomorrow.

In a note on the title of her 1968 collection of reviews and short essays *Kiss Kiss Bang Bang*, which she found on an Italian movie poster, Pauline Kael argued that these two words, *kiss* and *bang*, are "perhaps the briefest statement imaginable of the basic appeal of movies. This appeal is what attracts us, and ultimately what makes us despair when we begin to understand how seldom movies are more than this."[2] Paolozzi's *Yours till the Boys Come Home* is a violent visual collision of kiss and bang, sex and machine—a fetish for the age that will attract the connoisseur of the movies, those lovers of film whom we endow with a Parisian veneer of metropolitan sophistication by calling them "cinephiles."[3] These filmgoers tried to hold on to the film playing in front of them in order to retain and replay what it was that they had seen. The why and the how of this film viewing that refuses convention, that turns a truant and unruly eye toward the screen, is in part what this book explores.

This is a book about film culture and the movies that critics have variously labeled pulp, punk, trash, termite, and noir, films such as *Kiss Me Deadly*, *Shock Corridor*, *Fixed Bayonets!*, *I Walked with a Zombie*, *The Lineup*, *Terror in a Texas Town*, *Ride Lonesome*, and myriad other action movies. It is about the work of Otis Ferguson, Manny Farber, Lawrence Alloway, Pauline Kael, Raymond Durgnat, and their contemporaries. It is also about the legacy of less well known film scholars, such as Paddy Whannel, Jim Kitses, Colin McArthur, Alan Lovell, and their colleagues who worked in and around the British Film Institute in the

1960s. *Maximum Movies—Pulp Fictions* tells the story of how critics and scholars reinvented film culture and, for a short while, put American pulp movies of the 1950s at center stage.

These critics and scholars were working within and against critical traditions that managed and maintained a cultural hierarchy that assigned commercial arts to the lowest rung on the arts ladder. How a critic makes distinctions between the products of mass culture, of formulaic industrial media, became something of a shared international project during the 1950s and into the 1960s. Through a history of pulp, this book tracks the generative roots of that project, noting the differences in the approaches and objectives of the work carried out in Britain, the United States, and, to a lesser extent, France.

The broader context is the historically shifting terrain that explains differences in taste along class lines mapped out on a loosely constructed hierarchical tripartite frame of highbrow, middlebrow, and lowbrow. The specific terms of the identities involving these phrenologies are allusive, uncertain, and perhaps even unknowable. But what is certain is that attempts to categorize and define the parameters have absorbed an extraordinary amount of critical attention and produced some seminal and widely read essays. These studies include Clement Greenberg's "Avant-Garde and Kitsch" (1939), Leslie Fiedler's "The Middle against Both Ends" (1955), Norman Mailer's "The White Negro" (1957), Dwight Macdonald's "Masscult and Midcult" (1960), and Susan Sontag's "Notes on 'Camp'" (1964). Key historical accounts of the emergence and disintegration of a cultural hierarchy based on the notion of brows, include Lawrence Levine's *Highbrow/Lowbrow*, which examined the materialization of a binary high-low culture in America that stabilized around the beginning of the twentieth century; Richard Ohmann's *Selling Culture*, an account of the making of the middlebrow during the second decade of the twentieth century; and Michael Kammen's *American Culture, American Tastes*, a historical overview of the stratification of American taste.

Kammen has argued that the points of distinction between the three brows began to break down during the 1930s and became extraordinarily blurred in the postwar years with the massification of popular culture, advertising, and television.[4] It is this period, between the 1930s and 1970s, with which this study is concerned, in particular, the dialogue that went on between high and low culture, a dialogue that was based on an antagonism toward the middlebrow. An exemplar of this form of cultural commentary, one that assumes capital in terms of its rejection of the middle, is found in a letter written in 1949 by Raymond Chandler to his literary agent: "I am at home with the avant garde magazines and with the rough tough vernacular. The company I really cannot get along with is the pseudo-literate pretentiousness of, let us say, the *Saturday Review of Literature*. That sums up everything I despise in our culture."[5]

Chandler's distaste for the middlebrow is suggestive of a wider unease with middle-class values shared by subgroups within that particular social membership. Discussing the work of the American historians of cultural hierarchies, taste communities, and canons, Michael Denning has noted that their focus was almost wholly on the "tension between fractions of the middle classes, and particularly on the cultural power of the emerging professional and managerial classes." He asks whether it is possible to move beyond a "debunking of the authorized standards and judgments of taste and value to a mapping of the popular aesthetic and the cultural values of the working classes." The problem with achieving this aim, he argues, is that the critical activity of the bourgeois cultural theorist is commensurate with the acquisition of cultural capital as propounded by Pierre Bourdieu in *Distinction: A Social Critique of the Judgement of Taste* (1984). Denning cites Bourdieu's claim that the "struggles which aim . . . to transform or overturn the legitimate hierarchies through the legitimating of a still illegitimate art or genre . . . are precisely what creates legitimacy."[6]

In terms that mimic many of the critical positions discussed in the following chapters, Bourdieu wrote that "middle-ground" arts such as "cinema, jazz, and even more, strip cartoons, science fiction or detective stories are predisposed to attract the investments" from those who have cultural capital or those seeking it. "These arts, not yet fully legitimate, which are disdained or neglected by the big holders of educational capital, offer a refuge and a revenge to those who, by appropriating them, secure the best return on their cultural capital."[7] The upshot of this, according to Denning, is that class formations and cultural commodities become inexorably linked; in Bourdieu's formulation the process of accumulating cultural capital accounts for all cultural activity.

As the cultural theorist Andrew Ross has argued about the shifts in debates about mass culture, the classification of tastes and acts of discrimination on the part of intellectuals was carried out as "part of the reorganization of consent in the Cold War period along lines of cultural demarcation that would still guarantee and preserve the channels of power through which intellectual authority is exercised. Cultural power does not inhere in the contents of categories of taste. On the contrary, it is exercised through the capacity to draw the line between and around categories of taste; it is the power to determine what it contains at any one time."[8] While class and education play an important role in the hegemonic defined by Ross and others, cultural power is also rendered by gender.

The high critical regard in which the pulp authors and filmmakers discussed in *Maximum Movies* are held is underpinned, I argue, by the critic's and artist's shared stake in a masculinity that runs shy of emotional entanglements and openness and takes succor in a misogynistic worldview that values male comradeship above all else. At the heart of the pulp fictions, maximum movies, and their critical reception is the fact that these stories are produced in the main for men by men. They are celebrations of, and often retreats into, a male ethos. In the chapters that follow, the middlebrow is time and again defined as feminine and as a space of undifferentiated consumption. In the prosperous postwar years masculinity had to come to terms with cultures of consumption that had been, and still were, overwhelmingly defined as a sphere of female activity.

As the business and cultural historian Thomas Frank has noted, however, in the 1950s material goods were increasingly marketed toward male consumers. Advertisers appealed to this group in terms that have clear parallels with the rhetoric used by young cinephiles in France, Britain, and America when declaring the superiority of their taste in movies. Frank shows how, as the 1950s wore on, advertisers used a core theme of nonconformity and the commodification of deviance, articulated through vocabularies of transgression. To encourage men to become active consumers, advertisers suggested that the act of consumption was in and of itself a radical action, which counterintuitively defined the buying of a new suit, pack of cigarettes, or bottle of whisky as an act of individual rebuke to the dominant culture of consensus and standardization. The end result produced the oxymoronic "hip consumer"—in whom the "disgust with the falseness, shoddiness, and everyday oppressions of consumer society could be enlisted to drive the ever-accelerating wheels of consumption."[9] We now live in an age where, as Frank writes, "commercial fantasies of rebellion, liberation, and outright 'revolution' against the stultifying demands of mass society are commonplace almost to the point of invisibility in advertising, movies, and television programming" (4). "By the middle of the 1950s," Frank continues, "talk of conformity, of consumerism, and of the banality of mass-produced culture were routine elements of middle-class American life" (11).

The contradictory pull of consumerism as trap and release created the desire in more discerning and discriminate consumers for an object of consumption that transcended commercial exchange, that was deemed to be authentic, and therefore offered an authenticating experience. For many that experience was best found in the cheap and tawdry, but vital and lively, appeal of pulp culture—a realm of primitive attractions that seemed a world apart from the sophistry and sophistication of Madison Avenue. In his notes for a lecture on contemporary art given in 1958, Paolozzi wrote: "It is conceivable that in 1958 a higher order of imagination exists in a SF pulp produced on the outskirts of LA than the little magazines of today. Also it might be possible that sensations of a difficult-to-describe nature be expended at the showing of a low-budget horror film."[10] What might those sensations be, and to what can they be ascribed? How might lowly pulp science fiction invert an established cultural hierarchy by supplanting the avant-garde journal and becoming part of the higher order of things? Paolozzi concluded his speculative deliberation by asking the question: "Does the modern artist consider this?" If the examples I have given in the following chapters on the dialogue between high and low culture are a fair sampling, then the answer to his question must be in the affirmative; the modern artist, and his or her fellow traveler, the critic, did indeed consider this state of things.

Chapter 1 begins in the 1950s with Lawrence Alloway and Manny Farber and ends in the 1970s in Britain with the establishment of the academic discipline of film studies. This introductory chapter examines the shift from critical to theoretical perspectives on American pulp movies. Alloway's critique of the inappropriateness of employing a distanced contemplative approach drawn from the study of high art to engage with the popular arts is matched with Farber's ideas on underground film and termite art, Robert Warshow's interest in the "immediate experience" of watching the movies, and Raymond Durgnat's wedding of pulp and poetry. These 1950s and early 1960s critiques are filtered through a review of their precursors: Mayer Levin, who wrote about "punk" movies in the 1930s; Otis Ferguson on the common language shared by the movies and its audience; and James Agee on the appeal of pulp films, with screenplays that were "slapped together in a week." The chapter then turns to Arthur Mayer and Jonas Mekas, two central figures in New York's film culture. The former was an exhibitor and distributor of horror and B movies aimed at an exclusively male clientele, as well as an importer of European neorealist dramas. The latter was an avant-garde filmmaker, exhibitor, distributor, and publisher who also wrote film reviews for the *Village Voice*, many of which extolled the virtues of the humble B movie. This mix of the low and the high, pulp and art, hit critical mass with the publication of Pauline Kael's 1969 essay "Trash Art and the Movies."

The debate on lowbrow American movies in the 1960s moved into the realm of education in the 1960s, particularly in Britain, where a proactive Education Department at the British Film Institute, alongside the Society for Education in Film and Television, publishers of *Screen Education* and *Screen*, promoted the use of popular film in teaching liberal studies in schools and colleges. Through these two organizations there emerged a generation of film scholars who would decisively change the direction of British film culture and have a considerable impact on the study of film in North America. Working briefly through the influence on British scholars of F. R. Leavis, French film criticism and structuralism, the chapter concludes by considering the changes in film culture following the events of May 1968. These events led to the politicization of the emerging discipline of film studies; the maverick filmmakers, and the genres and films that displayed, in Farber's memorable phrase, "a bit of male truth" were abandoned for more "progressive" genres and auteurs and became objects of opprobrium.

Chapter 2 examines the boom in pulp magazine publishing in the 1920s, through the downturn in the 1930s and into the 1940s, when the pulps gave way to the new mass medium of paperback books. The chapter traces the shifting meanings in the use of *pulp* as first a term of disdain before becoming a marker of distinction, against which the quotidian and mediocre can be better identified. Beginning with a discussion of the anonymous artisans churning out countless words aimed at the mob, moving through the canonization of Hammett and Chandler by highbrow and middlebrow readers and critics, the chapter ends with an examination of the legacy of Mickey Spillane's fiction, which to this day remains unassimilated by alternative literary canons used to confront an aloof official culture. The scorn and contempt heaped on Spillane and his fiction was matched by a concomitant revaluation of hitherto critically dismissed forms of popular culture. It is this dichotomy of entrenchment alongside a more open attitude in some quarters to popular culture that forms the historical and immediate context for understanding the extraordinary critical reception of Robert Aldrich's film adaptation of Spillane's novel *Kiss Me, Deadly*.

Chapter 3 is the book's keystone, containing new and significant research on the production, exhibition, and critical reception of *Kiss Me Deadly* (Robert Aldrich 1955) and the other Spillane adaptations produced by Parklane Pictures in the 1950s. Paying close attention to American, French, and British critical reactions to the film, including censorship records and analysis of film scripts, the chapter examines *Kiss Me Deadly*'s ambivalent status as commodified trash *and* vanguardist art. One of the traditions that informed the new film criticism published in France during the 1950s was surrealism, which found its most marked expression in the celebration of Aldrich's film. Championed in the film journals *Cahiers du cinéma* and *Positif* as the thriller of tomorrow and as a marvelous expression of violent poetry, *Kiss Me Deadly* intrigued critics, who reveled in its visual disjunctions and narrative incoherence, the subversion of its source material, and transcendence of its generic base. Questions concerning narrative compression and the maximizing of conventions run throughout the chapter.

Critical reception in America and Britain was initially less open to the appeal of a Mickey Spillane adaptation, so they cited it as an example of the unacceptable face of popular cinema and as a brutish nonsensical nightmare. Either way, Aldrich would take much of the credit for the film's perceived paroxysmal energy, but other authors should also get credit, including Mickey Spillane. Derided from all corners, Spillane is here given the acclaim he deserves for his pulp tale and the amphetamine whirl of his storytelling that the filmmakers tried to match. The chapter also argues that a core difference between the source novel and its adaptation is the manner in which the filmmakers dissembled the proletarian certainties manifest in Spillane's hero by remodeling him as a contemporary exemplar of an idealized masculine consumer. In making this argument, I consider, through the use of blues and jazz and their sites of performance, the film's American specificity—its particular culture of consumption.

For the British, any rewriting of film culture would have to deal with class politics and the stultifying effect of a leaden cultural tradition. American popular culture, and Hollywood in particular, offered glamour, commonality, and a vision of the future that seemed endlessly seductive to a postwar audience raised on austerity. But Hollywood was also to be feared as the embodiment of a capitalistic and rapaciously imperialistic culture. The contradictory position in which British cinephiles were implicated was obscured by their acts of critical distinction that validated the work of directors they perceived as at odds with the Hollywood machine and whose films deployed characters that dealt with contradictions they themselves faced, none more so than the films of Samuel Fuller—"American primitive."

What does it mean to call Fuller a "primitive"? Chapter 4 answers that question alongside an account of the critical evaluation of his work in France and America. There then follows a consideration of Fuller's films, particularly as they were received in Britain during the 1960s and 1970s. Most critics worked with the oxymoronic construction of Fuller as an "intelligent primitive." I argue, however, that his work should not be viewed through the filter of high culture that constructs him as a hybrid—part Samuel Beckett, part Mickey Spillane. Instead, his work is best appreciated alongside other examples of sensationalist fiction, such as the comic book art produced by EC in the 1950s. A counterreading to the critical consensus would be that Fuller always had one foot in the gutter, and the other foot never reached higher than the sidewalk, certainly no higher than the cuff on Beckett's pant-leg. In this examination of Fuller's aesthetic I consider how he became one of the key figures through which British cinephiles were able to work out their ambivalent relationship with American popular culture—a culture that was at once attractive and distrusted. In the process these children of Marx and Coca-Cola helped pull filmmakers like Fuller from out of Farber's underground and into the daylight.

The shared international project of the 1950s and 1960s that oversaw the transvaluation of pulp, whether it was a film adaptation of a Spillane thriller or a war film written, produced, and directed by Fuller, had a late revival in the 1980s when the pulp novels of Jim Thompson were republished, first by independents and then by mass-market publishers, in Britain and the United States. This publishing activity was followed, in the early 1990s, by a Hollywood fad for Thompson. Thompson's rediscovery in the 1980s was carried out by a readership raised on the negationist rhetoric of punk. What attracted these young-adult readers was not only the novels' violent rejection of the empty promises of consumer culture, or the idea that Thompson's stories had a punk-like disregard for bourgeois notions of good taste, but also the contradictory idea that cheap, industrialized, pulp fiction written during the 1950s contained an authenticity that could not be found in contemporary consumer culture. In the process of the wider dissemination of Thompson's novels, however, his fiction moved from being a lowbrow's entertainment, to a highbrow's *objet trouvé*, to, finally, middlebrow art-house fare exemplified by the film adaptations of *The Grifters* (1990) and *This World, Then the Fireworks* (1997).

Jim Thompson adaptations were part of a focused reclamation by Hollywood of pulp writers in the 1990s for films that were marketed as "neo-noir." Behind this simple classification, however, lies a complex history of pulp novels, the critical status of pulp writers, and their relationship to discourses of film categorization. The explicit conjunction of film noir and pulp fiction in the marketing and consumption of neo-noir forms the core of Chapter 5. This focus will enable a link back to the work done on Spillane and Fuller, and a move forward to the bond between critical practice and film production, as exemplified in the Jim Thompson adaptations and the idea of neo-noir.

Alloway argued that the film critic needed to assume the same position in relation to his or her object of study as that taken by the habitual filmgoer. The book's conclusion considers the implication of such a stance by examining the idea of hiding out in the cinema, safe from one's pursuers, free, momentarily, from the draw of middle-class respectability and from domestic responsibilities and the feminine sphere of influence.

This book makes no claim for comprehensiveness in its coverage of the critical moments and movements that have helped frame our understanding of pulp, lowbrow culture, and maximum movies, and in the pages that follow I recognize that many other film scholars have passed an inquiring eye over some of the same material that I examine. The studies of Jeffrey Sconce on paracinema, Joan Hawkins on horror and the avant-garde, and Greg Taylor on cult and camp, for example, have obvious affinities with my project, as does James Naremore's classic study of noir.[11] But the compass of my research is distinct. Sconce and Hawkins are essentially dealing with marginal cinemas, while my case studies are now part of an academic canon shaped to a large extent by the legitimating project of cult and noir studies of the disreputable or dissident. In this sense my understanding of film culture owes much to Taylor and Naremore, but the particularities of my analysis of Spillane, Fuller, and Thompson, and of the critical contexts that have informed the consumption of pulp novels and films, draws on a wider field of cultural criticism than Taylor's object of study and is less generically specific than Naremore's research. My hope in *Maximum Movies— Pulp Fictions* is that the overlaps and parallels with this body of scholarship, alongside many points of divergence, will help to further illuminate our shared enthusiasm, perhaps even love, for the cinema, pulp or otherwise.

1

Position Papers

In Defense of Pulp Movies

There are few things in any art or art-industry more discouraging to think of, more inimical to the furtherance of good work or to the chance to attempt it, than the middle-brow highbrows. Half a brow is worse than no head.

–James Agee, *The Nation* (December 16, 1944)

Myth has it that the Independent Group (IG), the British critical and artistic community formed in the 1950s at the newly established Institute of the Contemporary Arts, found its inspiration in a trunk full of American magazines and other ephemera brought back from the States by one of its key members, John McHale, of whom Mark Wigley writes:

> He visited the United States in 1955 and returned to England a year later with his partner, the artist Magda Cordell. They brought back a huge trunk filled with American magazines, catalogues, Elvis Presley records, and odd bits and pieces of what we would call today "pop" culture. In fact, the term is unthinkable outside that very trunk. Richard Hamilton promptly cut advertisements out of those magazines and used them to construct his famous collage "Just What is it That Makes Today's Homes So Appealing?" that was the centerpiece of the 1956 *This is Tomorrow* Exhibition and has been canonized as the first significant work of Pop Art.[1]

The trunk is a twentieth-century treasure chest brought back from the New World and filled, not with pirate booty, but with something equally fantastical and equally full of the promise of adventure. The magazines, catalogs, and comic books are a visual index to a culture of plenty that in austere postwar Britain suggested tomorrow's world today.[2]

No doubt there was such a trunk, and its concentration of American imagery inspired discussion and works of art, but the members of the IG did not need the trunk's contents to know what was happening in the United States and what would eventually happen in Britain. The signs were all around them. One member, Nigel Henderson, caught the sense of the old and the new in his photograph of a dilapidated magazine and bookstore in London's East End, circa 1949–52. Crude hand-painted signs advertise the biggest selection of American comics in East London, the magazines' sensational seductions striking a contrast with the Dickensian location in which they are presented. The documenting of the "modern flood of visual symbols," of which Henderson's image was but one among many, was a core activity of the IG.[3] In their early writings and artworks there is a terrific sense of anticipation in the promise made by American popular culture, but elsewhere, for example in Geoffrey Wagner's *Parade of Pleasure: A Study of Popular Iconography in the USA* (1954) and in Richard Hoggart's *The Uses of Literacy* (1958), there is an equally keen sense of foreboding, a fear that a vital British culture will be swamped by a great tide of vulgar American imagery.

Like Henderson, Hoggart made a record of the shops that offered the promise of cheap American thrills. These shops, he wrote, are "littered and overhung with paper-backs in varying stages of disintegration, since they operate a system of exchanges." This "trash," in all but name, is subdivided into easily recognizable genres: "Crime, Science fiction, and Sex novelettes."[4] Glancing over the pulp science fiction titles that appealed so strongly to the "juke-box boys," Hoggart wrote:

> Again the same flat paper with glossy covers. This is the sort of science fiction which preceded, and presumably goes unaffected by, the elevation of some writing on similar themes into a subject for serious discussion in the literature weeklies. The manner and situations are alike extremely limited. In most stories there is a nubile girl, dressed in what a costume-designer for a second-class touring revue might be expected to consider a "futuristic" outfit. This usually means a very short and pleated white skirt, and an abbreviated top incorporating some sort of modernistic motif. This is "sex stuff" with zip-fasteners instead of the old-fashioned blouses and skirts; vicarious fornication (with no details) on a spaceship moving between Mars and Venus.[5]

He begins his dismissal of science fiction by noting that there is an interest and a debate going on about this genre in the "literature weeklies," something similar to the debates on crime stories that had once distracted the literati, but Hoggart's critique is aimed at the mass of stories that sit beneath the critical horizons of middlebrow reviewers.

As the art historian Graham Whitham has noted, "Science fiction in the 1950s was a genre consigned to a literary ghetto by the guardians of established taste. To some extent it was this situation which attracted some members of the

Independent Group whose aim was to be iconoclastic. Science fiction provided them with a wealth of suitably irreverent references that Lawrence Alloway, for one, delighted in parading before the intransigent ranks of traditional aesthetes."[6] But it was not just its provocative potential that drew IG members to science fiction. It was also because it "proposed the new and the immediately impossible." It was another direct link to a culture of plenty, particularly the American variety of science fiction, and it was, as Alloway pointed out, "one of the channels open to erotic art in our half-censored culture."[7]

Alloway and Paolozzi sought out American science fiction films at the London Pavilion cinema, an activity that sat well with Alloway's love of science fiction magazines: "I first read science fiction (SF) as a teenager in the early 1940s," he wrote, "when American pulp magazines reached England in fairly large numbers, as cheap bulk cargo or ballast or something, and I began to search for earlier publications."[8] Discussing the way Paolozzi's art derived from his improvisation with materials at hand, whether they belonged to the mass media or the fine arts, Alloway noted the impact the artist had on his ideas:

> He and I used to go quite a lot to the London Pavilion in Piccadilly which in those days was showing Universal horror films . . . so he was someone who had this itchy creativity on a continuous basis, always bombarded by mass-media imagery. And the example of seeing this happen to someone, I think sort of relaxed me and made it easier for me to go to the lecture at the Tate Gallery in the afternoon and go to the London Pavilion as soon as I could get out in the evening. He's been influential, I think, in setting up this notion of the fine art–pop art continuum—the touchability of all bases in the continuum.[9]

Hoggart divided science fiction into two realms—the first had pretensions to transcend its pulp roots, while the second appealed to the masses with its combination of sex stuff and zip fasteners. But as Alloway would argue, this is a crude formation, one that is unable to account for the levels of specialization practiced by readers of genre fiction. He argued that the mass media are not only a means of standardized learning, as surmised by Hoggart, but are instead consumed by groups, and individuals within the group, who are differentiated from the mass.

The media, Alloway believed, are "subject to highly personal uses." To illustrate his point, he quoted from the letters page of *Science Fiction Quarterly*, where the correspondent ponders the meaning of a front cover illustrated by the commercial artist Luros: "I'm sure Freud could have found much to comment, and write on, about it. It's [sic] symbolism, intentionally or not, is that of man, the victor; woman, the slave. Man the active; woman the passive. Man the conqueror; woman the conquered. Objective man, subjective woman; possessive man, submissive woman! . . . What are the views of other readers on this?

Especially in relation with Luros' backdrop of destroyed cities and vanquished man?" In response to the correspondent's erudition and pointed evaluation of the magazine's illustrated cover, which he does not pose as in anyway unique, Alloway wrote:

> The commentary supplied by the reader, though cued by the iconography of *Science Fiction Quarterly*, implies clearly enough his personal desire and interest. However, it is no greater a burden of meaning that he puts on the cover than those attached to poems by symbol-conscious literary critics. The point is that the mass media not only perform broad, socially useful roles but offer possibilities of private and personal deep interpretation as well. At this level Luros' cover is like a competitor of the fine arts, in its capacity for condensing personal feelings. . . . Both for the scope and their power of catching personal feeling, the mass media must be reckoned as a permanent addition to our ways of interpreting and influencing the world.

According to Alloway the mass media provide lessons, or guides to life, but this should not be construed as a simple top-down model. "The entertainment, the fun, is always uppermost. Any lessons in consumption or in style must occur inside the pattern of entertainment and not weigh it down like a pigeon with *The Naked and the Dead* tied to its leg. When the movies or the TV create a world, it is of necessity a *designed* set in which people act and move, and the style in which they inhabit the scene is an index of the atmosphere of opinion of the audience, as complex as a weather map." The popular arts are not one thing, Alloway would protest; they are "in fact highly specialized," with a "multitude of audiences within the great audience."[10]

In an overview of the work of the IG, Barry Curtis wrote that "the new elements of pop culture produced a scenario of both ends against the cultural middle ground occupied by most critics. They envisaged a future both more technologically rational and imaginatively fantastic. They were interested in the new identities created for the reception of new pleasures and in an aesthetic of use and assimilation which was generally complicit with, and expert in, the terms of mass culture."[11] For members of the IG there was no contradiction inherent in being an expert in mass culture. In the minutes of the Institute of Contemporary Arts annual meeting held in July 1954 it was recorded that "Richard Hamilton suggested that discussions could be held about the films released to local cinemas, as these had an enormous influence, and were amongst the most significant things in film today. . . . Mrs Richard Hamilton asked whether a policy decision had been taken in the film section: were the ICA to stick to 'Caligari and all that' (film society fare) or would discussions be held on the commercial cinema?"[12] The iconoclastic potential in commercial film within the context of an art institution is self-evident in this little act of provocation.

Although all the members of the IG held an interest in the movies, only Alloway developed a coherent theory of film as a popular art. Writing at the beginning of 1964, he called for a descriptive criticism of film that would account for popular cinema's "specific kind of communication (high impact, strong participation, hard to remember), or in the technology and organisation through which the movies reach us."[13] Throughout the 1960s Alloway published a small number of short critical pieces on American cinema that stayed true to those principles.[14] This work culminated in 1969 with the programming of a series of film screenings of American action movies at New York's Museum of Modern Art. His notes for the screenings were expanded and then published by MoMA in 1971 as *Violent America: The Movies, 1946–1964*—a richly illustrated book.[15] The monograph consists of five essays, which consider the issues of realism, expendability, iconography, the industrial context of film production, and a fulsome rejection of a catharsis theory of violence and the arts. Across these essays he supports his arguments by citing as evidence an extraordinary number of films. This active consumption of movies suggests Alloway was a habitual filmgoer, like millions of others, but he was also a singular critic with an uncommon insight into the aesthetics of popular movies.

Most of the thirty-five films screened at the time of their original release were inconspicuous genre pictures, though they are now some of the most valued and analyzed examples of American filmmaking. Titles in the screening program included *Out of the Past* (1947), *The Big Heat* (1953), *Kiss Me Deadly* (1955), *Written on the Wind* (1956), *Touch of Evil* (1958), *Seven Men from Now* (1956), *The Steel Helmet* (1951), and *In a Lonely Place* (1950).[16] The program was not intended to offer further critical or institutional validation of individual films— to proclaim a particular film as a distinctive work of American art, worthy of the cultural esteem that follows a screening at one of New York's premier art establishments. Instead, Alloway sought better to understand American iconography by examining examples of popular art in the context of the culture in which they were produced and consumed.

Alloway's reputation as an art critic rests primarily on the fact that he was the first in print to use the term *pop art*. Alongside pop art's relationship to other media, he also applied the term to the movies in the late 1950s and early 1960s, but, by the time he reset his ideas for inclusion in *Violent America*, the idea of "movies as pop art" had vanished. His critical method had not significantly changed, but the currency of pop art had. When he had first deployed the term in 1957/1958, he had meant it as a description of mass communications: "It was an expansionist esthetics, aimed at relating art to the man-made environment of the 50's. Advertising, color photography and color reproduction, (big screen) films, (early English) TV, automobile styling were regarded on equal terms with the fine arts; not the same, but equally interesting."[17] The British proponents of pop art were, he noted, accused of being pro-American, but this

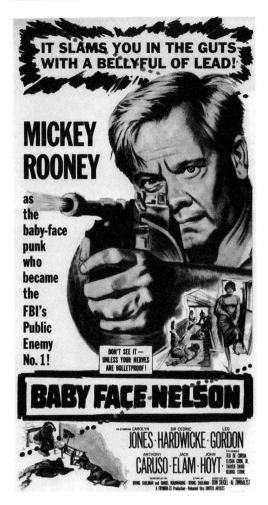

2. Press ad for *Baby Face Nelson* (1957).

was to conflate industrialization with America. All technologically advanced nations produce industrial art, but because the United States was the most fully realized industrial nation, it was producing the most admired pop art: "pop art was pro-urban and accepted the media's roots in mass production, at a time when traditional esthetics in England was mostly pastoral or universalizing. Pop art, in its original form, was a polemic against elite views of art in which uniqueness is a metaphor of the aristocratic and contemplation the only proper response to art."[18]

As understood by the IG, and articulated by the artist John McHale, the new media landscape of the 1950s represented an acceleration of everyday life that required "an array of symbolic images of man which will match up to the requirements of constant change, fleeting impression, and a high rate of obsolescence. A replaceable, expendable series of icons."[19] Initially, then, pop art was this series of short-lived, interchangeable, images. "It's [sic] users were art-oriented," wrote Alloway, "if not themselves artists, and interested both in extending esthetic attention to the mass media and in absorbing mass-media material within the context of fine art."[20] Writing to his fellow IG members Peter and Alison Smithson in 1957, the artist Richard Hamilton sketched out a table of pop art's characteristics:

Popular (designed for a mass audience)

Transient (short-term solution)

Expendable (easily forgotten)

Low cost

Mass produced

Young (aimed at youth)

Witty

Sexy

Gimmicky

Glamorous

Big business[21]

From 1961 to 1964 the meaning of pop art shifted, according to Alloway, to privilege the idea that it represented "art that included a reference to mass-media sources." During 1965 and 1966 the meaning again shifted, and it was now applied to "fashion, films, interior decoration, toys, parties, and town planning."[22] Pop art, then, moved from an aesthetics of consumer goods, through the appropriation of that series of icons by fine artists, to this new art's doubling-back into consumer culture. Alloway illustrated how the term's mobility mitigated against its original meaning by drawing on the history of Batman, which began as a comic strip, and then became a subject of painting, before becoming the camp hit TV series that proclaimed a self-awareness of its own "pop art" status. "Pop art" can no longer represent a sense of the wider culture where Batman and fine art coexist as equally interesting but distinct media, but, Alloway insisted, the original project begun by the IG to make "a descriptive account of the whole field of communications, in which we live and [of] which art is a part" remained valid. If he felt the term itself was now redundant owing to the shifts in meaning that it had undergone, Alloway still practiced a form of pop art criticism, which in practice he understood to be inclusive and speculative, showing a healthy distrust of the elitist disposition toward formalist and contemplative aesthetics.[23]

Assigning equal value to the elite and popular arts did not mean that differences were not recognized. The popular arts are defined by their topicality;

hence they are marked by transience and obsolescence as much as they are by immediacy and the present. Repetition and modification are key features that are "geared to technical changes which occur, not gradually, but violently and experimentally."[24] Redundancy, not permanence, is one of their defining factors. This does not mean the popular arts are any less interesting than an accepted work of art. In counterpoint to the fine arts, it is the ephemeral expendable qualities of popular art that make it so arresting. Through his inclusive approach to culture, Alloway presented an expansive view of modern communications, where "the new role for the fine arts is to be one of the possible forms of communication in an expanding framework that includes the mass arts."[25]

And the movies are a mass art. Alloway liked to link Hollywood with Detroit, noting how the film industry's seasonal novelties did not differ significantly from Detroit's annual style changes, which "were sufficient to entertain us with a comedy of newness but not radical enough to disrupt continuity with earlier models."[26] Like automobiles, movies had built-in obsolescence. That is, he argued, film is an obsolescent art form: expendable, inherently ephemeral, and largely forgettable (or hard to remember). Films offer the promise of transient immediate pleasure; they can be recalled only in vague outline or in the retention of a moment, never in their entirety.

In her dream portrait of Hollywood films of the 1940s, written in the early 1950s and published at the end of the 1960s, Barbara Deming assured her readers they had nothing to fear of false impressions drifting into her narrative. She did "not rely upon memory. At each film I took lengthy notes in shorthand—a very literal moment by moment transcription."[27] But for the habitual cinemagoer the uniqueness of the film viewed was less important than the repeatable pleasure of watching the movies. Alloway argued, however, that in terms of "continuing themes and motifs, the obsolescence of single films is compensated for by the prolongation of ideas in film after film"; thus, a film critic's "judgments derive from the sympathetic consumption of a great many films."[28]

The concept of film as an obsolescent art was crucial to Alloway's aesthetic; it was an idea he had worked out in tandem in the mid-1950s with Reyner Banham and other members of the IG. Banham proposed that consumer demand, changing technology, and taste led to an expendable aesthetic: "The addition of the word *expendable* to the vocabulary of criticism was essential before . . . [popular culture] could be faced honestly, since this is the first quality of an object to be consumed."[29] Furthermore, there was little point in claiming that mass-produced objects followed the classical verities—that a luxury car, for example, displayed timeless, classical qualities—because the cycle of style changes, technological advances, and consumer taste will soon enough prove this to be false.[30]

The movies are an industrial product produced for a mass audience; therefore, the study of popular film demands that the critic recognize that films do not stand alone but are produced and consumed in runs and sets, groupings that may be understood in terms of generic qualities, or the casting of stars, or iconographical elements, or the shared exploitation of topical issues. Rather than the discrete film, the continuities across groups of films, which audiences recognize, become the principal focus of critical attention. Change and stasis characterize Hollywood's film production so that by the 1940s and 1950s, Alloway argued, we are "witness to a maximum development of conventions." Alongside an aesthetic of obsolescence, the maximization of conventions is a key to Alloway's conception of how the movies work. "In the movies we are faced with figures that embody in terms of contemporary references maximum states of age, beauty, strength, revenge, or whatever."[31] Discussing formulaic fictions he noted that violence as "motivation gives the maximum definition to a story, a principle common to magazine fiction and violent movies" (11). The pulp or action movie concerns itself with the maximum state of being, and what matters is what generates intensity (37).

Condensed narratives, alongside heightened iconographic properties, such as those involved in casting, are linked to formal strategies intended to speed things up. On *Kiss Me Deadly* he wrote, "The film is jammed with character actors, Greeks and Italians, cops and gunmen, doctors and janitors, chicks and desk clerks. They are stereotyped but the stereotypes are so numerous and emphatic that they add up to a real crowd. They are presented on the small black and white screen with a dense but easy patterning. It is a kind of deliberate revival of the brisk and eventful style of small screen black & white movies of the 1940s which by 1955 was somewhat under pressure from the long takes and tranquil spaces of the big screens" (84–85). The "brisk and eventful style" of the action film with its "stepped-up violence" has, Alloway noted, developed an aesthetic of discontinuous editing, "as if Soviet montage has been revived via television commercials . . . so that a gunfight, for instance, becomes an anthology of stances, wounds, falls, made tolerable to the public by not dwelling on bullet impact (except for glimpses of galvanic body reactions) or exit wounds (except for glimpses of torn clothing and spurts of arterial blood)" (23, 25). A similar set of maximized conventions—characters, events, and formal and stylistic concerns—is also evident in Don Siegel's *The Lineup* (1958): "The opening is typical of the best handling of action. The whole thing feels as though it takes no time at all. It is a montage based on accelerated action, not on temporal delay nor symbolic reinforcement in the manner of Soviet films. It is the compression of continuous action as in the final gunfight in the bar in *The Killers*" (89). This compression produces the maximum movie.

During his first trip to the United States, in 1958, Alloway visited the abstract artists he so admired. In a letter home he wrote that he had "lunch with Rothko yesterday. . . . I spent all afternoon with him and learned a great deal about his art and background which was most exciting. He is charming and resourceful as a conversationalist—but without being trivial"[32] He met Franz Kline at the Cedar Bar: "he was drunk, affable, non-committal." He also met the art director of *Mad* magazine at the same watering hole and spent the next day at the magazine's offices, where he was introduced to the editor and secured back copies. Alloway's fine art/pop art continuum was not just a theory; it was the world he lived in.[33]

This was also the world that the abstract artist and film critic Manny Farber inhabited. Farber was adept at making distinctions between the products of the mass media in general and film in particular. Farber's interests ranged across American and European cinemas, the avant-garde and the commercial, but he is best known for his critical forays into American genre cinema. In his estimable account of the critical work and influence of Manny Farber and Parker Tyler, Greg Taylor noted that for Farber the act of discernment must be "creative and individual, never guided by formula."[34]

Like Alloway, Farber valued the ephemeral in the popular arts: a "great segment of fine Hollywood work isn't interested in Big Art, but in making a contemporaneous 'point' that, by the nature of its momentary truth, dies almost the moment the movie is released."[35] Films that announced their own importance gave off an air of the "solemnity and emptiness of a small-town library room" and invariably attempted to suggest a connection between the troubles confronting the protagonists with those "bothering each spectator in the theater. For this reason, many people, including the critics of *The New Yorker* and *Time*, think the movies are full of 'ideas'—'disturbing,' 'offbeat,' and even 'three-dimensional.'"[36] The well-intentioned film, that directed by Sidney Lumet, for example, is Farber's *bête noir*, coming on like "a high-powered salesman using empty tricks and skills to push an item for which he has no feeling or belief" (113). The trite pretentiousness of the Hollywood picture that made a direct appeal to a middle-class sensibility, Farber labeled "corrupt."

Filmmakers such as Lumet, Elia Kazan, Martin Ritt, and Paddy Chayefsky "have all but destroyed background interest, the gloved fluidity of authentic movie acting, and the effect of a modest shrewdie working expediently and with a great camera eye in the underground of a film that is intentionally made to look junky, like the penny candies sold in the old-time grocery. In place of the skilful anonymity of *Pickup on South Street*, *The Lusty Men*, or *The Thing*, there is now a splintering and a caterwauling that covers gaping holes with meaningless padding and plush" (123). "Background" and "underground" provide the terrain over which Farber's critical eye freely roams and enters. In his terms the more a film strives for cultural legitimacy, the more it is corrupt. Farber's aesthetic proposes a world turned upside down, where the culturally illegitimate—a film about a pickpocket and a prostitute, a modern-day cowboy movie with a rodeo setting, and a science fiction film set in an arctic wasteland featuring an alien

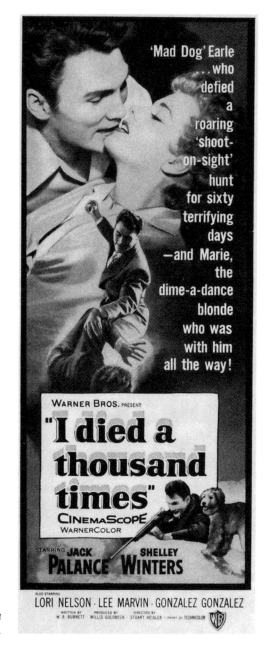

3. Press ad for *I Died a Thousand Times* (1955).

monster—have a greater claim on the truth of how things are than does legitimate, respectable, and consensual culture.

Farber's iconoclastic instinct was finely honed by the time his best-known essay, "White Elephant Art vs. Termite Art" was published in *Film Culture* in

1962. Most of that essay is concerned with pricking the balloon of artistic pomposity that carried some of the most celebrated filmmakers of the early 1960s—Tony Richardson, François Truffaut, and Michelangelo Antonioni. He believed they produced "masterpiece art, reminiscent of the enameled tobacco humidors and wooden lawn ponies bought at white elephant auctions decades ago."[37] These filmmakers aspired to "pin the viewer to the wall and slug him with wet towels of artiness and significance" (143). Good works have "no ambitions towards gilt culture but are involved in a kind of squandering-beaverish endeavor that isn't anywhere or for anything" (135). He calls this labor "termite art," work that does not attract the "spotlight of culture . . . so that the craftsman can be ornery, wasteful, stubbornly self-involved, doing go-for-broke art and not caring what comes of it" (136). Termite art aims at "buglike immersion in a small area without point or aim, and, over all, concentration on nailing down one moment without glamorizing it, but forgetting this accomplishment as soon as it has been passed; the feeling that all is expendable, that it can be chopped up and flung down in a different arrangement without ruin" (144).

The producer of termite art is more akin to a mechanic than to an artist, closer to someone like the hot rod customizer, pinstriper, gunsmith, knife maker, motorcyclist, and 1950s hipster Von Dutch—the "Leonardo da Vinci of the garage"—than he is to the fine art painter or sculptor. As Von Dutch said of himself: "I ain't no artist. There's a difference there. Y'see, artists distort everything or feels that he can distort everything. But a craftsman has to have a discipline that an artist can never get into because he's too busy telling someone that the picture he drew is the way he wants it. With a disciplined craftsman, it's gotta be a certain way."[38] Skill, technique, craft, and discipline allied to a vernacular or industrial art—motorcycle customization or the movies—represent "meaningful" masculine endeavors.

The New York critic Donald Phelps put the following spin on Farber's worldview and the particular attention he gave to filmmakers such as Anthony Mann, Samuel Fuller, and Robert Aldrich: "the common denominator of these artists . . . is not their masculinity (although manliness is an essential component of their work) but their dedication to their art; not as a replica of themselves, but as an emanation of themselves, a current of that behavior which at once links them to the world and dissolves them among the things of the world. Manny Farber has discerned and embodies this dedication."[39] Against all the "polishing," "bragging," and "fake educating" that went on in Hollywood, Farber argued that there was a group of filmmakers who had "tunneled" inside the action movies at which they excelled, producing "underground" movies.[40] These directors accepted the role of "hack so that they can involve themselves with expedience and tough-guy insight in all types of action: barnstorming, driving, bulldogging. The important thing is not so much the banal-seeming journeys to no-where that make up the stories, but the tunneling that goes on inside the classic Western-gangster incidents and stock hoodlum-dogface-cowboy types . . . private runways to the truth" (17).

Hawks, Wellman, Walsh, Mann, Karlson, and Aldrich—these were directors that Farber labeled "underground." They made "faceless movies, taken from a half-polished trash writing, that seems a mixture of Burt L. Standish [writer of juvenile sports stories], Max Brand [Western writer], and Raymond Chandler" (ibid., 16). In other words, they made pulp fiction in which the "small buried attempt to pierce the banal pulp of underground stories with fanciful grace notes is one of the important feats" (19). These grace notes—"a mean butterball flicks a gunman's ear with a cigarette lighter. A night-frozen cowboy shudders over a swig of whisky. A gorilla gang leader makes a cannonaded exit from a barber chair"—are "just bits of congestion," an opportunity for an underground director to take a chance with clichés and forc[e] them into a hard natural shape" (20). But what Farber found really significant in the underground film is the manner in which a scene is opened up, "the strategies that play movement against space in a cunning way, building the environment and the event before your eyes. In every underground film, these vigorous ramifications within a sharply seen terrain are the big attraction, the main tent" (22).

In an essay from 1959, "Underground Magic, Eccentric Vitality, and Artful Direction Salvage Banal Stories," Farber wrote: "Since every film is the product of technicians who are situated in different spots of the universe in relation to art, business and talent, the *real* fascination of a movie isn't the sum total of aesthetic effects, but the underground channels created by each artist pursuing his path. When considered only as whole works somewhere between dud and masterpiece . . . films not only shrink in interest but are too easily pigeon-holed." The critical act Farber was proposing was not the search for a masterpiece, or the dismissal of a dud, but the recognition that "each movie has an iceberg's hidden resources—the continuity of interest represented by each technician's following or veering from a battle-scarred path that has been 'long abuilding' and seems more crucial than the generalization of any single picture."[41]

What Alloway and Farber were interested in was the "immediate experience" of the movies, an experience that was quite distinct from a contemplative consumption of art. In this attitude they were paralleling another New York critic, Robert Warshow, who, in a withering critique of a complacent and arrogant bourgeois distaste for the popular arts, found in forums like the *New Yorker*, set out the grounds for the wholesale rejection of the worldview encountered in such journals: "The *New Yorker* has always dealt with experience not by trying to understand it but by prescribing the attitude to be adopted toward it. This makes it possible to feel intelligent without thinking, and it is a way of making everything tolerable, for the assumption of a suitable attitude toward experience can give one the illusion of having dealt with it adequately." Warshow understood the study of film to be dominated by sociological and aesthetic theories, but he saw neither strand as being a particularly fruitful engagement with the movies: "The sociological critic says to us, in effect: it is not *I* who goes to see the movies; it is the audience. The aesthetic critic says: It is not the *movies* I go to see; it is art."[42] Discussing Farber's similar rejection of such sensibilities, Phelps wrote, "The clamorous geography of this world informs everything he writes, or paints, and still more important—so does his sense of himself as a pedestrian witness to this world—as anything but Cortez."[43] This is to say as much as Warshow did when he wrote that a "man watches a movie, and the critic must acknowledge that he is that man."[44] In the best of their critical writings Alloway, Farber, and Warshow became that man.

Since the publication of Farber's essay "Termite Art," the uncovering and tracking of the trails left by "termite-tapeworm-fungus-moss-art" has become a major critical endeavor, but Farber's work was not without precedent.[45] The most important, and immediate, influence on Farber was the 1930s jazz and movie critic Otis Ferguson, who wrote the bulk of his film criticism for the *New Republic*, from 1933 to 1942. In his dispatches from New York's cinemas he presented a view of European imports and Hollywood's quotidian productions that met them on their own terms. As with his jazz criticism, Ferguson's film reviews were pitched as three-way conversations between himself, the filmmakers, and their audience. In jazz and the movies, he believed, one could hear the voice of the common American. Accordingly, the movies had a democratic calling: "For the most beautiful thing about the movies is that they are still so close to their public that good work is usually appreciated on the spot."[46]

In his review of *The Roaring Twenties* Ferguson praised its familiar dimensions and recognizable features: "Somebody—the director, the writer, or both—did some very fine things to keep this story human: just the hint of a feeling rather than the blowing of it in your face like soapsuds, the clasped hands on a table, the single word and turn and cut, the pace of a scene determined by its mood" (Ferguson 278). When they were at their most effective the movies shared a language with their audience, which was expressed in those moments where technique, performance, dialogue, and story coalesce to re-create the textures, tones, and facts of everyday life: "If you think back to *It Happened One Night*, you will remember that it wasn't the plot, which was corny, or the dialogue, which was the sort to snap the brim of a very old hat very smartly. It was a trick of building a whole thing out of little ordinary things, all caught in the shifting eye of the camera" (ibid., 23).

Like Farber, Ferguson cherished films where the protagonists were given physical problems to solve, where they had something tangible to test themselves against. Although by no means exclusively, the movies he tended to champion dealt with "truck drivers, linesmen, floorwalkers, train dispatchers, fighters and promoters, and the working press—the movies wade right into them. Doctors and nurses and district attorneys too . . . rather than go nagging along with a thousand more modern instances, I will remind you of a film called *Ceiling Zero*, which I couple with *Grand Illusion* whenever I think of the best expression of men in their calling, whether at odds or together" (Ferguson 10–11). When the movies reneged on their democratic principles they became affected, envious of the high standing of the other arts, pretentious, and therefore of no use to Ferguson.

Against the film that craved cultural respectability, he preferred the lowly calling of a crime melodrama such as the "*Lady in the Morgue*, a routine Crime Club job on a Jonathan Latimer novel, and manufactured out of Universal's shoestring at that. . . . It has humor and action and keeps moving busily along; and if it isn't so much, you at least aren't pestered by its trying to be. Humor and action and moves busily along—and that, if you think back to Ince and the Keystone lot, was why movies were born in the first place" (Ferguson 221–22). For Ferguson the "art" of the movies was never capitalized, never the uppercase *A*. He had a particular distaste for film adaptations of literary or theatrical properties that paid too much respect to their sources. "Art," he wrote, "is often most healthy when it doesn't stick out all over everything like a bagful of nails" (229). For this reason he was particularly generous in his praise for the well-made genre film: "*The Adventures of Sherlock Holmes* . . . is not the sort of thing to be considered a Work of Art: my point is simply that it is an exciting story told with more real movie art per foot than seven reels of anything the intellectual men have been finding good this whole year or more" (271). He disliked overly long movies and stood by the truism that movies should move: "Generally, the film holds together enough to make nice fast watching, solving one of the old old problems in one of the old old ways" (247).

The common touch of American culture, the craft and technique of the movies that can produce a movement of scenes and people responsive enough to pick up on the mercurial dimensions of everyday life, come together in the figure of James Cagney; who might stand as an exemplar of Ferguson's aesthetic:

> He is all crust and speed and snap on the surface, a gutter-fighter with the grace of dancing, a boy who knows all the answers and won't even wait for them, a very fast one. But underneath, the fable: the quick generosity and hidden sweetness, the antifraud straight-as-a-string dealing, the native humor and the reckless drive—everything everybody would like to be, if he had the time sometime. But always this, always: if as a low type he is wrong, you are going to see why. In spite of writers, directors, and the decency legions you are going to see the world and what it does to its people through his subtle understanding of it. (Ferguson 278–79)

Ferguson was not alone among his contemporaries in his enthusiasm for an unpretentious masculine strain in American movies. The novelist and critic Meyer Levin shared his aesthetic:

> I rarely walk out on a picture, and never want to walk out on a simple pro-gramme picture. It is only the more pretentious cinema efforts, the ones that try to be something besides just another movie that may stimulate me to walking out. Such pictures attain a kind of individuality, and if it happens to be the kind of individuality that rubs me up the wrong way, the spell is broken and I want to walk out. But even in the most obnox-ious picture, I can feel the basic, physical hypnosis of the medium. I want to sit and let the thing roll on and on. . . . They [run-of-the-mill pictures] roll along, and you would be really shocked if they should roll out of the routine. It would be like a pulp story turning Faulkner. . . . You are will-ingly hypnotized, and each time the trance is deeper, because you have comfortably given up suspicion, you know the litany, you know the ritual will never be betrayed. That's the movie in its most essential form; it's just a punk picture and I like it.[47]

In this formulation the movies are a type of street-level public art—everyday, democratic. "Punk" pictures presented a corrective to the pretentious, high-blown, and, not coincidentally, feminine cultures of consumption that these male critics were pushing against.

Following on the heels of Ferguson and Levin was James Agee, who also liked films to make a strong appeal to, in Farber's phrase, "a bit of male truth." Reviewing *Dillinger* (Monogram, 1945), Agee wrote: "admirably terse, it provides a tinnily entertaining, cinematically energetic antidote to the two-hour doses of pure unflavored gelatin now alarmingly on the increase. Significantly, it was made quickly on very little money, as pictures go, and for a humble but reliable audience—the general equivalent of the audience which reads pulp magazines. Its overall cost was $150,000. It was shot in 21 days. The screenplay was slapped together in a week."[48] Compressed in both playing time and shooting schedule, the ideal film with masculine appeal is fast, energetic, functional, and eco-nomic. It is stripped back and streamlined, nothing extraneous, no unnecessary embellishment, no feminine trimmings.

In an article for the *Hollywood Quarterly* written in 1947, the New York film exhibitor Arthur Mayer wrote of the need for more "B" movies and of the dire effect the end of block-booking was having on the production of innovative movies: "Untrammelled by either huge costs or the necessity of 'protecting' an investment in a featured player, [B movies] provided a field for occasional experiments in thematic material, and a testing ground for new directors, writ-ers, cameramen, and actors. Out of these 'B's' came much that was appalling, but a saving fraction that made for progress and higher standards."[49] Mayer's defense of the Hollywood production and distribution system, with its "fumbling" and "crawling" progression, echoed those heard by critics such as Farber, Agee, Levin, and Ferguson. Creative and inventive solutions can follow the imposition of tight budgets, formulaic narratives, and restricted production values when craftsmen with ambitions to do "good" work, not to make great art, are presented with the opportunity.

The context of the viewing experience helped fashion Farber's habit of viewing movies with a truant and unruly eye, feeding back into the films he connected with as if there was a symbiotic loop linking critic, film, and audience.[50] In his 1946 review of *The Killers*, Farber wrote, "Besides its brutality, it has noise, the jagged, tormenting movement of keyed-up, tough, flashy humanity that you get from a walk through Times Square."[51] The *demimonde* of Times Square was also the perfect audience to watch underground movies with: "The hard-bitten action film finds its natural home in caves: the murky, congested theatres, looking like glorified tattoo parlors on the outside and located near bus terminals in big cities. These theatres roll action films in what, at first, seems like a nightmarish atmosphere of shabby transience, prints that seem overgrown with jungle moss, sound tracks infected with hiccups. The spectator watches two or three action films go by and leaves feeling as though he were a pirate discharged from a giant sponge."[52]

Farber's authentication of his filmgoing experiences, and the acts of discrimination between Hollywood's commercial products, is a form of slumming, a crossing of the proverbial tracks. Like the white patrons of the 1920s and 1930s who went uptown to Harlem to the black-and-tan clubs to consume a more delirious, spontaneous, invigorating, physical spectacle than could be found in the sphere of *cultural* sophistication below 110th Street, going underground, Farber gets his movie fix in cinema's urban terminal zones.

In the 1950s, west of Broadway, where the first-run houses, the Roxy, Loew's State, and the Paramount, were located, there was a strip of theaters, each of which specialized in a certain type of movie: "The Times Square presented westerns. The Hudson offered violence and action-genre films. The Victory offered war movies, the Empire domestic, non-military violence (e.g. Fritz Lang's *The Big Heat*, 1953), the Lyric showed non-advertised first runs. The Selwyn ran second-run box-office flops, and the Liberty less successful, third-run mainstream misses. The Apollo specialized in foreign films, and the Rialto 'art,' mostly horror and soft-core sex."[53] These theaters were at the heart of Farber's underground.

In the 1930s the New York theater district, concentrated in and around Times Square, entered a period of economic decline that would not be halted until the 1990s. The 1939 WPA guide to New York noted that on "Forty-second Street west of Broadway, once the show place of the district, famous theaters have been converted into movie 'grind' houses devoted to continuous double feature programs of burlesque shows."[54] The theater historian Brooks McNamara writes, "As huge, elaborate movie palaces like the Paramount and the Roxy arose on Broadway and Seventh Avenue, the old Forty-second Street houses could no longer compete and were forced to lengthen their hours and lower both their prices and artistic sights."[55] All the Forty-second Street theaters had midnight screenings, and many stayed open until 3:30 a.m.

At the intersection of Forty-second Street and Broadway stood the Rialto, which had been run as a cinema specializing in horror and action since 1933. Arthur Mayer, a former Paramount employee and public relations operative for Mae West and Marlene Dietrich, managed the theater. At the Rialto he "instituted the profitable policy of playing nothing but bad pictures." He recalled, "The type of picture we featured was rated strictly masculine fare. . . . It was a source of gratification, morally and financially, to see so many male patrons assert themselves by patronizing the Rialto and not meekly following their women into the Valentino traps operated by my competitors."[56] The Rialto could be entered at street level and via the subway, making it Manhattan's only truly "underground" cinema.[57]

Ferguson provides a singular description of a Forty-second Street–type cinema and its audience:

> The Globe is one of those Broadway fleatraps which hawk at modest prices the pick of the refuse left in the distributor's bin after every theatre exhibitor with any kind of decent pitch has had first, second, and third choice on everything from fair to awful. It has naturally built up its own kind of audience, a trampling, hoarse, and hoodlum pack off the garish sidewalks of what ranks today among the first gutters of the world, Broadway and Seventh, from Fortieth to Fifty-second. . . . You . . . find the picture starting half an hour later than schedule, part of which waiting time is taken up with a throwaway advertising short, and most of the rest of the time is devoted to sweat and suffocation and being walked over. If you can imagine a Turkish bath in a tight seat with all your clothes on, the steam coming from roiling vats of old underwear, you will know what fusty anachronism is ahead of you.[58]

During the 1960s, in his *Village Voice* column, the avant-garde filmmaker, publisher, and journalist Jonas Mekas wrote a number of pieces on Times Square cinemas: "Go to 42nd Street, where you can always find a Western. The Times Square Theatre, which shows Westerns exclusively, is always full, day or night. A sad, lonely crowd, made up usually of older people. It's like an old people's home, a hundred per cent male. The American Western keeps them company. They sit there, in the midst of all that poetry sweeping grandly across the screen, dreaming away."[59] And, like Farber, he cast this audience and its

4. Press ad for double bill of *Brute Force* and *Naked City* (1947/1948).

environs as an underground, a secret world of shadows and the forbidden: "I hear some people want to clear up 42nd Street. What would we do without our movie joints, our hamburgers, our secret places? Clean places! We need more shadows, that's what I say. There we can cultivate forbidden virtues and forbidden beauties. Man needs unnecessary, unclean corners" (75). Mekas saw little

contradiction in his love for cinema's more immediate pleasures and his participation in the avant-garde.

Discussing Mekas's use of the term *underground*, the film historian Juan A.
Suárez noted that it had "great critical fortune, due to its descriptive power and
its cultural history, which pointed to both the modernist and the avant-gardist
components of the movement."[60] By this he meant that it signified both a with-
drawal from and a burrowing into mass culture. By the late 1960s underground
film was believed to be a phenomenon that best described American avant-
garde film practice and exhibition.[61] In its anti-Art stance, its cultural illegitimacy, its evocation of the primitive, its willingness to investigate the lurid and
the taboo, this form of underground film would appear to find a rich complement in pulp films admired by Farber.

The films produced by underground artists such as Jack Smith, Andy Warhol,
and Kenneth Anger drew liberally from the common currency of Hollywood
archetype and myth—arch-reflexivity and exaggeration were endemic, symptoms of a camp sensibility. But this new underground also readily inverted the
gender certainties of underground film as established by Farber, just as his
underground transvalued Hollywood's films. As the 1960s progressed, the common ground of cultural illegitimacy shared by the two undergrounds induced
interesting production overlaps, mutually supportive exhibition practices, and
corresponding critical and scholarly pathways. And not the least of these is the
suggestion made by the avant-garde film historian David E. James that the
Farber-esque action film contested Hollywood from within while the avant-
garde did it from without.[62]

Mekas's anarchic tastes and open and eclectic approach to editing his
journal, *Film Culture*, produced some marvelous juxtapositions. The winter
1962/63 issue had Andrew Sarris's "Notes on the Auteur Theory," Kael's review
of Truffaut's *Shoot the Piano Player*, Jack Smith's homage to Maria Montez, and
Farber's development of his theory of underground movies in "White Elephant
Art vs. Termite Art." In the spring 1964 issue, which was largely devoted to
Anger's work, a letter to Sarris from Samuel Fuller was reproduced alongside
a production still from *The Naked Kiss* and a series of frame enlargements from
the film's opening scene. The images of a bald Constance Towers attacking the
camera are not out of place alongside the journal's more usual avant-garde fare,
and in retrospect, at least, the idea of Fuller touting his sexploitation film to
intellectuals like Sarris and Mekas does not seem at all strange.

The trancelike pull of "punk movies," as Levin called run-of-the-mill films
in the 1930s, is best experienced, he believed, in second-run theaters such as
the Sheridan Square in Greenwich Village, where an "expectant mood raised by
the advance promotion is no longer in effect." There, on almost "any evening,
you can run into some of the nation's highest thinkers, standing in line at the
box-office, to get their weekly or bi-weekly dosage."[63] Underground or punk

movies in a suitably nonbourgeois setting had a clear appeal to certain segments of the intelligentsia.

While on a "reviewer's holiday," and covering similar ground to that covered by Farber, Ferguson, Mekas, and Levin, James Agee chanced upon a screening of Val Lewton's *The Curse of the Cat People* (1944), which he watched with a "regular Times Square Horror audience." This is a "specialized audience, unobstreperous [*sic*—he surely meant they are 'obstreperous'], poor, metropolitan, and deeply experienced. The West Times Square audience is probably, for that matter, the finest movie audience in the country (certainly, over and over, it has proved its infinite superiority to the run of the 'art theater' devotees—not to mention, on paper which must brave the mails, the quality and conduct of Museum of Modern Art film audiences)."[64] The validation of a proletarian audience's taste over and above the acts of distinction performed by an educated elite may not have been quite the act of obscenity that Agee suggested would get the postmaster general hot under the collar, but it may have provoked a reaction from his readers who would not generally be inclined to attend a cinema specializing in horror movies.

Uncovering the "Muck" school of American comedy personified by Ernie Kovacs, Lenny Bruce, and *Mad* magazine, Phelps, who followed Farber as he had followed Ferguson, suggested this form of humor could best be appreciated by a visit to "one of the Movie Row caverns around Times Square; watch the frequent reactions of the audience to any film prolific in scenes of sadism, rough-house sexual fummadiddles or simple larceny; and gage these reactions against the reactions which Archer Winsten or Bosley Crowther has informed you are mandatory to such films."[65] By aligning himself with the proletarian Times Square movie audiences, like Farber, Ferguson, and Agee before him, Phelps was displaying a contemptuous attitude to middle-class values—here personified by the *New York Times* critic Crowther. As with like-minded critics, Phelps understood that west of Times Square, down Forty-second Street was where the *real* audiences were to be found.[66]

In a 1953 review for *The Nation*, Farber defended the Forty-second Street audience:

It is a custom among professional pipe smokers to offer romantic estimations of American moviegoers. The latest evaluation appeared in the *New Leader*—a tongue-in-cheek description of the action-movie fans who attend shabby theatres west of Times Square. It was a classic case of what happens when a critic turns sociologist. Mr. Markfield found that the largely male audience for action and horror pictures was made up of a desperate crew—perverts, adolescent hoodlums, chronic unemployeds, and far-gone neurotics—who possessed an impeccable taste in good, unpretentious off-beat films. These moviegoers shuddered or tittered, snored or shrieked obscenities. But somehow, while unable to control their bodies and emotions in the slightest degree, they were movie critics who simply couldn't be fooled by the expensive or pretentious.[67]

Farber concluded his defense of the action-horror crowd by noting the difference between his and Markfield's dallying with the proletariat. Farber wished "to encourage moviegoers to look at the screen instead of trying to find a freak show in the audience."[68] Farber and his fellow intellectuals, who loved roughneck movies, were no more than a small but vocal clique. The larger part of the audience west of Times Square probably did not read *The Nation* but probably did read Mickey Spillane. Spillane sometimes had his hero watch a Forty-second Street horror movie: "The lead feature had an actor with a split personality. One was man, the other was ape. When he was ape he killed people and when he was man he regretted it. I could imagine how he felt."[69] Mike Hammer's appreciation of movies was rather more literal than Farber's.

In 1952 Farber wrote, "The reason movies are bad lies in this audience's failure to appreciate, much less fight for, films like the unspectacular, unpolished 'B,' worked out by a few people with belief and skill in their art, who capture the unworked-over immediacy of life before it has been cooled by 'Art.' These artists are liberated from such burdens as having to recoup a large investment, or keeping a star's personality intact before the public; they can experiment with inventive new ideas instead of hewing to the old sure-fire box-office formula."[70] The idea that the low-budget film and creativity had something in common was a felt presence in 1950s film criticism. In "In Defense of Action Films" Mekas wrote, "You fools who look down on Westerns, who go only to 'art' films, preferably European—you don't know what you are missing. You are missing half of the cinema, you are missing the purest poetry of action, poetry of motion, poetry of the Technicolor landscapes."[71]

In 1963, when Pauline Kael called the *Village Voice* critic Andrew Sarris and the British *Movie* critics to account for their boyhood devotion to "virile" filmmakers, she produced a critique that could more readily be laid against Farber, who preceded her objects of scorn in celebrating roughneck movies in roughhouse theaters. Unlike Farber, Kael does not bond with the brotherhood of the action-horror crowd: "These critics work embarrassingly hard trying to give some semblance of intellectual respectability to a preoccupation with mindless, repetitious commercial products—the kind of action movies that the restless, rootless men who wander on 42nd Street and in the Tenderloin of all our big cities have always preferred just because they could respond to them without thought. These movies soak up your time."[72] By 1969, however, Kael's position on action movies had shifted.

In her 1969 essay "Trash Art and the Movies," in an echo of Farber, Ferguson, et al., Kael argued, "The lowest action trash is preferable to wholesome family entertainment. When you clean them up, when you make movies respectable, you kill them. The well-spring of their *art*, their greatness, is not being respectable. . . . If we have grown up with the movies we know that good work is continuous not with the academic, respectable tradition but with glimpses of something good in trash, but we want the subversive gesture carried to the domain of discovery. Trash has given us an appetite for art."[73] Kael's support and promotion of trash movies as a rude yet vital alternative to "respectable" forms of cinema, which she understands as being embodied in the idea of "family entertainment," is caught up in the belief that certain examples of low-brow entertainments have the potential to subvert the legitimate arts, or at least to reject their easy pieties and complacent certainties. Like pulp and punk, Kael's trash movies are venerated because an enervating middlebrow, domesticated, feminized culture of good taste has not emasculated them.

A New York film critic who did believe in the principles of good taste, John Simon, attempted to put Kael's endorsement of trash movies into some kind of perspective in the introduction to his 1971 collection of film criticism. There had been, he noted, a change in the status of film and film criticism in recent years; symptomatic of that change was the debate over whether it was "movies" or "films" that were being discussed:

> When a group that was to become the National Society of Film Critics pondered at its first meetings what name to settle on, some members, and notably Pauline Kael, argued for the term Movie Critics instead of Film Critics. . . . There is, obviously, no harm in calling films movies, or cinema, or flicks, or anything else. Nevertheless, "movies" is a diminutive of "motion pictures" . . . [and] a diminutive is not what one usually applies to an art. . . . The implication is that we go to the movies purely for fun, and to hell with the highbrows, scholars and other squares who would try to turn a movie into Art.[74]

What concerned Simon was the loss of a sense of distinction, proportion, and value. The movement into the critical fray of advocates for the "movie" meant, he argued, that buffs were threatening to overrun the asylum: "For the movies are the cheapest and most accessible playground for the acquisition of meaningless expertise, and the fellow who can rattle off the filmography of George Cukor or Douglas Sirk is no better than the guy who memorizes baseball batting averages, but usually much more pretentious" (4). Particularly reprehensible, Simon believed, are the fallacies of auteurism that gave greater value to the "atrocious" work of Edgar G. Ulmer and the "abysmal" direction of Samuel Fuller than it does to films that attempt to deal genuinely and openly with profound matters (3, 8).

By 1971 Simon was at best fighting a rearguard action against the transvaluation of pulp films; indeed, he was not just kicking back against his contemporaries, such as Kael and the *Village Voice* critic and auteurist advocate Andrew Sarris. Even if it was unknown to him, the "perverse" overvaluation of pulp film went back, beyond Ferguson, to at least the second decade of the century. Simon was railing against a critical position with a long history of provoking proponents who held a firm belief in notions of good taste. An archaeologist of pop modernism, Juan A. Suárez has uncovered an interest in pulp cinema in the pages of the Dada-inflected avant-garde journal *The Soil*, published in New York between 1914 and 1920. In this journal writers spoke out against the dominance of the photoplay to the detriment of "visual motion" and celebrated the action serial, where performers were valued for their athleticism and movement rather than "their ability to convey subjective density." Suárez records how the debate on motion pictures was carried over into the pages of *Broom*, another New York Dada-influenced journal, where a cheaply made serial is championed over and above lavish spectaculars. Moreover these serials had to be watched in neighborhood theaters, far from glamorous first-run houses. Without any apparent cultural capital, the action serial was valued for its "lack of pretension and [its] physicality . . . for the speed and excitement of the improbable narrative: 'characters dashed out of places and in again, men grappled, tumbled off freight cars, and rolled down embankments.'"[75]

This provocative view of cinema was something that the iconoclastic British critic Raymond Durgnat would no doubt have enjoyed. Recalling an interview given by Sarris, which began "with a sustained defence in intellectual depth of his auteur theory, and concluded by confessing that what really kept him coming to the cinema was its girls," Durgnat noted that here was the "beginning of wisdom. . . . Here, however shyly, the old Adam peeps out from behind the *pince-nez* of culture, and the bland, shining mask of 'objectivity' cracks to reveal a human expression."[76] Pulp erotica, in other words. The prurient appeal for critics of Hollywood's movies was allied to American film's style and form, which Durgnat described as "fast, bold, terse, flexible and clear. Its sharp cuts and bold reverse angles express a philosophy of life as fact confronting fact, face confronting face, in a series of collisions and challenges, a philosophy of dynamic action-reaction, viewing life as a sequence of decisions tending to some purpose. It has the limitations, but it has also the meanings and merits, of any 'classicism'" (76–77).

Hollywood's particular "classicism" derived, he believed, from a "wedding of poetry and pulp." He writes, "Our implication is that some pulp-movies are very much more considerable than others, that the mythic can be distinguished from the cliché, that, through the myth, movies communicate with people's *real* doubt and feelings, that such movies are in a very real sense 'good' art as opposed to others which are in a very real sense 'bad' art. This isn't to elevate the subversive possibilities of entertainment above its reinforcing of social attitudes" (268–69). Durgnat's critical position on the movies may be summed up by his belief that "the whole point of appreciating a good film which happens to be couched in the idiom of a pulp thriller is that you don't lower your normal standards an inch, you're no more indulgent to Bond than you would have been to Liberace or Rin-Tin-Tin" (75). Durgnat works outside of the tension between middle-class puritan and the unregenerate masses (155). He searches for the poetry in commercial cinema, which he finds in its permutations of "fact, drama, the 'Surreal,' dream, magic and the supernatural powers at their play. Perhaps we too readily assume the mass media's lack of, and antagonism towards, poetry" (238). Durgnat understood the poetry of pulp to consist of the exploration of irrationalities (224).

What is being repeated across all of these accounts is the expressed desire for an authentic experience, for the truth that lies hidden inside a falsifying culture of consumption. The emasculating experience that these critics believed they faced when confronted by this everyday culture was best resisted by burrowing deep into its subterranean depths, where in dark shadows and dimly lit caverns a masculine culture could be found. This underworld was explored and mapped by skilled critics who had developed an acute, razor-sharp, ability to discriminate between the products of the popular arts, to find the authentic, to recognize certain male truths, and to detect acts of feminine deception. In short, they sought to identify, justify, and promote a male ethos as a barrier against the stultifying effects of the middle-class culture that otherwise defined and contained them.

When Simon was writing his defense of film's potential as an art form, it was not yet clear what direction film culture would move toward. Since the late 1940s, the steady influx of European art movies into the American market worked as an extraordinary counterweight to any perceived critical overvaluation of commercial movies. But what would finally resolve the issue, or at least strike it mute, was the growth in film studies as an academic discipline. From the mid-1970s, film scholars, not critics, led the debate over the value and function of American movies. This shift in authority was most pronounced in Great Britain.

In her 1996 essay "Americanitis: European Intellectuals and Hollywood Melodrama," Laura Mulvey revisited her own history as a film scholar in the context of an emerging film studies culture, discussing in particular the 1960s generation of cinephiles' fascination with Hollywood. American film was, she wrote, "energetic and cathartic, a cinema of the machine age, streamlined and commodified, able to produce and repeat successful formulas, stories or stars, as Detroit might produce motor cars. This cinema stood in direct opposition to high cultural values encrusted with the weight and authority of tradition. European intellectuals took up American cinema partly in a spirit of political polemics with the traditions and values of their own culture."[77] Mulvey was part of a group of film critics and scholars who sought to revitalize British film culture through establishing the importance of studying American genre films. At the heart of this endeavor was the Education Department at the British Film Institute.

Under the leadership of Paddy Whannel, the Education Department grew rapidly during the 1960s, as did the parallel organization the Society for Education in Film and Television (SEFT), which published *Screen Education* and *Screen*. Through these two organizations there emerged a generation of film scholars who would decisively change the direction of British film culture and have a considerable impact on the study of film in North America. Scholars linked to the BFI or SEFT in the 1960s and 1970s included Laura Mulvey, Alan Lovell, Ed Buscombe, Sam Rhodie, Richard Combs, Stephen Heath, Colin McCabe, Jim Kitses, Jim Cook, Pam Cook, Stuart Hall, E. Ann Kaplan, Ian Christie, Colin McArthur, Geoffrey Nowell-Smith, Claire Johnson, Christine Gledhill, Sylvia Harvey, David Lusted, Ben Brewster, Jim Hillier, Tom Ryall, Douglas Pye, Elizabeth Cowie, John Caughie, Steve Neale, and Paul Willeman. Initially the Education Department concentrated its efforts on encouraging the study of films in schools and further education colleges, particularly in liberal and general studies courses aimed at recent school leavers, who as part of their employment were expected to attend college one day a week.[78]

If the study of film was to appeal to school pupils, or day-release students, it was essential, Kitses argued, to work with films they would "respond to and find meaningful in terms of their experience." This meant dealing with the commercial cinema. In his 1966 primer on teaching film to young people, Kitses wrote about the difficulties involved in getting students to talk about film in ways that were very often antithetical to their consumption of movies. In one particularly telling transcript of a class that used Kubrick's *Paths of Glory* as the focus of study, the students debate what they expect from the film experience:

TEACHER: Why do we go?

CHORUS: Entertainment.

CHRISTINE: Education.

GILLIAN (SCORNFULLY): Depends on what you're being educated in.

CHRISTINE: It does educate you because it makes your mind work . . .

WENDY: Who wants to think? You can think anytime.[79]

It is no great exaggeration to claim that encouraging student interest, without alienating them from the learning process, was the crucial problem that drove many of the most important developments in the study of film in Britain in the 1960s.[80] At the core of this public-funded project was a desire to engage in an educational film program that was in line with left-leaning working-class values: a desire equal to and commensurate with the American quest to find "a bit of male truth" in the activity of filmgoing. Such was the energy and resolve behind the project to expand access to film studies that, beginning in 1973, the BFI took the program to the very citadels of bourgeois learning when it began sponsoring university lectureships, first with Robin Wood's appointment at Warwick and, in following years, Richard Dyer's post at Keele, Peter Wollen's at Essex, Charles Barr's at East Anglia, and Ben Brewster's at Kent.[81]

The importance of American cinema within this extraordinary development in film education, and the debate over its value, can be gauged by looking at a small booklet published by the British Film Institute: Alan Lovell's *Don Siegel: American Cinema*. The study was produced to coincide with a retrospective of the director's films programmed at the National Film Institute. It included a translation of a *Positif* interview with Siegel, some follow-up questions posed to Siegel by Lovell, a filmography, and Lovell's critical account of Siegel's films. Also included was the response to a questionnaire that had been given to a selection of British film critics and scholars. The purpose of this survey was to weigh critical attitudes to popular American cinema.[82] By the time the booklet had had a chance to be read and debated, however, the world had moved on. In an update published seven years later Lovell noted the irony of the date of its initial appearance, April 1968. The seismic events in Paris the following month and the cultural change wrought in their wake threw the debates around American cinema into sharp relief; by the mid-1970s it was impossible for progressive-minded critics and scholars to write about film and ignore the regressive politics of the Hollywood machine.[83]

With this context in mind Lovell looked back on the project with which he and his fellow critics had been involved. He suggested that three intellectual currents had informed the debate up until that point in April 1968. The first was the fundamental intellectual influence of F. R. Leavis, whose ideas on literature and the "Great Tradition" provided a context for the debates on popular culture and the arts carried out in the work of Raymond Williams, Richard Hoggart, Stuart Hall, and Paddy Whannel. Their shared project, if such it can be called, was to counter the deadening influence of mass culture, though, by the time Hall and Whannel took up the debate, the focus had shifted from evaluating the best that a culture can offer to "the problems of value and evaluation in the media."[84] The second intellectual current was the work of the French theorists and critics at *Cahiers du cinéma*, and the emphasis on the concept of mise-en-scène and the critical attention directed toward formal analysis in order to articulate a director's themes and values.[85] In the shape of the ideas of Claude Lévi-Strauss and Roland Barthes, structuralism formed the third current of influence.

According to Lovell these critical positions presented the possibility that the study of film might become more "intellectually formidable and less restricted by the accidents of personal temperament" (5). Whether given over to subjective readings or to more objective analysis, the aim was to produce an evaluative criticism that no longer paid "tribute to the conventional prestige of high culture" (5). Leavis may have started this revolution in attending to the evaluation of culture, but, by the time his ideas had filtered down to British cinephiles, his attempt to maintain a cultural hierarchy was being seriously undermined, even with the contradiction that by "using the notion of the 'talented artist' as its [film studies] central critical category it assimilated the American cinema to orthodox ways of thinking about the arts" (6). This contradictory cleaving to tradition and revolution characterized much of the key activities in British film studies in the 1960s and 1970s.

On the effects of the events of May 1968 Lovell wrote:

> The combination of the erosion of the cinema as a form of mass entertainment with a greater political awareness in film criticism changed the attitude towards Hollywood films from a positive to a negative one. The problem of the popular appeal of mass culture didn't pose itself so insistently. . . . Increased political awareness, particularly that generated by the Vietnam war, redirected attention to Hollywood's ideological role. The consequence was that Hollywood resumed the position it had in the original mass culture debate—it was the enemy to be combated.[86]

The shocks of 1968 did not take immediate effect: work in progress on studies of Hollywood directors and genres continued to be published in journals and small monographs, most notably in the BFI-sponsored Cinema One series, which between 1967 and 1976 published works on Joseph Losey, Billy Wilder, Buster Keaton, Rouben Mamoulian, Samuel Fuller, Douglas Sirk, Orson Welles, Val Lewton, Elia Kazan, John Ford, and George Cukor, alongside two genre studies of the western and one on the gangster film: Philip French's *Westerns*, Jim Kitses's *Horizons West*, and Colin McArthur's *Underworld USA*.

Kitses and McArthur were mainstays of the British film culture community that developed around Whannel and the BFI, and their studies are brought together with the stated aim, according to McArthur, of showing "that the supposed constraints on the artist working within a commercial/industrial structure such as Hollywood may be better described as disciplines. The necessity of working within narrative and genre, with prescribed stars, a strong producer's hand and forceful collaborators, may lead not to a diminution but to an intensification of the artifact's force and range through the ironing out of its purely coterie elements."[87] Don Siegel is presented as his exemplar, but McArthur also covers the crime films of Fritz Lang, John Huston, Jules Dassin, Robert Siodmak, Elia Kazan, Nicholas Ray, Samuel Fuller, and Jean-Pierre Melville, alongside short pieces on the background, development, and iconography of the crime film genre. McArthur's identification of the role of genre as "disciplining" the auteur is used with the understanding that it enables a modification of auteurist criticism that will enable him to engage in a more profound evaluation of individual films.[88] Despite McArthur's call on the determining role of genre on certain films and directors, his objective, as with auteurism, was to isolate examples and individuals, to define the best that was on offer.

Kitses followed a similar path, advancing the idea that filmmakers were working within an "American *tradition*" and that the conventions of the form are a "gift" provided for its practitioners.[89] *Horizons West* is subtitled "Studies of Authorship *within* the Western" (my emphasis). Kitses was looking to find a balance between individual achievement and structural conventions.[90]

In a 1973 review of the impact of auteur theory on the study of film, Ed Buscombe built on the work of McArthur and Kitses: "The test of a theory is whether it produces new knowledge. The auteur theory produced much, but of a very partial kind, and much it left totally unknown." Asking how things might move forward, Buscombe outlined three areas with which film studies needed to occupy itself: (1) the effect of cinema on society, (2) the effect of society on cinema, and (3) the effect of films on other films; "this would especially involve questions of genre, which only means that some films have a *very* close relation to other films. But all films are affected by the previous history of the cinema. This is only one more thing that traditional *auteur* theory could not cope with. It identified the code of the *auteur*; but was silent on those codes intrinsic to the cinema, as well as those originating outside it."[91] Buscombe's position no longer depended on the need to establish a filmmaker's artistic worth, however contextualized, in order to validate the study of popular cinema. This was a course developed further by Steve Neale in his monograph *Genre* (1980).

Neale sought to negotiate the theoretical discourses that had become established as the new orthodoxies of film studies. His objective was to "relocate the discussion of and importance accorded to genre, hence to rework, replace and to a large extent transform the basic terms and concepts used in and promoted by that discussion."[92] But what Neale hoped would become an opening gambit in a revitalized debate about film and genre became instead an end point. Throughout the 1980s his work was repeatedly referenced in scholarly articles, yet it was rarely extended or challenged in any substantive way.

This lack of debate was further evidence that, post-1975, work on American commercial cinema, at least as it was once defined by Whannel, Kitses, Lovell, and McArthur, was now of only marginal interest to the new discipline of Film Studies. The plethora of monographs on American directors exemplified by the Cinema One and Studio Vista series had come to a halt by the late 1970s.[93] During the 1980s, British interest in American action movies found a shadowy home in the back pages of the *Monthly Film Bulletin*, under the editorship of

Richard Combs, but when commercial imperatives amalgamated the journal with its sister publication, *Sight & Sound*, in 1992, there was no alternative British outlet for such critical work.

Since his days at the BFI, Combs's criticism has been published in *Film Comment*. Outside of editing a booklet on Robert Aldrich (1978), he has yet to produce a book-length study of the films and filmmakers championed so eloquently over the years, nor has there been a collection of his criticism. Whannel died in 1980, and though leaving a marked influence on his colleagues at the BFI, he published little on film after his work with Hall in 1964. Following the Siegel booklet, Lovell has published intermittently on documentary film, film acting, and most recently contemporary Hollywood but nothing on the postwar action film. After writing *Horizons West*, Kitses left the BFI and returned to his native country, the United States, to teach. He did not publish on film again until 1996, a gap of seventeen years, when he became one of the first contributors to the BFI's Film Classics series with his study of *Gun Crazy*.[94] Alongside writing film reviews during the 1970s for the socialist weekly the *Tribune*, McArthur refocused his interest on questions of film and national identity in his studies of Scottish cinema, but he returned to American genre films, like Kitses, with a contribution to the Classics series with a volume on Lang's *The Big Heat*.[95] The series was originally edited by Ed Buscombe, who had entered the orbit of Whannel and Kitses at a BFI summer school in 1967, dedicated to the study of the western. Buscombe produced one of the key essays on genre theory for *Screen* in 1970 and worked in the education and publishing departments of the BFI from 1974 to 1996. He did not produce a substantial work on an American genre until the publication in 1988 of the encyclopedia *The BFI Companion to the Western*.[96]

Given the fervor that these advocates of American action movies displayed in the 1960s and early 1970s at the BFI summer schools, the Edinburgh Film Festivals, and in the pages of *Sight & Sound*, *Monthly Film Bulletin*, *Movie*, and *Screen*, the cessation of research and publishing from them on westerns, gangster films, and other genre movies through much of the 1980s until the present day is extraordinary, yet it is also, given the direction film studies took, not at all surprising. These were men writing about male-oriented films that they had grown up with, that had helped shape their being. In an essay on the western and film criticism, Douglas Pye wrote:

> Among the key changes to the analysis of popular cinema in the mid seventies were those associated with gender and spectatorship, particularly in the work of feminist critics interested in exploring the place of women—as characters, directors, stars, audiences—in the Hollywood of the studio period. As this work developed, it focused on melodrama and film noir rather than genres of male action, and with the emphasis

on the exploration of fields relatively untouched by previous criticism and the reconceptualisation of whole areas of representation and of a generic form, the Western was largely abandoned—it became in effect the ghost town of genre criticism.[97]

Work that appeared on the western and other male-oriented genres since the heyday of the 1960s and early 1970s has invariably focused on questions of identity politics, Mulvey's hugely influential article on visual pleasure is symptomatic of this turn to politics, and it is noteworthy that she aimed her criticism squarely at the films of the key auteurs: Hawks, Hitchcock, and Sternberg. "Visual Pleasure and Narrative Cinema" was published in *Screen* in 1975; in a follow-up essay, published in 1981, Mulvey turned her attention to the western in the guise of *Duel in the Sun*.[98] In an interview Mulvey conducted with Peter Wollen on British film culture in the 1960s (with a particular focus on the influence of Paddy Whannel), she noted:

> If it had not been for the background of cinephilia the "Visual Pleasure" critique would never have been possible. It was a critique that was enabled by cinephilia and a deep love of Hollywood. . . . We felt, by the early 70s, that there was a new world beginning in which the Hollywood we had loved no longer existed. Secondly, it was harder to combine a political allegiance to the left and an allegiance to the culture of the United States. The political spectrum was changing by the late 60s and early 70s. There was the Vietnam War. As our political allegiance shifted towards the Third World there were also more opportunities to see its cinema. And then the idea of a radical avant-garde began to emerge, for instance, at the London Film Makers Co-op. The actual possibility of making films was appearing on the horizon, a whole new horizon of 16 mm.[99]

At the time, this shift in consciousness opened up seemingly insurmountable gaps between entertainment and art. Yet, in retrospect, the gap might more profitably be seen as a continuum. The acts of provocation against middle-class values and the feminine sphere proffered by cinephiles were political acts, even if they were produced in order to shore up "a bit of [working-class or anti-middle-class] male truth." The politics of this generation of male critics and scholars was writhen with contradiction—radical in its affront to middle-class notions of good taste yet deeply reactionary in its celebration of a masculine ethos. Mulvey and other feminists moved cinephilia away from a male-dominated environment toward an engagement with commercial cinema that held identity politics as its principal focus of engagement. One result of this was an eventual plethora of studies on the gender politics of action or male-identified genres, notably Constance Penley's *Close Encounters: Film, Feminism and Science Fiction* (1991), Carol J. Clover's *Men, Women, and Chainsaws: Gender in the Modern Horror Film* (1992), Jane Tompkins's *West of Everything: The Inner Life of Westerns* (1992), and Yvonne Tasker's *Spectacular Bodies: Gender, Genre, and the Action Cinema* (1993). Beyond the shared object of analysis, what the feminist film critics and male cinephiles have in common is an antagonism toward a repressive conservative middle-class status quo.

2

A Genealogy of Pulp

Black Mask to Mickey Spillane

Bad taste leads to crime.

–Sherlock Holmes in *The Story of the Bald-Headed Man*

Like punk, pulp has made the long journey from being a noun for organic matter to becoming a term of disdain, before becoming a marker of distinction against which the quotidian and mediocre can better be recognized. When it meant something other than a moist, slightly cohering raw mass, *pulp* was shorthand for the products of the mid-twentieth century's fiction factories. Its roots were in the proletarian story forms of the nineteenth-century dime novel, formulaic fiction that fed the maw of the newly literate urban working class.[1] Sensational literature was set on the new frontiers of modernity: in space, beneath the waves, in the Wild West, in the jungles of Africa, or on the streets of Chicago. Cowboys, detectives, explorers, adventurers, soldiers, aviators, spacemen, and mechanics were the heroes of popular fiction.[2] *Pulp*, used as a term to describe a particular type of magazine fiction printed on cheap paper stock and bound in a brightly colored, action-filled cover, only entered into the popular vernacular in the late 1920s.[3]

In an August 1929 edition of the *New Republic*, in an article titled "Magazines for Morons," the one-time pulp editor Alvin Barclay outlined pulp's attraction: "A wood-pulp magazine is one of the most diluted forms of pabulum obtainable in America. It is just a half-rung below the average Hollywood movie. For that reason it is, aside from the newspaper, the favorite reading matter of a huge proportion of the reading public."[4] John Locke locates the earliest use of *pulp* to describe a particular story form to a 1929 issue of *Writers Markets and Methods*. The first citation of pulp to indicate a type of popular fiction in the OED is from 1931, in *Frontier* magazine: "We need some outlets for the work, with pay, of young and enthusiastic writers; something to keep them away from the 'pulp' and 'slick paper' magazines."[5] The contrast made between pulp and "slick-paper" publications is important. The latter were aimed at a middle-class

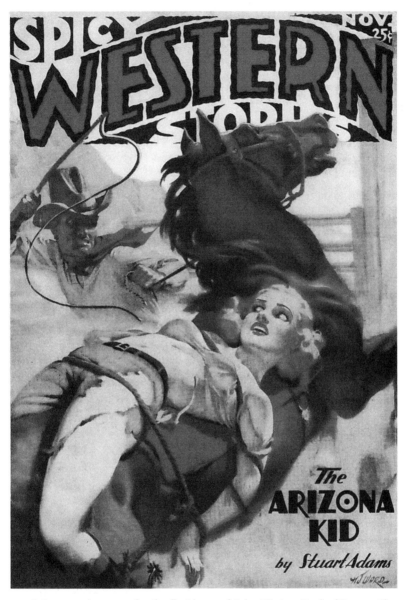

5. Pulp magazine cover for the first issue of *Spicy Western Stories* (Nov. 1936).

market, such as the million-selling periodicals *Saturday Evening Post* and the *Ladies' Home Journal*. They were printed on good paper stock, heavily illustrated, and offered a wide range of articles, features, commentary, and fiction; these up-market magazines were fully capitalized with large staff numbers and supported by mass subscriptions and significant advertising revenue.[6]

In contrast, pulp magazines were printed on cheap paper stock, aimed at working-class readers, contained relatively few advertisements (certainly none from large corporations), and sold in the thousands, not in the millions like the slicks.[7]

As the literary historian Sean McCann notes: "Nearly every aspect of pulp publishing was shaped by . . . minor budgets."[8] Only at the high end of the pulp market, for example in the case of *Black Mask*, did name recognition of an author pay dividends for the publisher. Most contributors wrote under a number of guises, and because they were paid by the word they wrote a great deal of formulaic fiction quickly, without finesse. Though the writers saw themselves as craftsmen, they were in fact akin to factory laborers: writing to fixed deadlines, being paid by the quantity not quality of their work, which was produced within rigid guidelines determined by market-tested narrative formulas, and using stock characters and situations. In a 1935 article in *Writer's Digest* the pulpster Alfred Burke made a direct link between his occupation and industrial labor:

> The sweatshop isn't confined to the clothing manufacturing trade. Its methods have crept into publishing. I shouldn't say it [is] exactly like that. For those methods were current twenty, forty years ago. But a new technique has been brought in. Take the house names deliberately built up so that when its original user has been sucked dry, a fresh fish can take up the pen and continue under that name. Some of the oldest house names have appeared over the work, literally of dozens of writers, many of whose real names have never been known to the public. One of them loses his job, goes to another publisher, tells him he has been writing under such-and-such a house name. the answer he gets is a bored: "So what? Your own name is just as new as anything we got in the house. Lowest rates or shut the door behind you."[9]

Writing about the link between production and product with pulp's predecessor, the dime novel, Bill Brown has noted, "The technology that produced the Western was completed by the narrative technology of the Western itself—a set of interchangeable parts, a standardized structure, and a regularized rhythm of crisis and resolution, event and explanation."[10]

When the bottom dropped out of the sci-fi market in the late 1950s, Robert Silverberg turned to paperback pornography, producing 150 novels between 1959 and 1964 at fifty thousand words per title. Discussing the industrial-like assembly of formula fiction, he writes, "One way I managed to keep up this amazing level of output was to assemble a sheaf of what I called 'modules'— prefabricated sex scenes that I could simply plug into any book. Plots and characters had to change from book to book, of course, but under the highly restrictive rules we were forced to use there were only so many ways to describe what my people were up to in bed, and so I extracted relevant scenes from my books—a basic seduction scene, a copulation scene, a voyeurism scene, a rape scene, a Lesbian scene, and so on—and recycled them into the new manuscripts in the appropriate places as needed."[11]

The final print offspring of the original pulps, men's adventure magazines of the 1950s and 1960s, similarly recycled elements, particularly the visuals. One historian of "the sweats," Steven Heller, writes, "The cuckolded husband one month could be a gay paedophile the following year; a nymphomaniac wife might return as a communist hooker seducing American soldiers," and so on.[12] But more than this essentially superficial recycling, the pulps repeated stories and images with only minor variation to take into account questions of topicality and the need to produce at least the superficies of distinctiveness. In doing so, stock figures, archetypal scenarios, and visual tropes were produced that might best be summarized by pulp's metonym of the bound white woman in a state of distress and dishabille being assaulted by a dark-skinned villain. Factory-made, with standardized, interchangeable parts, pulp's creative machine was a literal pulp engine, which *Webster's New International Dictionary* (1932) described as a "machine with revolving knives or cutters for converting paper stock into pulp." One might imagine it this way: On the conveyor belt moving the dry paper stock toward the whirling blades of the pulp engine is the bound and gagged body of a young woman, her eyes wide open with fear. Feeding the engine is the story's mustachioed, dusky-hued villain, who laughs hideously as the cutters begin to rip into the woman's outer garments; disrobing her before it can rip her into small pieces. Enter the hero . . . *Deus ex machina.*

Pulp was factory-produced periodical fiction for a working-class readership, printed on low-grade paper stock, featuring sensational formulaic stories, marked by a high degree of seriality, ensuring that popular characters and situations reappeared with some regularity across issues. It was cheap, both to produce and to purchase. For its critics pulp was also an inferior, shoddy, form of fiction with cheap morals, exploiting and degrading its naive readers. In a 1932 letter to *Writer's Digest* an editor for Dell Publications confronted the issue of declining sales of the company's pulp titles and revealed the low regard he held for its readers: "The fact is that the buyers of pulps have been hardest hit by the Depression. They look longingly at the money they formerly spent for a magazine. Many of them don't have it. Had they the money they would buy the same magazines they always did. Their tastes have changed only slightly; the readers of pulps represent a distinct section of our population. Morons, if you like. They will always be with us."[13]

The casting of the pulps as literature for morons echoed the characterization aired earlier in the *New Republic*, which also characterized pulp readers as

6. A typical pulp magazine cover: *Dime Mystery Magazine* (Aug. 1937).

immature, a critique that will be repeated in many of the later accounts of pulp found in middlebrow journals:

> Wood-pulp literature caters exclusively to the adolescent mind. The first editor I worked under told me on the first day of my editorial

career: "Always remember that we are getting out a magazine for The Great American Moron!"

Since the stories are edited for mental children and persons suffering from arrested development, they are strictly moral in tone. However invidious they may be in suggestion, however harmful the influence of the unreal world they depict and the phantasies they foster, their surface is always repulsively virtuous.[14]

The pulps also had their defenders, however, not the least of whom were the writers who supplied the stories.[15] The literary market in which the pulps existed was, according to McCann, "intensely competitive and brutally labor-intensive," but it was "also proudly democratic."[16] Lacking the mediation and solicitation of advertising, the pulps stressed they had a unique relationship with their readers—a "publishing fraternity." McCann writes:

> The big slick magazines were studiously indifferent to that audience [high-school educated, skilled and unskilled laborers], and pulp writers and editors eventually took advantage of that fact by playing up their populist alienation from the world of mass-market consumerism. Defending themselves from recurrent charges of cheapness and sensationalism, "pulpsters" (the term was their own) gradually defined their world as a refuge of honest, manly labor, independent of the "terribly effeminate" world of solicitation and image-mongering that they saw in the slicks. The pulps were "honest and forthright," Raymond Chandler later claimed; their slick competitors, which "cater[ed] princi-pally to the taste of women," were "artificial, untrue, and emotionally dishonest."[17]

Reversing the terms on which value judgments could be made meant that the pulpsters took succor in the derogatory criticisms hurled against them by middle- and highbrow cultural and social guardians. If their fictions were ille-gitimate, then they were outlaws—just like so many of the heroes they created. If their stories lacked refinement and propriety, then they could take pleasure in the fact that they were offering a lusty masculine fare. If pulp pandered to the prurient instincts of its readers, feeding them lurid tales of vice and crime, it was, said its defenders, honest in its reflection of everyday life—these were stories pulled from today's headlines. If their fictions played to the base instincts of the lower classes, at least their wares were available to all.

Pulp was democratic, but it was also excessively masculine in its orienta-tion in action and hard-boiled variants. The literary historian Erin Smith writes, "Hard-boiled writing culture created an all-male imagined community that included writers, readers, and the he-manly heroes of this fiction. For some, reading pulp fiction was also a refusal to read slick magazines, which trafficked in genteel, feminine fare and placed consuming women at the center of American life, where producing men had once reigned."[18] As Smith noted, romance pulps with an intended female readership made up a significant sector of the market that was defined by heavily demarcated niche interests: war, boxing, football, different types of western stories, science fiction, and, of course, detective stories. Though no more than part of the mix during pulp's heyday, by the late 1930s detective pulp magazines represented close to a quarter of the two hundred or so pulp titles in distribution.[19] Detective stories also drew a more distinctive audience than science fiction and western tales, or at least a more remarked-upon readership.

In the *New Republic* Barclay claimed that all was not equal in pulp publishing; its sales may not have been as great as western stories, but the mystery and crime yarn held a claim on the attention of the more erudite and elite members of society: "The detective stories are the intellectual kings of the wood-pulp realm. One magazine can boast that it was the relaxation of Wilson and Roosevelt; and it now adds Hoover to its list. Perhaps this is why detective magazines do not have the biggest circulations. Readers of crime and mystery stories, being of more educated tastes, are likely to buy their entertainment in book form."[20] And their interest would contribute to the impression that the pulps were forums primarily for hard-boiled detectives.

This was a view that was easy to sustain in the postwar years, when the popularity of pulp magazines had waned, surpassed by the new publishing phenomenon of the paperback. The fact that pulp's most renowned practitioners, Dashiell Hammett and Raymond Chandler, both *Black Mask* alumni, had gone on to successful careers as novelists published by one of the preeminent houses of the day, Alfred Knopf, was not immaterial. Making the move into the world of the New York moderns, Hammett wrote to his editor at Knopf that he had hopes of "adapting the stream-of-consciousness method, conveniently modified, to a detective story."[21] Chandler, too, had such aspirations for his work:

> I am engaged and have always from the very beginning been engaged in the effort to do something with the mystery story which has never quite been done. . . . The thing is to squeeze the last drop out of the medium you have learned to use. The aim is not essentially different from the aim of Greek tragedy, but we are dealing with a public that is only semi-literate and we have to make an art of a language they can understand.
>
> In doing this I must accept certain handicaps. No snob appeal, no uplift, no apparent social significance. Very easy to deprecate, just another hardboiled mystery, and so on. But it's a funny thing, to get anywhere you have to interest the extreme intellectuals. Our target is not the mystery addict. He knows nothing, remembers nothing. He buys books

cheap or rents them. It all goes in one ear and crosses the vacuum to the other. Circumstances compel both of us to have an eye to the dollar; but only one eye.[22]

And, of course, both Hammett and Chandler were much admired and respected in intellectual circles, a fact that gave a belated respectability to the pulps, but it would be wrong to think that they were representative of pulpsters. Both wrote for *Black Mask*, a journal established by H. L. Mencken and the drama critic George Jean Nathan as a way of providing financial support for their "Magazine of Cleverness," the *Smart Set*. Mencken and Nathan had already known success in the pulp market with *Parisienne* and *Saucy Stories*, so a mystery pulp was the obvious next step. The periodical was subtitled on its first appearance on April 1919 as *An Illustrated Magazine of Detective, Mystery, Adventure, Romance and Spiritualism* (the latter genre was soon dropped and replaced with the western. The subtitle would continue to evolve over the years). Before the magazine was a year old, they sold the title for a very lucrative profit, though it still had some way to go before it overtook the sales of its key competitor *Detective Story*. Carroll John Daly and Dashiell Hammett began writing for *Black Mask* in 1922; they were followed the year after by Erle Stanley Gardner and then, in 1925–26, by Raoul Whitfield and Frederick Nebel, and, most significantly, by a new editor, Joseph Thompson Shaw, in 1926.

Hammett's work matured under Shaw, who also added new talent to the stable, including Horace McCoy, Paul Cain (no relation to James M. Cain), and Raymond Chandler. By 1930 circulation of the magazine had risen from 66,000 in 1926 to a peak of 103,000. Shaw lasted a decade as *Black Mask*'s editor; he was succeeded by Fanny Ellsworth, who engaged the talents of Cornell Woolrich, Max Brand, Frank Gruber, and Steve Fisher, all of whom would become significant authors during the postwar paperback boom.[23] This extraordinary array of name talent was not matched by any other pulp; some perspective on this can be gained by the following figures given by the pulp fiction historian William F. Nolan: "Prior to World War II, 25 million readers devoured 200 million bimonthly and monthly words ground out by more than 1,300 pulp writers. In any given month, some 200 pulps in all genres (war, western, romance, adventure, science fiction, etc.) crowded the stands."[24] Anonymity best characterizes pulp authorship. Of the thirteen hundred writers referred to by Nolan, how many are now remembered, let alone read? Outside of the cult appeal of Woolrich, McCoy's quartet of novels, Cain's collection of pulp stories *Seven Slayers* and his novel *The Fast One*, only Chandler and Hammett of the *Black Mask* authors are widely known and still read.

The respectability that Hammett and Chandler gained for American hard-boiled detective fiction took on a particular force during the heyday of America's paperback revolution in the early 1950s, when Mickey Spillane sold

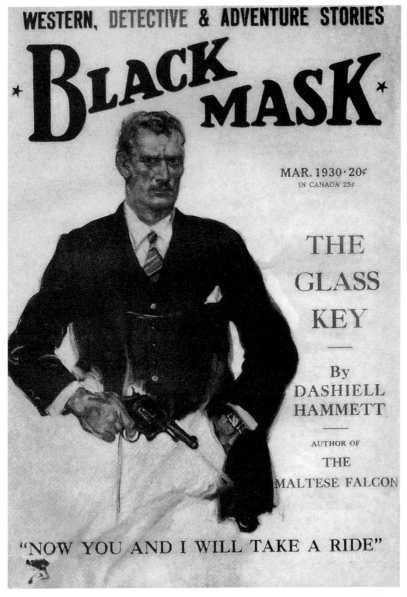

7. Pulp magazine cover of *Black Mask: Western, Detective & Adventure Stories* (March 1930), featuring Dashiell Hammett.

seventeen million copies of his "sensational mystery thrillers" featuring the detective Mike Hammer.[25] The rapid development of the paperback industry began with the foundation in 1939 of the Pocket Books company. In his study *Two-Bit Culture* the historian of paperbacks Kenneth C. Davis wrote that "like Hollywood and television, this undertaking was another amalgam of that

peculiar American genius for combining culture, commerce, and a little technology. After 1939, the world of books—like the world itself—would never be the
same" (12–13). Pocket Books were innovators on price (individual titles sold at
twenty-five cents, one-tenth of the average price of a hardback), on format
(plastic-laminated covers measuring 4¼ by 6½ inches), and in choice (republi-
cations of a range of authors from Shakespeare to Agatha Christie by way of
Dorothy Parker and James Hilton—classics, genre fiction, and best sellers were
all included in the first ten titles they published).

Republication of classics and new fiction that had been first sold in hardback editions would continue to be a mainstay of the paperback industry, but
this new industry also quickly began to solicit readers by offering original stories,
unique to the format. After Pocket Books, the leading publishers were Bantam,
New American Library, Dell, Avon, and Popular Library. Between them they
accounted for 148 million out of 200 million paperbacks published in 1950.[26] These
phenomenal sales figures inevitably attracted the attention of the chattering-
classes. As an example, Davis provides a quote from a 1951 issue of *The Nation*:

> Last year, the stupefying total of 214,000,000 paper-bound books was
> published in this country, as compared with 3,000,000 in 1939. Most of
> them were sold and the probability is that a larger proportion of them
> was read than of hard-cover books, many of which are bought as
> unwanted gifts or as book-club prestige items for the coffee table.
> Whether this revolution in the reading habits of the American public
> means that we are being inundated by a flood of trash which will debase
> farther the popular taste, or that we shall now have available cheap
> editions of an ever-increasing list of classics, is a question of basic
> importance to our social and cultural development. (146)

Competition for sales placed an extraordinary emphasis on the cover art to
attract potential readers. Vibrantly colored illustrations of sexually suggestive
and/or violent scenes could adorn a reprint of a classic, or a serious sociological
report on the nation's youth, as it could a paperback original mystery thriller.
The public sale and consumption of paperbacks, sold in drugstores, train and
bus terminals, and newsstands, inevitably caught the attention of moral
guardians. Pulled into the postwar moral and social panics that figured juvenile
delinquency, rock 'n' roll, comic books, the Kinsey Report, and communism, as
the country's ruination. Paperbacks were first attacked by local censorship
bodies; then in 1952 the House of Representatives authorized an investigation of
the paperback, magazine, and comic book businesses to determine the extent
of "immoral, obscene, or otherwise offensive matter" or "improper emphasis on
crime, violence, and corruption" (Davis 219). A statement made on the opening
day of the hearing set the tone: publishers were accused of "the dissemination
of artful appeals to sensuality, immorality, filth, perversion, and degeneracy,"

aided by the "lurid and daring illustrations of voluptuous young women on the covers of the books" (Davis 220). If they were not censored, the "moral damage" done to the nation's youth in its consumption of these obscene fictions would, it was argued before the House, inevitably lead to juvenile delinquency. Davis believed that political fear in the specter of communist conspiracies was one of a number of barely suppressed motives behind the hearings; another was the period's "almost compulsive sexual repression." He noted that both local and national censorship drives had substantial religious backing (230). But beyond the political and moral imperatives of the censors there was also an overt agenda to maintain sharp cultural and, thereby, social distinctions.[27]

In a robust defense of the paperback industry, Victor Weybridge, editor at New American Library, argued that paperbacks for first time offered to the everyman "entertainment, information, instruction, and inspiration that formerly were only available to the well-to-do." "Let me repeat," he told the House, "reprints are not new books; they are books you have seen before at four to twenty times the price. Reprint fiction deals with sex and sin to the same extent as the trade fiction of which it is a reproduction, and no more." Shifting his response to criticism of the paperbacks' content, Weybridge argued that a "large proportion of the better fiction being written today, and therefore a substantial proportion of the fiction appearing in reprint form, belongs to the realistic or naturalistic school, depicting life in realistic detail as sordid and ugly in those aspects where life *is* sordid and ugly." On the issue of the paperbacks' cover illustrations he more forcefully stressed the question of taste and distinction as it applied to the hearings: "in the case of the great majority of covers, the only issue is one of taste. I do not believe that it is the function or the intention of Congress to legislate in matters of public taste. These are matters to be settled by the force of public opinion, operating in a free market place."[28]

Despite such sterling defenses mounted by the industry, the committee's majority report maintained its tone of condemnation of a business founded on "artful appeals to sensuality, immorality, filth, perversion, and degeneracy" (Davis 235). Congress did not act on the committee's recommendations, and there were no further moves by the federal government to censor the industry. Local and national bodies, however, particularly those organized through the Catholic Church, continued to actively seek to "purge" the paperback racks.[29] The effect of this agitation resulted in a shift to more sedate and "tasteful" covers. Davis wrote, "The cover artists who had come out of the pulp school of illustration were giving way, and a relative sophistication was replacing the harsh realism and blatantly deceptive covers of a few years before" (240).

Beyond the populist appeal of the House investigation and moral crusade of groups such as Brooklyn's Decent Literature Committee of Our Lady Help of Christians Roman Catholic Church, the supposed deleterious effects of paperback fiction on its readership were much discussed in middlebrow

8. Cover illustration for Lionel White's *The Killing*, a 1956 Signet film tie-in. There is no equivalent bondage scene to that depicted here in either the novel or Kubrick's film, and the illustration would be reused on other pulp paperbacks.

9. Mickey Spillane, *One Lonely Night*, 1952 Signet paperback edition. Sex, sadism, and
Mike Hammer.

forums. Central to these discussions were the work and sales figures of Mickey
Spillane, the writer singularly responsible for maintaining, in the transition
from magazine to paperback fiction, the notion of pulp as an inferior form of
sensationalist writing aimed at the masses.

The crude and simple appeal of Spillane's stories and their phenomenal sales were castigated in the contemporary equivalent of the slicks, in middle-brow forums such as *Life* and *Good Housekeeping*. In 1955 the latter published a lengthy article titled "The Crime of Mickey Spillane," in which the opening paragraph neatly condenses a sense of bourgeois revulsion at Spillane's appeal to the lower orders:

> Some years ago, while in bed with the flu, I found in a stock of 25-cent books brought home by my wife a mystery story called, I seem to remember, *The Big Kill*, by an author named Mickey Spillane. After a few dozen pages I began to smile at the amateurish efforts to make dirty words sound important. After a few more pages I flung the book across the room in revulsion. Reading about brutality, bestiality, and dirty sex might have been Mr. Spillane's idea of recreation; it wasn't mine. To me his backdrop of blood and lust was sickeningly tedious. Moreover, the happenings in the books were unbelievable, and the writing so bad I couldn't see how even a fifth grader could bear it.[30]

Noting the extraordinary sales of these books (125,000 hardback copies, 26 million U.S. sales of the paperbacks), the writer also noted the, to-date, three movie adaptations: "They were released by United Artists, complete with lurid and suggestive poster art, for the edification of movie-going children of all ages." Spillane's "Melodramas-in-mayhem" are condemned for their sadism (displayed in individual acts, but also in the novels' repetitive cycles of sex and violence), the absurdity of the stories, the glorification of revenge, the hero's antisocial attitude, and his attacks on figures and institutions of authority: "In other words the books appeal by direct action to every low, brutal, cruel, sadistic, lawless impulse that humanity has been trying to master for thousands of years in the effort to maintain civilisation."[31] These criticisms are remarkably similar to those aimed earlier at the pulp magazines, including the inevitable infantilization of the readers of such fiction.

In his 1953 polemic, *The Game of Death*, which warned of the devastating effects of the cold war on "our children," the journalist and communist Albert E. Kahn included horror and crime comics, the movies, and Mickey Spillane, alongside living under the shadow of the bomb, the fear instilled in children by civil defense rehearsals, the scandal of underfunded schools, military training, prison policy, and institutional racism, as among the great ills that threatened America in the postwar age. The chapter called "Niagara of Horror" begins with a quotation from Spillane: "Kill, kill, kill, kill!" Citing the *Life* article "Death's Fair-Haired Boy," Kahn runs through the usual litany of Spillane's crimes against society, but he concludes by noting, rather uniquely, that Spillane had begun his apprenticeship in the "literary formula of 'sex and sadism,'" working as a comic book writer.[32] The core of the chapter discusses the deleterious effect of horror

and crime comic books on children, drawing deeply from the work of Dr. Fredric
Wertham, who at that time embodied the public image of the socially engaged
psychologist or sociologist—the expert. Kahn then turns his attention to television before concluding with an attack on Hollywood as being equally complicit
in the corruption of young minds:

> Before the intent gaze of the nation's youthful movie-goers there unfolds
> an endless phantasmagoria of gangsters and convicts battling police offi-
> cers, cowboys butchering Indians, American GIs slaughtering enemy sol-
> diers, Federal agents shooting down "Moscow spies," homicidal maniacs
> killing various victims, husbands murdering wives and *vice versa*. With
> rare exceptions, the hero of these gory productions is distinguished from
> the other characters solely by the fact he is stronger and tougher, can
> shoot faster and straighter, and has greater proficiency in the arts of
> boxing, wrestling, rough and tumble and jiu jitsu. Almost invariably, the
> dramatic climax comes when the muscular Aryan-type hero kills or beats
> into a bloody pulp the villain, who is frequently a foreigner, Communist,
> Oriental, or dark-skinned native of some colonial region. (110–12)

The effect of all this visual and aural violence on the nation's youth is clear and
unanswerable: "The niagara of horror and sudden death with which young
Americans are being inundated day and night through motion pictures, TV,
radio and comic books is not only training them to regard acts of brutality,
violence, and homicide as a natural, every-day part of life. It is also conditioning
them to commit such acts" (116).

Reviewing the "cultural picture" America presented in 1952, Bernard Iddings
Bell, like so many of his peers, lit upon the work of Spillane as an index of the
cultural malaise facing the country, a malaise that suggested a lack of maturity
among the citizenry: "The most popular novelist in America today, if one may
judge by the number of copies sold, is a meretricious brute of a fellow, almost
ludicrously savage in his substance and his style. He writes tales of violence that
is near to madness plus a degenerate sexuality."[33] Bell believed that the "common man's" liking for Spillane revealed that American culture was "childish" and
based on "greed for goods, on avidity for sensation, on a search for enervating
comforts, on conformity to a type set by subhuman urbanization, on a divorce-
ment of the people from the soil, on eager response to the propagandists."[34]

Writing in a November 1954 edition of the *Saturday Review*, Christopher La
Farge, in his essay "Mickey Spillane and His Bloody Hammer," echoed the points
raised by Bell, Kahn, and others: "What is phenomenal about it is that a series of
books can be written in what is supposed to be the form of fiction, but is not
truly fiction, but rather a wholly unadmirable kind of wish-fulfilment on both
an immature and a potentially destructive level, and be immediately successful
on a scale far beyond average. . . . Normally one would say that it was silly to

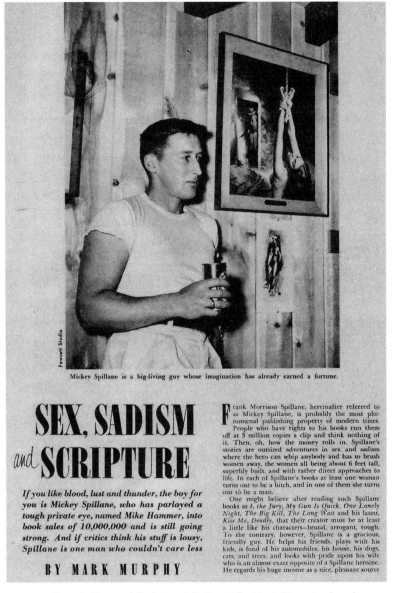

Mickey Spillane is a big-living guy whose imagination has already earned a fortune.

SEX, SADISM *and* SCRIPTURE

If you like blood, lust and thunder, the boy for you is Mickey Spillane, who has parlayed a tough private eye, named Mike Hammer, into book sales of 10,000,000 and is still going strong. And if critics think his stuff is lousy, Spillane is one man who couldn't care less

BY MARK MURPHY

Frank Morrison Spillane, hereinafter referred to as Mickey Spillane, is probably the most phenomenal publishing property of modern times. People who have rights to his books run them off at 3 million copies a clip and think nothing of it. Then, oh, how the money rolls in. Spillane's stories are outsized adventures in sex and sadism where the hero can whip anybody and has to brush women all being about 6 feet tall, superbly built, and with rather direct approaches to life. In each of Spillane's books at least one woman turns out to be a bitch, and in one of them she turns out to be a man.

One might believe after reading such Spillane books as *I, the Jury, My Gun Is Quick, One Lonely Night, The Big Kill, The Long Wait* and his latest, *Kiss Me, Deadly,* that their creator must be at least a little like his characters—brutal, arrogant, tough. To the contrary, however, Spillane is a gracious, friendly guy. He helps his friends, plays with his kids, is fond of his automobiles, his house, his dogs, cats, and trees, and looks with pride upon his wife who is an almost exact opposite of a Spillane heroine. He regards his huge income as a nice, pleasant source

10. "Sex, Sadism and Scripture," in *True: The Men's Magazine* (1952).

write a critical article about a lot of books so badly written. . . . Their writing is turgid or grotesque or childish or simply the worst kind of lurid. Or it is plain revolting." What made this particular piece of criticism unique is that La Farge did not make any grand claims about the effect this fiction had on unformed minds, at least not directly; instead, he believed it "reflects" an "attitude already held by the public—an attitude which has grown to the extent that is at the least inimical to the basic principles on which our country has so far operated. Mike Hammer is the logical conclusion, almost a sort of brutal apotheosis, of McCarthyism: when things seem wrong, let one man cure the wrong by whatever means he, as a privileged savior, chooses."[35]

La Farge, like so many middlebrow critics, also highlighted the errors in Spillane's writing, particularly "grammar and use of words ('they huddled in recessions of doorways'), inconsistencies (like the 'cold, impartial jury' weeping)," which occur "*ad nauseam.*" Spillane dismissed his critics as hypocritical "long hairs" who, *Good Housekeeping* reported him as saying, "decry the vulgarity in [my] books while praising Faulkner, Hemingway, and Steinbeck for describing the 'same things' more artistically. . . . Nobody likes my work except the public. . . . I'm not an author and never pretended to be. I'm a commercial writer. I write what the people want to pay for."[36] But, responded *Good Housekeeping*, the "very opposite is the case. . . . His grammar and usage, for one thing, are atrocious. He uses a good many words he does not actually know the meaning of."[37] *Life* magazine covered similar territory in a lengthy profile of Spillane: "Some critics—shackled by old-fashioned regard for the English language—have suggested that while Mickey Spillane can type, he certainly can't write. It is undeniably true that Spillane, in the white-hot, gut-wrenching heat of the chase, occasionally plays hell with syntax. Sometimes he even invests his participants' knees with personality, as in *Vengeance Is Mine*, where he wrote, 'I dove toward the origin of the snorts and crashed into a pair of legs that buckled with a hoarse curse.'" Spillane, however, remained unabashed by such criticisms: "I write scenes, pictures you can see, and the story moves."[38]

Central to the marketing of Mickey Spillane was an appeal to readers of girly and lowbrow magazines—*Vue, Real, Tops, Pageant, Picture Scope, Foto-rama, Male, Quick, The Male Point of View, Focus, Lowdown, Cavalier, Bold,* and *True: The Man's Magazine.* Here, among the cheesecake poses of burlesque queens—and articles such as "The Suburbs How Sinful?," "Is Science Changing Your Sex Life?," "Why Some Women Hate Sex," "How Your Sex Glands Work," "How Russia Built a Vice Town," "I Have a Date with the Executioners," and "Sex Is Better at Home"—can be found articles by and about Mickey Spillane, including "Mickey Spillane Spicy Mayhem," "The Test of Mike Hammer," "Mickey Spillane: Does Sadism Pay Off?," "Mickey Spillane: Men's Room Scribbler," "Mickey Spillane: Sex, Sadism and Scripture," "Mickey Spillane's Dames," "The Ever Loving Ladies of Mickey Spillane," and "Spillane's Dames in the Flesh." The latter three pieces are photographic spreads linked to the recently released Spillane adaptation *The Long Wait.* "The Ever Loving Ladies of Mickey Spillane" provides poses of Dolores Donlon, one of the female leads in the film, as ten characters from Spillane's novels: "These ten girls are about the best little booksellers in the trade. All of them arose, full-breasted and yielding, from the fertile mind of mystery writer Mickey Spillane, [and] they coaxed 14 million quarters out of American readers."

STAR
OF THE
MONTH

Tempting Dolores Donlon
warms the flinty heart of
her boy friend, a gangster in
United Artists' film treatment
of Mickey Spillane's *The Long
Wait.* For a peep at how she,
and her sisters-in-crime, fan
the ardor of Spillane hero
Johnny McBride, turn the page.

11. *Bold* magazine (July 1954) features Dolores Donlon as its centerfold. She is a female lead in *The Long Wait* (1954).

Beneath each picture is a line or two from one of the novels: "Her breasts fought the dress . . . valiantly."[39] The charms of Dolores Donlon are also featured in *Picture Scope*'s "Spillane's Dames in the Flesh," where she appears as one member of the "quartet of cuties who step from the pages of *The Long Wait* and onto the screen": "She was oozing out of a Bikini suit like toothpaste out of a tube." That's the description of a typical Spillane dame, and there are four such lovelies in *The Long Wait*, a film version of the book by the same name.[40]

MARY BELLEMY (*I, The Jury*): "She wore a sheer pink negligee that was designed with simplicity as the motif . . . she passed momentarily in front of the light streaming in from the window and I could see through everything she had on. And it wasn't much. Just the negligee."

CHARLOTTE (*I, The Jury*): ➔ "Her hair was almost white . . . a smooth forehead melted into alive, hazel eyes framed symmetrically in the curves of naturally brown eyebrows studded with long, moist lashes. Her breasts fought the dress . . . valiantly."

142

12. *Pageant* magazine's (July 1954) exploitation of Spillane's dames.

LILY (*Kiss Me Deadly*): "Her body was a tight bundle of lush curves under a light terrycloth robe. Lovely Lily, with my .45 in her hand."

JUNO (*Vengeance Is Mine*): "She met me at the door, a smiling goddess in a hostess coat of iridescent material that changed color with every motion of her body."

CONTINUED

Writing in 1953, the New York intellectual Dwight Macdonald added his voice to the general sense of despair about the state of the nation's well-being, though he also included in his list of the despised the "homogenized mass-circulation magazine," such as *Life*: "It appears on the mahogany library tables of the rich, the glass end-tables of the middle-class and the oilcloth-covered kitchen tables of the poor. Its contents are as thoroughly homogenized as its circulation."[41] Homogenized culture, he argued, "destroys all values, since value judgments imply discrimination. Mass Culture is very, very democratic: it absolutely refuses to discriminate against, or between, anything or anybody. All is grist to its mill, and all comes out finely ground indeed" (62). Macdonald saved his most withering critique for Middlebrow Culture, what he would later call "midcult," which "threatens to engulf everything in its spreading ooze" (63–64).

Mass and middlebrow culture, he argued, produced passive consumers, adultized children, and infantilized adults; it trivialized the serious and corrupted tradition; the creators of mass culture were "art workers . . . as alienated from their brainwork as the industrial worker is from his handwork" (65). At the center of Macdonald's condemnation was a short analysis of the way science had been misused in popular fictions from Frankenstein to Hiroshima, from Sherlock Holmes to Mike Hammer. Where the detective's art of ratiocination once appealed to readers "accustomed to think in scientific terms" (67), contemporary versions of the detective story had cheapened and despoiled the form. The uncovering of the criminal, which had once been the point of the story, was now just a "mere excuse for the minute description of scenes of bloodshed, brutality, lust, and alcoholism" (68). He concluded this section of the essay with a dire prognosis: "A decade ago, the late George Orwell, apropos a 'sensationalist' detective story of the time, *No Orchids for Miss Blandish*, showed how the brutalization of the genre mirrors the general degeneration in ethics from nineteenth-century standards. What he would have written had Mickey Spillane's works been in existence I find it hard to imagine" (68).

Orwell's essay was written in 1944; in it he compared Raffles, the amateur cracksman, with James Hadley Chase's heroine in *No Orchids for Miss Blandish* in order to account for the "immense difference in moral atmosphere between the two books, and the change in the popular attitude that this probably implies."[42] Chase was an English novelist, but his story had an American underworld setting. Orwell lumps *No Orchids* in with American crime fiction in general, of which, "quite apart from books, there is the huge array of 'pulp magazines,' graded so as to cater to different kinds of fantasy, but nearly all having much the same mental atmosphere. A few of them go in for straight pornography, but the great majority are quite plainly aimed at sadists and masochists. [They are] sold at three pence a copy under the title Yank Mags" (159). In a footnote Orwell suggested that the pulps were imported into Britain as ballast, which he thought "accounted for their low price and crumpled appearance. Since the war the ships have been ballasted with something more useful, probably gravel" (164). Leaving aside the onanistic proclivity of the readers of "Yank Mags," Orwell's link between contemporary crime fiction—as distinct from that produced by Conan Doyle, Poe, or E. W. Hornung (the author of the Raffles tales)—and pulp is a further example of the seemingly inexorable conflation of hard-boiled American crime fiction with pulp.

Writing six years after Orwell's essay, the American literary critic Edmund Wilson also had his say about detective fiction in the much anthologized "Who Cares Who Killed Roger Ackroyd?"[43] In the essay Wilson noted that his contribution belonged to something of a contemporary vogue for critical commentary on the form, and he cited recently published articles by Jacques Barzun, Joseph Wood Krutch, Raymond Chandler, Somerset Maugham, and Bernard De Voto.[44] Wilson remained thoroughly unimpressed by the genre, though he found much to admire in Raymond Chandler, who, he judged, did not belong with the writers of "old-fashioned" detective stories but was instead a first-rate exponent of the adventure novel, though nevertheless a "long way below Graham Greene" in his achievements in that genre. If Spillane had appeared among the detective fiction Wilson was judging, it would, I suspect, only have confirmed the critic's belief that the genre was at best a form of subliterature: "With so many fine books to read, so much to be studied and known, there is no need to bore ourselves with this rubbish."[45]

Wilson's peer in literary criticism, Malcolm Cowley, however, did tackle Mickey Spillane:

> I am not used to having Jack the Ripper presented as a model for emulation and I confess that Mike Hammer frightens me. It has been argued that the stories have no relation to American life; that they put together the ingredients of the Western novel, the pursuit thriller, the comic strip and the animated film cartoon in a cockeyed fairy story that has no more social significance than the fun house at Coney Island. The publishers, I suppose, would like to accept this explanation: what fun! . . . What frightens me about these fairy tales is that they are entirely too close to one side of American life in 1952. . . . Mike Hammer helps to show—like the comic books and some of the animated cartoons—that the sadism is there, in the midst of our elaborate and internally peaceful culture.[46]

Cowley explored the misogynistic impulse behind the sadism in Spillane's fiction, a perceived symptom of a culture gone awry that was considered at greater length in Gershon Legman's 1948 booklet *Love and Death*. Gershon's thesis considered the "absurd contradiction" that "murder is a crime. Describing murder is not. Sex is not a crime. Describing sex *is*. Why?": "The penalty for murder is death or lifelong imprisonment—the penalty for writing about it: fortune and lifelong fame. The penalty for fornication is . . . there is no actual penalty—the penalty for describing it in print; jail and lifelong disgrace. . . . Is the creation of life really more reprehensible than its destruction?"[47]

Legman takes to task the gratuitous portrayal of sadism in comic books, film, and crime novels and the "uncontrollable letch for death." According to Donald Phelps, the "theme which nudges us throughout Legman's essay is the threat to our culture of a violence which underlies even the violence [of the] bludgeonings, murders, and mutilations which Legman itemizes. The primary violence is the violence of bad art; the violence of unremitting contempt."[48] Legman aims his opprobrium at the heads of slumming intellectuals: "Least innocent, because they are most aware, are the amateurs of murder—the writers especially—the feuilletonist clergymen, the pansy intellectuals, the homicidal housewives and pseudonymous college-professors, all swilling happily through paper straws at their hot cathartic toddy of blood. Least guilty, because stupidest, are the professionals—the word-mongers: publishers and their hacks—hip-deep in murder strictly for the dollar, the merest puppets of the *Zeitgeist*. And they will tell you that only the public is responsible, only the reader is culpable."[49]

Consciousness of the role of class in the production and consumption of pulp was particularly marked in British critiques. In his study of working-class British culture, *The Uses of Literacy* (1957), Richard Hoggart decried the debasement of that culture by the commercial entertainment industries. The "shiny barbarism" of the mass entertainments appealed to the young and impressionable, those without family and work commitments and responsibilities: "This regular, increasing, and almost entirely unvaried diet of sensation without commitment is surely likely to help render its consumers less capable of responding openly and responsibly to life, is likely to induce an underlying sense of purposelessness in existence outside the limited range of a few immediate appetites. Souls which may have little opportunity to open will be kept hard-gripped, turned in upon themselves, looking out 'with odd dark eyes like windows' upon a world which is largely a phantasmagoria of passing shows and vicarious stimulations."[50]

Hoggart's criticism centered on the selling of "sex in shiny packets" to the "juke-box boys" who read "comics, gangster novelettes, science and crime magazines, the newer style magazines or magazine/newspapers and the picture dailies" (247). These readers are boys "aged between fifteen and twenty, with drape suits, picture ties, and an American slouch. . . . Their clothes, their hairstyles, their facial expressions all indicate [they] are living to a large extent in a myth-world compounded of a few simple elements which they take to be those of American life" (248). Hoggart traced the origin of the "sex-and-violence" novel back from Mickey Spillane to James M. Cain's *The Postman Always Rings Twice* (1934) and produced a list of imitation pulp titles to illustrate the formulaic nature of the stories—"Sweetie, Take It Hot"; "Sweetheart, Curves Can Kill"; "No Talk from Tombstones"; "Lady, It's Cold Down There"; "Death-Cab for Cutie"—alongside the observation that the "authors are usually American or pseudo-American" (259). Hoggart's critique of contemporary mass culture was in keeping with the broader concern among the period's British social guardians with the "Americanization" of everyday life: a "gangster" culture that lacked moral order, celebrated the trivial, the vulgar, and the garish:

> Most mass-entertainments are in the end what D. H. Lawrence described as "anti-life." They are full of a corrupt brightness, of improper appeals and moral evasions. To recall instances: they tend towards a view of the world in which progress is conceived as a seeking of material possessions, equality as a moral levelling, and freedom as the ground for endless irresponsible pleasure. These productions belong to a vicarious, spectators' world; they offer nothing which can really grip the brain or heart. They assist a gradual drying-up of the more positive, the fuller, the more cooperative kinds of enjoyment, in which one gains much by giving much. (340)

Hoggart understood the clipped phrasing, the "bittiness" and fragmentation of the pulp crime stories to be a debased consequence of Hemingway's influence.[51] To underscore how far removed pulp stories are from more legitimate forms of literature he compared a "typical gangster-fiction novel" with some of the more brutish scenes from Faulkner's *Sanctuary* (1931). Faulkner's "language stretches and strains to meet the demands of the emotional situation. . . . We see the horror as it is, without intermediate moral comment, but we see it for what it is only because of this larger sense, embracing and surrounding it all the time, of an order without" (268).

The contrast with pulp fiction is stark and immediate: "With the gangster-fiction writing we are not aware of a larger pattern. We are in and of this world of the fierce alley-way assault, the stale disordered bed, the closed killer-car, the riverside warehouse knifing. We thrill to those in themselves; there is no way out, nothing else; there is no horizon and no sky. The world, consciousness, man's ends, are this—this constricted and overheated horror" (268). The moral relativism taken by Hoggart operates between an example of modernist literature that inhabits a pulp story and an unreflexive formulaic example of mass fiction. It is a relativism with which Edmund Wilson would have been comfortable and which presupposes a highly educated response to literary values. Most critiques of pulp in general, and of Spillane in particular, found a more readily available comparison within the genre itself. In a review of the film adaptation of Spillane's first novel, *I, the Jury*, a British film censor wrote: "But for the nasty hints, the story would have had a Raymond Chandler–type toughness which has its devotees among the most respectable sections of the population,

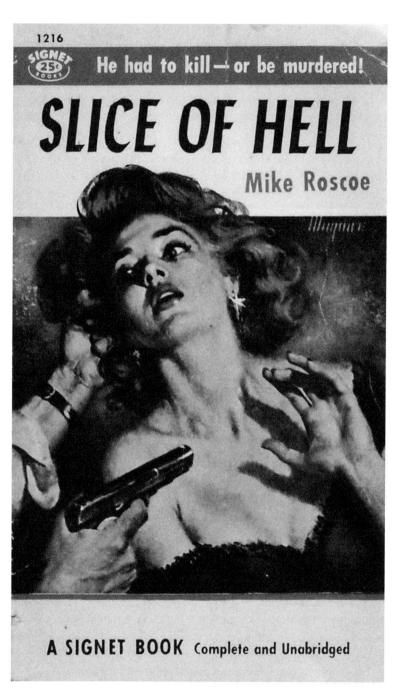

13. Mike Roscoe, *Slice of Hell*, 1955 Signet paperback. Roscoe was one of many Spillane imitators. Like the jacket illustration for *The Killing*, this one is from a Robert A. Maguire painting.

including Dons and other peaceable people."[52] The reference to Chandler as the acceptable face of literary "toughness," whose supporters can be counted on to include among their number members of the educated elite and the well-behaved middle classes, casts Spillane as completely alien to bourgeois mores and values. A reviewer in the British weekly magazine *Picture Post* underlined the moral turpitude of Spillane's fiction, compared to Chandler's:

> The film, *I, the Jury*, gives hints to the hungry on murder, prostitution, physical violence, torture, perversion and nymphomania. This delectable mixture is thrown on celluloid as it was originally thrown on paper—without apparent effort or talent. And Crime Pays, for hero Mike Hammer, devoid of even the dregs of moral fibre, gets away with every felony in the book, including premeditated murder. The subject matter recalls Raymond Chandler, but where Chandler writes about a moral demi-monde, Spillane seems to be writing *for* it. In the words of an American critic, Spillane's books are "daydreams for the frustrated and the sick." By filming this swill, its producers have finally come into the open as to the kind of audiences they are addressing.[53]

Even Chandler concurred on the demerits of Spillane's fiction: "Pulp writing at its worst was never as bad as this stuff. It isn't very long since no decent publisher would have touched it. . . . This Spillane stuff, so far as I can see, is nothing but a mixture of violence and outright pornography. He and his publishers have had the courage, if that is the correct word, to carry these a little further than anyone else without interference from the police. I can't see anything else in it. This sort of thing makes the home boys with their libraries of elegant erotica seem rather nice people."[54]

In April 1954 Scotland Yard appeared at the offices of Spillane's British publisher, Arthur Baker, and seized copies of *I, the Jury* and *Kiss Me, Deadly*; the director of public prosecutions was preparing a case of obscenity against Spillane. Earlier in the year Baker had written to his American colleagues and warned that a number of local magistrates had confiscated and ordered copies of Spillane's novels destroyed. The obscenity charge never reached the courts, but in helping Baker to mount his defense, the editors at Signet inadvertently noted the streak of anti-Americanism inherent in the threatened prosecution: "I realise that American attitudes of approval of Mickey might actually boomerang, if a prejudiced attack would endeavor to portray Mickey's works as examples of libertine American criminality."[55]

The concern that Spillane's appeal was principally with and to the demi-monde, the working class, was also echoed in American reviews, though their concern was often recast as a fear for America's vulnerable young: "there is some danger that its only appeal will be to that sector of juvenility who already are worrying the sociologists."[56] Some filmmakers also concurred. *Marty*, which won the Academy Award for best picture in 1955, has a scene where Marty's pals sit around flipping through a girly magazine and discussing the merits of Mickey Spillane: "Boy, does that Mickey Spillane know how to handle women." Male, working-class, and still living with their mothers, these are juveniles, despite the fact they all look to be pushing toward middle age. The distaff side to *Marty*'s middle-aged delinquents was showcased in Fritz's Lang's *The Blue Gardenia* (1953); a young pulp romance addict changes her preferred genre when she and her roommates become embroiled in a murder. Lang shows her reading a pulp novel written by the wonderfully named Mickey Mallet. The novel, *My Knife Is Bloody*, has a suitably lurid cover.

The crime writer James Ellroy has recalled his juvenile experience of reading Spillane: "I stole some Spillane paperbacks. I read them and got titillated and scared. I don't think I followed the plots very well—and I know it didn't hinder my enjoyment. I dug the shooting and the sex and Mike Hammer's anti-communist fervor."[57] In a thriller with a circus setting, *Ring of Fear* (1954), Mickey Spillane plays himself and is introduced interrupting a worker on a concessions stand who is absorbed in the reading of *My Gun Is Quick*. After the inevitable double take, the worker blames Spillane for ruining his life; he now spends too much time reading and too little time selling coffee. Whether or not these representations are a caricature of Spillane's core readers, they were recognizable to his publishers. In a private letter between his trade and paperback editors, the cliché of the broad appeal of the mystery story is parodied; his audience, it is said, ranges from "high-brow intellectuals down through the man on the street, possibly even to the man in the gutter."[58]

In his consideration of the influence of sensational fictions on antebellum literature—Melville, Poe, Whitman, Hawthorne—David Reynolds wrote that "there emerged a body of popular adventure fiction which, in its darkest manifestations, featured some of the most perverse scenes in literature. In much of this seamy fiction, popular writers forged a distinctly American irrational style whose linguistic wildness and dislocations were also visible in the grotesque American humour that arose during this period."[59] It was, he argued, a "style of intentional narrative discontinuities, oddly juxtaposed imagery, confusions between dream and reality, and feverish emotions creating distortions of perception" (202). This is a more than adequate description of Spillane's fiction and is suggestive of the firmly established tradition on which he draws, yet this aspect of his work is endlessly effaced in contemporary criticism, lost to the overarching concern with the work's topical connections and its perceived adverse effect on readers.

Writing in the debut issue of *New World Writing* (1952), the first mass-market literary magazine, Charles Rolo, however, put together a sterling defense of both detective fiction in general and Spillane in particular. He noted that "last year, one out of every four works of fiction newly published and reprinted in the United States was a murder mystery. The total sales of mysteries was around 66,000,000 copies." And apart from Edmund Wilson, the genre's appeal has touched "great men and great minds," including chiefs of state, men of letters, college presidents, generals, and scientists: "What charms has this unreal, mechanical brand of fiction which soothes the troubled breast of low-brow, highbrow and middlebrow? What do we find in its corpse-strewn cosmos that makes an escape so refreshing?" His hypothesis is that the murder mystery is a "metaphysical success story," and his evidence is provided by the fiction of Georges Simenon and Mickey Spillane—"two writers who stand at opposite poles." Spillane's work, intellectually, approximates the "same world as the comic strip"; Simenon "has been mentioned as a candidate for the Nobel Prize." Both were phenomenally popular, but the comparison is strained and is not helped by a cynical reading of the essay that suggests it was commissioned by the editors of New World Writing, who also happened to edit Spillane's novels. Nevertheless, what is particularly interesting about Rolo's apologia is that he does not make an appeal to some hitherto hidden points of comparison between Spillane and that of more respected writers; instead, he sees Spillane as proudly belonging to a tradition of lowbrow story forms: "In a crude way, Mickey Spillane is something of an innovator. He has hopped up the hard-boiled murder mystery into a shocker which combines features of the western, the ani-mated film strip, the pulp sex story, William Steig's 'Dreams of Glory' cartoons, and the sermons of Savonarola."[60]

The image of Spillane as a writer working unreflexively inside his chosen genre—as opposed to, say, Chandler's critical ruminations on the genre through his hero Marlowe; or Ian Fleming's James Bond stories, which exploit the genre yet disavow its lowborn status through a hero who defends and celebrates an aristocracy of taste and class; or, say, the deadening mechanical repetition of the formula in the novels of Charles Wells, Mike Roscoe, Earl Basinsky, or any other Spillane imitator—is addressed by Stuart Hall and Paddy Whannel in their seminal study The Popular Arts (1964). Chandler, they write, "worked within his form, commanded it, making it work for him, rather than, as Fleming does, exploiting it in a calculated way, or, as Spillane does, allowing it to exploit him."[61]

In a chapter devoted to Spillane, Fleming, and Chandler, Hall and Whannel present a study of "that colourful and bizarre collection of pulp fiction in the newsagent's window—the crime comics, the mysteries, the Confidential-style police exposés, the prisoner-of-war-camp tales, the private-eye thrillers" (142). Although calling Spillane's books a virtual "nightmare of fascism" (148), they also pay him his due as a writer of popular stories:

> The Spillane novels succeed because of their boldness. They contain all
> the elements of the thriller novel, each raised to its most advanced form.

The style is tough throughout. Murder, violence and sex are intertwined in each narrative, and each episode is graphically realistic in treatment. The novels also contain that other ingredient, the transcending of authority and accepted moral codes. . . . Finally the stories are set off against a background of the corruption and vice of the big city, a constant theme in the thriller novel. These are essentially urban fantasies. (143–44)

There then follows an insightful critique of the politics of Spillane, but rather than end on a note of condemnation for both the content and the form of Spillane's fiction, the authors note that "a Spillane novel, whatever its faults, never seems to be coldly put together or manufactured out of stylistic spare-parts, like so many of its imitators. The emotions are strong and direct, they thrust forward into the narrative and carry it along. In their own way, they are compellingly written and imagined" (149). Hall and Whannel were concerned with how we evaluate the particular qualities of the *popular* arts: "the struggle between what is good and worth while and what is shoddy and debased is not a struggle *against* the modern forms of communication, but a conflict *within* these media" (15).[62] The worth of Chandler is not established against examples drawn from the high arts but from within the genre in which he wrote, just as the outstanding work of John Ford in the field of westerns must be judged against both the mundane and the overreaching, or the blues should be valued as *popular* music and its true worth measured against the *mass* music of, say, Liberace, not against the classics.

The effect of all this critical industry and consumer activity was that popular culture was being taken seriously. Regardless of variety, pulp takes a significant place, though its meaning is still in flux. It might be evoked to suggest that a particular body of work transcends its origins, such as Chandler's. It might be used provocatively as a means of expressing disdain for official culture. It might also be taken as a reproach to elite culture, to signal the redundancy of cultural hierarchies, or it might be condemned as fiction for morons. It might even be valued for and of itself.

Donald Phelps has made the case for considering pulp as pulp in his critique of Ernie Kovacs, Lenny Bruce, and *Mad* magazine, which he called the "Muck School of American Comedy." This form of comedy, Phelps argued, owes its "existence to an inert layer of disgust and passive resentment which lies like a pool of candle-wax in nearly every city-dweller's soul. This feeling is about as useful and creative as the contents of the occasional alleys between bar and novelty store along Sixth Avenue; and, I'd be willing to bet, inaccessible to any treatment in any conventional kind of serious art."[63]

The recognition that certain forms of cultural production are not responsive to critical practice forged in the furnace of debates on the high arts, rather than diminish the critic's role, might actually enhance his or her standing. In a 1960 *Sight & Sound* article on the theory then emerging from France, Richard Roud quoted Rene Guyonnet's provocative statement that genre movies, not art movies, best assessed a writer's critical skills: "Westerns and film noirs are perhaps the best test of the film critic because their value is so often a matter of form, technique, iconography: all the elements that separate the cinema from literature."[64] This was not, however, an arbitrary plundering of the trash bins of popular culture. As the film scholar Thomas Elsaesser pointed out in an essay on the French fascination with American cinema: "The cinephiles, like the surrealists before them, were ransacking popular culture for conscious or involuntary sublimities in the way of visual or emotional shocks and for that elusive quality of the 'insolite' by which imaginative authenticity could be gauged." The French cinephiles "stressed the subversive element in 'pop,' where Hollywood could provide additional fire-power in the revolt against bourgeois notions of appeasement, sobriety and taste in art."[65]

Writing in 1960, the same year as Roud's critique of French theory, Lawrence Alloway had the following to say about the difference between the French and the English consumption of American popular culture: "In Paris, on the contrary, acceptance of American movies and *Mad* is subject to both a surrealist filter and a language barrier. The result is that French intellectuals judge U.S. pop by a canon of strangeness and eroticism which is sheer fantasy. Luckily England is not subject to this exotic view: the balance of distance and access is just right for U.S. pop art to be real but not common, vivid but not weird."[66] These cultural distinctions between France, Britain, and the United States were most marked in the debates around the value of Robert Aldrich and A. I. Bezzerides's adaptation of the Mickey Spillane novel *Kiss Me, Deadly*.

3

A World of Small Insanities

The Critical Reception of *Kiss Me Deadly*

Beauty will be CONVULSIVE or it will not be at all.

–André Breton

In 1999 the Library of Congress selected *Kiss Me Deadly* (1955) to be included in the National Film Registry, thus preserving "a significant element of American creativity and our cultural history for the enjoyment and education of future generations."[1] The film's selection as a national treasure brings into relief the shift in critical positions that *Kiss Me Deadly*, in particular, and pulp films, more generally, underwent in the almost half-century between 1955 and 1999. The award of cultural legitimacy placed on the film by the Library of Congress was made in the knowledge that when *Kiss Me Deadly* was originally released, it was sold and received as a sensational crime movie. Based on the multimillion-selling pulp novel by Mickey Spillane, whose work had been roundly disparaged as brutish male fantasies, the film faired poorly with American critics when it was first appraised. Opinion against it was even more outspoken in England, where critics thought that the film was yet another example of degenerate postwar American culture that was then widely assumed to be undermining public morality. Over the channel in France, however, some critics found poetry among the blood-guts-sex-and-sadism. They argued that this was a movie directed by a genuine auteur, who had subverted the film's nauseous source material and revealed the hollowness of American capitalism and consumer culture. They claimed Robert Aldrich had produced the thriller of tomorrow. Over the years English and American critics would catch up with, and honor, their French counterparts by bestowing on the film the designation "film noir"—they too had found poetry in *Kiss Me Deadly*'s savage art.

In an essay published in the year following *Kiss Me Deadly*'s induction into the National Registry, Richard Maltby challenged the received wisdom that the film was a "subversive" text and an auteurist masterpiece. Maltby reclaimed the context of the film's production in order to engage "in a form of cultural history that tries to situate a complex artifact like *Kiss Me Deadly* more concretely

14. Press ad for *Kiss Me Deadly* (1955).

within the culture in which it was formed and in which it functioned as both a cultural and economic entity."[2] Moving through a history of paperback publishing and the debates on mass culture, Maltby continued his examination via an analysis of the exploitation and exhibition of *Kiss Me Deadly*. He paid particular attention to the adaptation process and the regulatory role of the Production Code Administration (PCA).

Maltby persuasively argued that the institutional framework determined the possibility of Aldrich's supposed subversion of his source material: "The

PCA's insistence on the movie's anti-heroic treatment of its protagonist required the attitudinal shifts that are, by critical convention, attributed either to Aldrich and Bezzerides as authors or to *noir* as a sensibility. Unable to discard the commercial value of the source material in an overt and explicit rejection of its protagonist, the production was obliged to resort to strategies of incoherence, contradiction and allusion. The subsequent critical repositioning of the movie provided a framework in which this breakdown of convention could assume interpretive malleability." The acts of interpretation Maltby was particularly keen to challenge were those that led to the film's canonization as an American art movie, an act of transformation enabled by the film's redefinition as film noir. The film moved, Maltby concluded, from cultural detritus to aestheticized object of veneration. "Commodified trash" was turned into "vanguardist art" through the process of critical intervention and appropriation. Maltby's essay is a necessary corrective to the excesses of auteurist studies of Aldrich and to the solipsism of so much noir criticism, but, despite the compelling force of his argument, it is far from the complete story of the film's ambivalent status as pulp *and* art.

Censorship did produce moments of incoherence, as Maltby argues, but this important trait in the film's varied reception history was already present in the source novel. Indeed, Spillane was roundly and often criticized for his failure to tell a coherent story. The author and his core readership were repeatedly condemned for their willingness to suspend disbelief in the face of weak plotting and characterization, and twice damned for the pleasure taken in *Kiss Me, Deadly*'s sensational story of an investigation into a criminal conspiracy, carried out at a terrific pace with the guarantee of frequent scenes of violence and erotic titillation. The filmmakers respected both the strictures of the production code and the base appeal of Spillane's fiction, including the tired plotting, broad characterization, and moments of willful incoherence.

The PCA worked to dilute, obscure, and expunge the sensational aspects of Spillane's novel, particularly its investigation into drug trafficking, which was transformed into an atomic conspiracy, but also, as recorded in a PCA memo, "its portrayal of Mike Hammer, private detective, as a cold blooded murderer whose numerous killings are completely justified. His taking of the law into his own hands and successfully bringing the criminals to 'justice' by killing them, is in complete violation of the Code" (Maltby). An anemic adaptation of a Spillane story, however, would be a hard sell. The filmmakers needed to ensure that an adaptation of his work delivered on the promise made in marketing materials of "white-hot thrills!" and "blood-red kisses!" Negotiating between these seemingly antithetical positions is what Maltby argues was the determining factor in the production of an unstable, unconventional, and incoherent text.

Critical accounts that ascribe the determination of the film to the creative agency of Aldrich, and scriptwriter A. I. Bezzerides, still have some validity, however. On one hand, there is no doubt that the filmmakers had little, if any, sympathy with Spillane's worldview as expressed through the character of Mike Hammer. Evidence to support this position is found not only in statements they have made in interviews, in interpretations of the film, but it is also there in extant versions of the screenplay. On the other hand, the filmmakers were engaged in the commercial exploitation of Mike Hammer. Bezzerides may have despised Spillane and his creation, as has often been attested, but he was also being paid to represent Hammer for the legion of readers who saw nothing untoward in the thuggish figure of a self-appointed law enforcer, judge, and jury. The contradictory position held by the filmmakers toward their source material helps explain changes in the characterization of Hammer from an unrefined man, at home in the bars and dives of New York, who uses his fists to uncover the conspiracy, to the narcissistic playboy living in a bachelor pad in Los Angeles who solves the mystery by reading a poem. These core changes cannot alone be explained by the intervention of the PCA.

Sex and violence are the common currency peddled by the seven Spillane novels and the four Parklane Picture adaptations—*I, the Jury* (1953), *The Long Wait* (1954), *Kiss Me Deadly*, and *My Gun Is Quick* (1957). *Variety* noted as much in its perfunctory review of *Kiss Me Deadly*: "The ingredients that sell Mickey Spillane's novels about Mike Hammer, the hard-boiled private eye, are thoroughly worked over in this latest Parklane Pictures presentation built around the rock-and-sock character. The combo of blood action and sex which has attracted b.o. in previous entries should repeat here."[3] The *L.A. Examiner* also focused on sex and violence as the film's primary attraction: "Not for children, not for the squeamish and certainly not for those seeking pleasant diversion. The story's appeal will in the main rest with those fans who simply dote on the Spillane brand of gory goings-on."[4] The *L.A. Times* concurred with *Variety* and the *Examiner*, but it also noted the superior production values over the earlier entries in the series and its sometimes coherent story line: "It attains the dubious distinction of being the best of the Mike Hammer series. Thanks to having had an at-least-reputable writing man, A. I. Bezzerides on the screenplay, it contains moments that are comparatively lucid and almost begin to make sense. An instant later, of course, the whole thing slips off base and we are groping in the dark again; but in Mickey Spillane's world, a world of small insanities, we are grateful for small favors."[5]

The lack of lucidity, and the senselessness of it all, was also noticed by the *Hollywood Reporter*, which is worth quoting at length to see how the reviewer grappled with the film's artistic ambitions and its violations of conventional storytelling:

> If this production had not been made so relentlessly "arty" it might have been thoroughly artistic. It contains many good things, including some exciting camera angles by Ernest Laszlo on locations that feature the

picturesque and seamy side of Los Angeles. Part of the score by Frank
DeVol is arresting and interesting. But at other times the sound track is
so cluttered with moans, screams and blatant broadcasts of horse races
and prize fights that it is almost impossible to concentrate on the dialogue
and the story. . . . A. I. Bezzerides has written some literate dialogue, but
when a heavy says, "Had I all the heads of Cerebus, I would bark at you,"
it gets so high-flown that it soars beyond the frontiers of thought and
common sense. Robert Aldrich has directed an arresting opening and a
hair-raising ending, but since he never gets either of them clearly related
to his story, the resulting murder mystery is even more mysterious when
everything is over than when it began. The production has everything
"On the Waterfront" had except the ability to coordinate its elements
into a connected and harmonious narrative.[6]

The review pulled into sharp focus questions around coherence, comprehen-
sion, and rationality as they apply to storytelling, but it also recognized, however
dismissively, the film's artistic pretensions. The question over how one inter-
prets and values the film's moments of incoherence and heightened stylistic
traits lies at the heart of responses to the film, particularly in France.

"There can be no doubt that the revelation of Robert Aldrich will be the
cinema event of 1955. When the year began we didn't even know his name,"
wrote François Truffaut in his review of Kiss Me Deadly. Indeed, 1955 was
Aldrich's year, so was 1956. Truffaut thought Kiss Me Deadly the most original
American film since The Lady from Shanghai. In the Christmas 1955 edition of
Cahiers du cinéma Jacques Rivette claimed Aldrich as evidence of the arrival of
the age of the auteur in Hollywood. The journal put three Aldrich films into
their "best of" list for 1955. Also in the Christmas issue Claude Chabrol made Kiss
Me Deadly the centerpiece of his essay on the evolution of the thriller. In 1956
Truffaut interviewed Aldrich for Cahiers, and the Cinémathèque paid homage
to the director with a season of his films. The cinema's curator, Henri Langlois,
echoing Rivette, considered "Aldrich to be living proof that an 'author' could
still exist in Hollywood."[7] In that same year Positif ran a major article on
Aldrich's work to date, and Cahiers du cinéma ran Jean Domarchi's article on
Marxist theory, which argued that Aldrich's films represented a radical critique
of capitalist society.

Domarchi made the case for an American cinema that has "tried to bring
on to the screen the fall of American man." According to Domarchi recent films
by Minnelli, Mankiewicz, Aldrich, Welles, Hawks, Lang, and Hitchcock all dealt
with the same subject: "the impossibility in the present state of things of an
effective and genuine morality, or if you like, the incompatibility of morality
(other than that of the police) and capitalist society." He continued: "The
denunciation of artificiality is found at its bitterest in The Big Knife and Kiss Me

Deadly." These films, like those of the auteurs listed above, are all the more punishing in their "critique of an extremely commercialized American consciousness . . . when their subject seems furthest from any social preoccupation that the critique goes furthest, touching the sensitive nerve of the new Leviathan which is American capitalist society." This quasi-Marxist explication of *Kiss Me Deadly* is the finest example of the "ideological subversion" of the film's source novel as we are likely to find.[8] Certainly, Spillane's absolute insistence on the inviolability of his hero's individual agency, and the violent imposition of his reactionary values on all and sundry, is completely antithetical to any communitarian ideals. So, for Domarchi to claim that the film is a critique of capitalism is to truly turn Spillane and Hammer on their heads.

Chabrol's description of *Kiss Me Deadly* as "the thriller of tomorrow" is based on the idea that it both subverts its source material and transcends its generic conventions: "freed from everything and especially from itself . . . out of the worst material to be found, the most deplorable, the most nauseous product of a genre in a state of putrefaction: a Mickey Spillane story. Robert Aldrich and A. I. Bezzerides have taken this threadbare and lacklustre fabric and woven it into rich patterns of the most enigmatic arabesques."[9] Domarchi claimed that the film is a political subversion of the novel; Chabrol further claimed that the film is a formal and stylistic subversion and transformation of its source.

Truffaut had not read the Spillane novel, as he understood it to be mediocre, anyway. He was more interested in the film as a film. To "appreciate *Kiss Me Deadly*," he wrote, "you have to love movies passionately and to have a vivid memory of those evenings when you saw *Scarface*, *Under Capricorn*, *Le Sang d'un poète* (*The Blood of a Poet*), *Les Dames du Bois Boulogne*, and *Lady from Shanghai*." *Kiss Me Deadly*'s "inventiveness is so rich that we don't know what to look at— the images are almost too full, too fertile. . . . You can only admire the extraordinary freedom of this movie, which surprisingly enough, may be compared in some ways to Jean Cocteau's *Le Sang d'un poète*, a favorite classic of the cineclubs."[10] Truffaut did not offer any direct points of comparison, though he clearly believed there was an affinity in the films' foregrounding of discontinuities, incoherencies, and oneiric configuration of time and space. The connection he was making, however, between a much respected art film and a commercial example of pulp cinema—art house and grind house—was equally an act of willful provocation, an act that was produced to upset sensibilities that rejected the "primitive" cinematic attraction of some forms of American cinema.

In his "Notes on a Revolution" Rivette wrote, "For years the cinema has been dying from intelligence and subtlety. Now Rossellini is breaking down that door; but you can also breathe in that gust of fresh air reaching us from across the ocean." The fresh air came with the films of Nicholas Ray, Richard Brooks, Anthony Mann, and Robert Aldrich. With these filmmakers as his evidence, Rivette claimed the age of the auteur in Hollywood had arrived. "Violence is their virtue; not that facile brutality that made Dmytryk or Benedek successful, but a virile anger that comes from the heart, and is to be found less in the script and the plotting than in the cadences of the narrative and in the very technique of the mise en scene." Reading their mise-en-scène as a rejection of the pieties of more "sophisticated" filmmakers, Rivette claimed that their "frequent recourse to a discontinuous, abrupt technique which refuses the conventions of classical editing and continuity is a form of the 'superior clumsiness' which Cocteau talks about, born of the need for an immediacy of expression that can yield up, and allow the viewer to share in, the original emotions of the auteur," which, in Aldrich's case, is "precisely the destruction of morality, and its consequences."[11]

The spirit of Cocteau, and the aesthetic of a "superior clumsiness" that Truffaut and Rivette discovered in Aldrich's early films, cannot have been far from the thoughts of the *Positif* critic Roger Tailleur's extraordinary appreciation of *Kiss Me Deadly*, a film he thought akin to a surrealist poem:

> . . . a procession of night and death: a collector of abstract art in his apartment-cum-museum, a girl running barefoot on a road at night, a suave-sounding chief of the FBI, an Italian mover, a few killers, a Greek mechanic with a booming voice, a noisy blonde girl on a bed in a hotel room, a black manager in his gym, looking a little purple from overexertion, a disfigured reporter hiding out in a room, a doctor in a morgue dissecting bodies, other killers and other girls around a billionaire's pool, a bel canto singer in a sordid apartment, the deceitful secretary at the Hollywood Athletic Club, a truck driver having dinner with his family at home, the female singer in a black nightclub, a few black cops.
>
> On the screen, the poem is the film itself, black and gray, brutal and blaring (a hysterical soundtrack, full of panting, shouting, punches, and explosions), a nightmare. For one of the keys to the film is the resolutely dreamlike nature of the story, which is the most obvious—and darkest— source of its violent poetry.[12]

The oneiric, violent poetics of *Kiss Me Deadly* that Tailleur unravels dovetails with the surrealist allusions in the *Cahiers du cinéma* criticism; this is not simply a happy coincidence.[13] Discussing the French auteurist critics of the 1950s, James Naremore wrote that "their charm lay in the fact that they were always dreamers of mass culture, looking for what André Breton has called 'moments of priceless giddiness.'"[14] The film was also given a positive notice in the surrealist literary revue *Bizarre*, which, like Domarchi, found the film profoundly moral, particularly in its attack on bourgeois propriety.[15] Surrealism's long-standing engagement with popular cultural forms that display an insolent disregard for the appropriateness of bourgeois notions of good taste provided a ready-made platform from which the cinephiles of *Positif* and *Cahiers du cinéma* could make their claims for *Kiss Me Deadly*'s unique appeal.

In *Pulp Surrealism* Robin Walz offers an extraordinarily rich guide to the popular culture from which, in great part, surrealism emerged. He writes that "the surrealists did not so much create as discover the surreality of their epoch. At the founding of their movement, the surrealists drew inspiration from currents of psychological anxiety and social rebellion that ran through certain expressions of mass culture, such as fantastic popular fiction and sensationalist journalism."[16] There was a shared understanding on the part of surrealists that in some forms of popular culture there was the potential for an insolent and provocative engagement with bourgeois mores and values by "displaying a flagrant disregard for cultural conventions and social proprieties" (3).

One element of the surreal that so enthralled was the manner in which the incoherence of popular fictions matched the incoherence of everyday life: "The surrealists were well aware that on an everyday basis commercial mass culture was not experienced as incomprehensible but as ordinary and banal." However, avers Walz, as "literary and artistic provocateurs, part of the surrealist project was to illuminate the extraordinary in a mass culture that might otherwise pass as quotidian" (9). The fictional crime series *Fantomas* best exemplified this process. According to Walz, *Fantomas* created "popular entertainment out of indeterminate identities, incoherences of time and space, technological gadgetry, and unmotivated violence." In the surrealists' hands these elements were released from "their bourgeois social moorings. . . . *Fantomas* operated outside logic and deduction, and it offered no moral or social restitution. Instead, it was a *récit impossible*, an impossible story of displaced identities, detours, paradoxes, and violence" (45).

Fantomas is the supreme example of popular culture that is surreal *before* the fact; however, by combining banal commercial objects with surreal artifacts, it is also possible to radically alter the perception of everyday products, to make them surreal *after* the fact. An example of the transformative potential of juxtaposition is evident in the program of films that supported the initial run of *Un chien andalou* in Paris, beginning in June 1929, at the avant-garde cinema Studio 28. According to a February 1930 report from the Paris-based *New York Times* correspondent, Morris Gilbert, the latest Parisian cinematic craze was for *Un chien andalou*, which he described as a "horror film"—"The horror does not depend on plot in any sense, since there is none; or on suspense, since there is none—except the fear in the audience that it may see again, before the picture is over, the same, or a worse, incident which passed across the film within the first two minutes of its unrolling. . . . From that point the film unfolds its incoherent path, dealing with pathological states and the presentation of varying degrees of putrefaction and carnality." *Un chien andalou* was not presented in isolation but alongside other films, thus creating the possibility for some marvelous associations:

[The] other features are extraordinarily attractive, from a point of view not only intellectual, but popular.

The first presentation is also a modernist film—*Vive la Foire* [directed by Michel Gorel and Daniel Abric, camera by Jean Dréville, 1930]—a picture without story or apparent sequence, dealing with the gayety, the life and manners of a French fair. This has moments of charm and none of boredom or disgust. Following it is a riotously funny—and very ancient—comedy of the genus Keystone, featuring Harold Lloyd in those antediluvian days before he wore spectacles.

The evening was brought to a close successfully, but with a certain conventionality, too, by a picture featuring William Boyd, a "cop" picture of New York. It was called here *14-101*—the number of Boyd's policeman's shield. Perhaps it had the same title at home.[17]

The Boyd film, directed by Donald Crisp, was called *The Cop* (1928) on its domestic release. It is not difficult to see in this particular compact of the popular (American comedy and crime films) and the avant-garde (a "modernist" actuality and a surreal film) a set of associations that will later enable the reading of *Kiss Me Deadly* as a marvelous incarnation of insolent popular culture.[18] This type of compact is what lay behind Truffaut's provocation of cine-club patrons in his linking *Kiss Me Deadly* with *Le Sang d'un poète*.

But while Truffaut and his peers reveled in the overlap between art and commerce that they had discovered in *Kiss Me Deadly*, elsewhere a different response to the film could be found. The reviewer for the British Film Institute's *Monthly Film Bulletin*, Gavin Lambert, noted the artistic aspirations of *Kiss Me Deadly*'s filmmakers and highlighted the film's play with incoherence, but unlike his French contemporaries he did not share a surreal tradition through which he could filter his response, so he found the compact of art and pulp unsatisfactory: "The latest Mike Hammer adventure is distinguished from its predecessors by an extraordinary arty style—bold, formalised low-key effects, tilted shots, extreme close-ups, complicated long takes, sometimes *outré* compositions. The meeting of 'art' and pulp literature is, at the least, curious. One cannot say that Robert Aldrich's direction lends clarity to a narrative already somewhat confused and difficult to follow—indeed, at times it further obscures it; but it does create an atmosphere of its own."[19]

Was the film, then, a marvelous mélange or an unsatisfactory combination of usually discrete elements? Either way, the apparent contradiction between the filmmakers' artistic pretensions and the story's pulp status is partly responsible for determining the film's reception as something akin to a dream. The *Motion Picture Herald* categorized *Kiss Me Deadly* as a "Phantasmagoria," which is commonly understood as a series of strange, bizarre, oneiric images, where a scene might encompass many things and many changes. Such a categorization put the film in a genre all its own. The generic term *melodrama*, which was usually used to categorize films like *Kiss Me Deadly*, was not deemed appropriate.[20]

The *Herald*'s reviewer considered that "Spillane's notorious brutalities seem forced and artificial, his sex is not pornographic, hardly even photographic, and the action is so disconnected as to leave an impression of nightmarish non-sense," hence, phantasmagoria.

Although the reviews in British and American popular and trade presses were generally negative, they were, nevertheless, selecting and emphasizing exactly the same aspects of the film as their French counterparts, most obviously the projection of a nightmarish nonsense, or, alternatively, a superior clumsiness. The opposing critical responses to the same phenomena appear to exceed the filmmakers' motivation for producing the film, which was to present an expedient exploitation of Spillane and his character, Mike Hammer. In attracting a diverse audience—cinephiles and Spillane's core readership—and in eliciting such divergent critical responses, *Kiss Me Deadly* "overspills the mold in which it has been cast." This is what J. H. Matthews understood had to happen in order for a commercial film to become available for surrealist misuse.[21] The French critics focused on the film's excesses, delighting in their discovery of a "subversive" American auteur, and willfully forcing through a connection between the film and the avant-garde, as represented by Cocteau, in order to promote their radical critical credentials and to provoke, and undermine, the critical establishment.

The idea that *Kiss Me Deadly* might pose as a surreal artifact would have appeared grossly pretentious to the film's original British and American reviewers. Yet a close examination of the trade press notices and other reviews of the film underscores the idea that it shared a similar state of incoherence, with "varying degrees of putrefaction and carnality," with films such as *Un chien andalou* or *Le Sang d'un poète*. But to recognize these traits as marvelous meant that one had to hold a view of culture that maintained that certain aspects of popular fictions could be potentially seditious—producing a troubling presence for the bourgeois consumer. British and American reviewers, however, obviously did not share the worldview held by their less regardful French counterparts. Like good bourgeois citizens, Anglo critics took umbrage with the film's direct appeal to the sensational ("The film has brought together a bevy of well-stacked, pistol-packed broads who are easy on the eyes, but murder on the nerves.") and roundly condemned it as rubbish.[22] That which the American and British reviewers found intolerable in the film became the source of the cinephiles' fascination.

The recognition that there are a number of distinct responses to the film's incoherencies needs to be understood alongside the fact that there are also a variety of explanations for what produced this effect. As demonstrated in Maltby's analysis of the PCA's records on the development of *Kiss Me Deadly*'s screenplay, narrative incoherence was a strategy employed by the filmmakers to enable them to make best use of the principal exploitable elements in Spillane's work—sex and violence—while remaining true to the letter, if not the spirit, of the Code. The British Board of Film Censors' (BBFC) file on *Kiss Me Deadly* has been destroyed, but contemporary British reviews note how local censorship had furthered the film's irrationality: "The censor has excised a few (presumably brutal) moments, making one scene almost incomprehensible."[23] The BBFC's file on *I, the Jury*, however, does still exist, and it helps to illuminate the issue of incoherence determined by regulatory intervention in the adaptation of Spillane's fiction. A BBFC examiner wrote: "I thought *I, the Jury* an unpleasant and senseless picture—no more than a vehicle for violence and crude behavior with a lacing of sex. The story was [so] confused (possibly made more confused by cutting) that it was difficult to follow the thread." The film is senseless on two counts: narrative incoherence and its apparent defense of antisocial behavior—"The most dangerous element seems to me the representation of the hero. To build up a hero figure of this type must be an encouragement to the adolescent tough, and the reiteration of his appeal to women makes it worse."[24]

A second BBFC examiner concurred:

> I saw this wretched film at the London Pavilion on Saturday, 12 December, 1953, not primarily to test audience reactions, but to see if I could get the story any clearer in my own mind. I still cannot tell it with any precision, but I must admit that the unpleasant qualities of the film emerge much more clearly when one no longer has to try and keep up with the story. . . . It is, however, an expert piece of censor-dodging, because, just as one thinks it is about something censorable for any category, it suddenly goes about on the other tack and pretends to be a straightforward tale of crooks and fences disposing of priceless jewels. . . . Perhaps we ought really to have seen this film twice and then banned it.[25]

Certainly censorship contributed to the sense of incoherence, and Aldrich and his collaborators would have been aware of this effect when they were in preproduction on *Kiss Me Deadly*. Like the source novels, however, the Spillane adaptations function on the basis that the narrative, character types, locations, and so forth are readily familiar to their intended audience. Audiences, such as the BBFC's examiners, who are unreceptive to the formula are apt to identify points of incoherence, when in fact the film might be perfectly logical within its own terms of reference. Moreover, while the censors clearly value narrative coherence, it cannot be taken for granted that the core audience for Spillane adaptations gives it the same value.

In *Kiss Me Deadly* Aldrich and Bezzerides effectively captured Spillane's manic movement from scene to scene, action to action, seduction to seduction, beating to beating, cigarette to cigarette, and killing to killing. This extract from the novel gives a good indication of the story's pacing:

> The bulging eyes flattened out, sick. "They're spending advance money along the Stem."

"Moving fast?"

I could hardly hear his voice. "Covering the bars and making phone calls."

"Are they in a hurry?"

"Bonus, probably."[26]

The speed with which he tells his story inevitably leads Spillane to take shortcuts in his plotting, which in turn leads to coincidence:

"Coincidence is out," I said.

"Naturally." His mouth twitched again. "They don't know that you're the guy things happen to. Some people are accident prone. You're coincidence prone."

"I've thought of it that way," I told him. "Now what about the details of her escape?" (51)

And coincidence in Spillane's fiction goes hand-in-hand with incoherence: "If ever there was a mess, this was it. Everything out of place and out of focus. The ends didn't even try to meet. Meet? Hell, they were snarled up so completely nothing made any sense" (77). Working with Spillane's gallery of types and stock situations, the filmmakers made sure they also remained true to the amphetamine whirl of his storytelling.

In a 1952 article in *True: The Man's Magazine* the journalist described Spillane in the act of creation: "Most professional writers double-space their copy as they type it so pencil corrections can later be made where necessary. Not so Spillane. He gets so excited when he writes that he single-spaces his typewriter so he won't have to interrupt himself as frequently to change pages. 'I hate to waste seconds putting another piece of paper into the machine.' He seldom corrects anything."[27] The emphasis put on the speed of writing matched Bezzerides's description of how he wrote the screenplay: "I wrote it fast, because I had contempt for it. It was automatic writing. You get into a kind of stream and you can't stop."[28] The difference is that Bezzerides is an intellectual, unlike Spillane. Spillane might practice "automatic writing," but he would not have been conscious of this fact. Bezzerides, however, knew about the surreal potential of automatic writing, producing in his screenplay a meeting of art and pulp that is wholly absent in the source novel.

Any need for narrative coherence in Spillane's fiction, and in the adaptation of *Kiss Me, Deadly*, must not be allowed to slow things down. Spillane tells his stories in a stepped-up, hopped-up fashion, with little regard to narrative coherence. As a critic from *Lowdown* magazine noted: "It's not easy to keep up with Mike Hammer while he is tearing through the night, making love intermittently and blasting down people. It is also confusing to keep track, in the same book, with which girl he is being torrid." And this is from an article that is generally supportive of Spillane. The critic finished with some advice for Spillane wannabes: "DO YOU WANT TO BE A SUCCESSFUL WRITER? Take your easy, four-free lessons in the men's room, pack a gun on every page, undress a girl with a zip, and send it off to a publisher."[29] But Spillane's success was not so simply reducible, nor was it easily duplicated. Even his publishers had a hard time explaining Spillane's popularity: "I don't think we can ever judge Spillane's appeal by logical mystery standards. His magic, in our market, seems to consist of a sort of existential vibration, to which the readers out yonder seem to be able to tune in."[30] His editor may as well have explained Spillane's appeal as something conjured up by voodoo. What Spillane's editors did acknowledge, however, was his ability to keep the story moving. In a letter to E. P. Dutton, Spillane's trade press publisher, the assistant editor at Signet, Marc Jaffe, explained what was happening in the latest round of rewrites for *The Long Wait*: "I'm afraid Mickey hasn't succeeded in making the finish any more plausible (for those who demand plausibility in a Spillane yarn), but the long and rather dull exposition of the plot is broken up and made a bit more suspenseful."[31] In this context, making sense is far less important than keeping things moving.

In a defense of Spillane in *New World Writing* (1952), Charles Rolo noted: "Spillane has, incontestably, a remarkable talent for keeping the action moving fast and furiously; and his climaxes (until you get to know his plotting) are packed with suspense and surprise—melodramatic beyond belief."[32] Suspense is a key feature of the stories, but it is not something that necessarily relies on logical plot developments; narrative plausibility is often forgotten in the rush to the finish. Discussing the follow-up to *I, the Jury*, Victor Weybright, editor-in-chief at Signet, wrote: "I think this book is right on the beam of *I, The Jury*, and, despite a pretty fantastic plot, has enough momentum and vibration to overcome any incredulity."[33] When Spillane's publishers were demanding a follow-up story to his second novel, *My Gun Is Quick*, the author offered them *Whom God Wishes to Destroy*, an old manuscript. It was a story about the kidnapping of a precocious child of a top-ranking scientist and featured the usual gallery of stock types: "Suspicious characters include various York relatives (one a very hot piece of feminine pulchritude); a nurse whom Mike knows as an ex-burlesque queen; a lesbian governess; a crooked local police chief; and minor individuals who move in and out of the plot wielding blackjacks and bosoms."[34]

The publishers did not think much of the story but believed it could be improved, particularly if Spillane would raise the age of the child and pull back on the descriptions of his prodigious talents—the child had taught himself to play concert standard piano in five days. Spillane preferred not to make any changes. New books were published, but after the delivery of *Kiss Me, Deadly*, which Spillane, his publishers, and many readers thought his weakest novel to date, no new novel-length material appeared, and the publishers looked to revive *Whom God Wishes to Destroy*. Weybright wrote to Spillane: "As you know Dutton have been holding this book until the time when its rather incredible aspects would be acceptable to your public. That time has certainly arrived, to judge by the trade and reprint sales of *Kiss Me, Deadly*, which is not nearly so strong a book as *Whom God Wishes to Destroy* or, for that matter, most of your other books."[35] The idea that Spillane's public cared little, if at all, for plausibility, particularly as they became more familiar with his work, is intriguing, but it is not unique to Spillane.

Lawrence Alloway noted an increased narrative velocity in postwar American action films in general, something akin to what occurs in Spillane's novels, and supported his argument by quoting M. C. Bradbrook, an authority on Elizabethan tragedy: "The Revenge plays had a fixed narrative and fixed characters; consequently the speed of the intrigue steadily accelerated, yet the people would not feel the incidents to be incredible, though their effectiveness depended on their being extraordinary."[36] Turning Alloway's equation around, the theater director John Landau described his 1955 production of John Webster's *The White Devil* as an "Elizabethan thriller": "Revenge is the end. The ingredients are murder, adultery, perjury, rape, the madman's laughter and the widow's tears. The vitality—Rupert Brooke named it the 'foul and indestructible vitality'—of these people intrigued Webster. They live in what might be called an Elizabethan Mickey Spillane world. Webster himself refers to his characters as 'glorious villains,' and the lives they lead as 'vain.'"[37]

Bringing this idea of the extraordinary and everyday events into nineteenth-century fiction, the historian of American dime novels Michael Denning wrote, "So a story to be a story had to be set in a contemporary time and knowable landscape, but its plot had to be out of the ordinary; 'everyday happenings,' according to this working woman's aesthetic, did not make a story. The story was an interruption in the present, a magical, fairy tale transformation of familiar landscapes and characters, a death and rebirth that turned the social world upside down, making proud ladies villains, and working-girls ladies."[38]

There is something of this transformation of the everyday in Spillane's fiction. Weybright called him a "comic strip extravagandist,"[39] and the editor defended Spillane's stories against criticism from Max Lerner, a columnist at the *New York Post*: "They portray, in an urban setting, a never-never land as fantastic as the pseudo-chivalry and sudden death in the milieu of the Western novels, which has now become so much [a] part of the national folklore that its extravagances are innocuously taken for granted. Spillane—primitive as he is—is playful; and in his composite game he has put together the ingredients of the western novel, of the pursuit thriller, of the comic strip, and of the animated film cartoon, into a sort of cockeyed fairy story—just about as socially significant as the fun-house at Coney Island."[40]

Lerner responded with typical bourgeois incredulity: "I find it difficult to regard his curious concoction of violence, sadism, and fetishisms as 'playful.' The fact that it is done as a formula means simply that he has not been creative but it does not change the impact of his work."[41] "Fantastic" in its depiction of the everyday for one critic, Spillane's fiction was for another simply banal in its everyday degradation.

Kiss Me, Deadly, the novel, and *Kiss Me Deadly*, the film (the coma mysteriously vanished in the translation from book to movie), have "impact." But again, how we conceive of and value that impression, and to whom we ascribe responsibility for its production, remains open to question. In his *Positif* piece on *Kiss Me Deadly* Tailleur noted how Aldrich had turned "the modern thriller into a compressed form of serials, which in former times used to have twelve or twenty-four episodes." Aldrich, he wrote, disposed of the genre's secondary characters "masterfully in two words, two gestures, sometimes fewer."[42] Whether or not Aldrich is responsible for these acts of extraordinary compression remains to be answered, but concentrated and maximized generic traits were a fundamental element of Spillane's fiction.[43]

Life magazine began its profile of the writer with Spillane telling his interviewer about a short story called "The Girl with Green Skin": "There's this girl, see—she's beautiful, she's stark naked, only she's all green."[44] Spillane is trying to illustrate his craft by telling a story, a simple story, because that is what he does. He is a teller of tales, a craftsman, or at least that is how he wants to be seen. In a 1953 edition of *MALE* magazine Spillane gave an illustration of how his fiction can be condensed down to a small number of key elements. The story is "The Screen Test of Mike Hammer," and it is produced in the form of a screenplay, accompanied by eight illustrative stills. The film lasts five minutes, it is said, and features three characters: Hammer, Helen, and a Bum. A kill-happy maniac is on the loose, and the police are using Mike Hammer's girl as bait. This is because, like Mike, she grew up on the same street as the killer, and the killer is out to kill everyone whoever lived on that street:

MIKE (*LOOKS OVER HER HEAD INTO THE DARKNESS*): The street. Putrid Avenue. Killer's Alley. They've called it everything. Just one street that isn't even alive and it can make murderers out of some people and millionaires out of others. One street, Helen. (*Long pause.* Mike *looks over her head.*) I can hear them, kid. They're closing in now. There's no place for the maniac to go now. (*Looks at her.*) Can you imagine a mind filled with a crazy obsession for a whole lifetime? Imagine hating a street so hard you wanted to kill everyone on it. One stinking street that makes up your whole background that you can never escape from. Can you imagine that, Helen?

HELEN: No, Mike . . . it's incredible. It's almost impossible!

Helen, however, as Mike already knows, is the real force behind the killings.

15. "The Screen Test of Mike Hammer," in *MALE* (July 1953).

HELEN (SCARED STIFF. CRYING): Mike . . . no . . . you . . . loved me. We were going to . . . be married. You . . .

MIKE: So we were in love. Should it make a difference? Fourteen dead people. Should it make a difference? So because I loved you I'll do you a favor, Helen. Nobody will ever know. . . .

HELEN: Mike . . . you can't . . . (*suddenly choked off.*)

MIKE'S VOICE: Don't pull your gun on me. So long, kid.

> *Camera catches* Helen, *her neck in* Mike's *hand, sinking . . . slowly on top of* Carmen. Mike *lets her fall, then flips cigarette on her back. Gun falls from her hand.*

> *Music up and out.*

Urban streets, many dead bodies, a mystery, a detective, a fatally attractive deceitful woman, and a denouement built on personal vengeance and rough justice—this is the essence of Spillane, his maximization.[45]

Spillane's influence is not difficult to locate in Peter Morisi's mid-1950s comic book stories of *Johnny Dynamite: The Wild Man from Chicago*, which read like perfect distillations of Spillane. The tales are full of pep and zip, with the one-eyed detective, who is visually modeled on John Garfield, sorting out hoods with both fists while sucking on a "chestie." The comic book historian Dan Nadel calls Morisi a "master of moment to moment storytelling . . . highly economical, and even refined."[46] The stories and art are certainly better than the Mike Hammer comic strip that ran in the dailies, which Spillane helped author, not least because they are closer to his fiction in their depiction of a squalid, brutal, misogynistic world.[47] A world is summed up in the cover blurb: "Meet Johnny Dynamite—his code: never trust a dame! Once he forgot! Just once! His lousy memory cost him an eye! The dame did it—but she paid with her life. With Johnny it was an 'eye for an eye.'" Johnny Dynamite was a maximized version of an already maximized character, Mike Hammer—an accelerated form of storytelling for an accelerating culture.

One of the finest illustrations of this concentration of elements is "The Girl Hunt" sequence in *Band Wagon* (1953), where Fred Astaire and Cyd Charisse assume the roles of archetypical Spillane characters within a series of tableaux linked by a dreamlike logic. The authors of *Panorama du film noir américain*, Raymond Borde and Etienne Chaumeton, found the sequence extraordinarily effective in its acts of compression:

> The ballet in *The Band Wagon* . . . is more than a parody, even a subtle one: a final concession to our past, it has the savor of those fated love affairs and wan nights of which all passive adventurers dream. A bit like Yves Salgues's poem "Clarinet Lament." From the cinema angle it's also one of the most extraordinary shorts in talkies, and, if the print were to disappear, one would wish to preserve this reel in some imaginary cinematheque. . . .

> . . . Sure, Minnelli has been inspired by a facile and banalized Surrealism. This ballet is a success, for all that. Never had the noir series been grasped "in its very essence" with such lucid complicity.[48]

16. *Dynamite* comic book, published by Comic Media, 1954. Johnny Dynamite, the one-eyed detective, was modeled on Mike Hammer. "His code: Never trust a dame! Once he forgot! Just once! His lousy memory cost him an eye! The dame did it—but she paid with her life. With Johnny it was an 'eye for an eye.'"

Like Tailleur, in his *Positif* review of *Kiss Me Deadly*, in their appreciation of "The Girl Hunt" sequence Borde and Chaumeton create a list of moments from the film that has the appearance of a surrealist poem, "a procession of night and death": "Rod Riley, a private eye, a tough guy, traverses the sleeping city. Somewhere, a trumpet solo pierces the night. A gorgeous, slender blonde falls into Rod's arms, terrorized. A man advances, gesticulates. He'd like to talk. Boom!" (110). And on it rolls. The acts of compression in Spillane's own work, in "The Girl Hunt," and *Kiss Me Deadly* are equally apparent in the two previous entries in the Spillane cycle of adaptations. *I, the Jury*'s story is every bit as simple as *Kiss Me Deadly*'s and equally confused and confusing, with Hammer intuitively solving the mystery of who killed his best friend, without any evidence to lead him to his conclusion.

The film is filled with the kind of generic compression enjoyed by the French supporters of *Kiss Me Deadly* and introduced a marvelous gallery of underworld types: pool hustlers, a bootblack in a top hat, a punch-drunk ex-fighter, a blind newspaper seller, an informer dressed up as Father Christmas, a nervous bartender, numbers runners, a femme psychiatrist with a hot line in negligees, nymphomaniac twins, homosexual art dealers, a barber, a dance instructor who gives private "rumba" lessons, flatfoot cops, dumb newspaper reporters, and a wise police captain. These are precisely the kinds of characters played by featured and bit-part actors who have been lovingly compiled in Ian and Elisabeth Cameron's rogues' gallery *The Heavies* (1967)—a pocketbook-sized digest of biographies, filmographies, and short descriptive passages on, among many others, the likes of Elisha Cook Jr., Gene Evans, Wesley Addy, Jack Elam, Jack Lambert, and Ralph Meeker, all of whom appear in one or more of the Spillane adaptations.[49]

The hoods, heavies, and fall guys that these actors portray populate a world that the French poet, novelist, and journalist Blaise Cendrars has called "gangsland":

> The passage between the reality of the street and the blazing artificiality of a bar happens so easily, and so unexpectedly. . . . You feel a sense of vertigo. Suddenly, you are hanging on to your table for dear life, like a wreck tossed about a tidal wave of dancing couples in a hot-jazz club. The first shot of alcohol down, overwhelmed by the abstract décor, nothing can help you figure out where you are, or how you got there.
>
> Are you in Shanghai? In Buenos Aires? In a New York "speak-easy"? Or are you in Paris?
>
> Without being aware of it, you have landed, simply and completely, in *gangsland*—a cynical and triumphant spectacle of neon lights in a miserable little room, where nothing is a mystery, but everything is disturbing.[50]

The tightly confined compositions, the claustrophobic spaces within which much of the action takes place, help to create the disturbing or phantasmagorical

17. Publicity photo for *I, the Jury* (1953). Mike Hammer (Biff Elliot) slugs it out with a hood in the Bradbury Building.

side of *I, the Jury*. Dull, flat surfaces patterned with grotesquely oversized shadows define most of the living and working spaces. The world between those interiors and the outside, the corridors, stairwells, and elevators, is equally barren and cramped. Only the skylit atrium of the Bradbury Building, with its cast-iron staircases and open-cage elevators, offers any contrast to the restricted interiors, but then the shots of the atrium are filmed from such disorienting high angles that vertigo replaces claustrophobia.[51] Outside it is night and raining. Each of the film's key images, according to the scholar Will Straw, takes on the appearance of the cover of a pulp paperback.[52]

In a press release it was announced that Mickey Spillane was to help out on scripts and dialogue "so that the film version will remain faithful to the published works." The film's producer, Victor Saville, it noted, anticipated "little problem in screen adaptation of the hard hitting novels of Spillane. Mr. Saville pointed out that all the novels were originally written very much like a movie scenario." There is no evidence that Spillane worked on the screenplay, but the shooting script does, rather uniquely, quote directly from his novel when describing the appeal of Charlotte Manning.[53] Composed exactly along the lines of the paperback cover of the Signet edition of the novel, the final scene shows Mike Hammer, dressed in trench coat and hat, holding his gun on Charlotte Manning as she undresses. The viewpoint is from over his shoulder, looking down the line of his gun. The point of view reverses that established at the beginning of the film, when the instructions in the screenplay demanded that the title be superimposed across the screen "as though it were A BULLET SHOT OUT OF THE SCREEN AND AT THE AUDIENCE."

In an interview given in the late 1990s, Spillane explained: "Sex and violence are punctuation marks in a story. The whole thing isn't written about sex and violence. There's a story involved."[54] Even by Spillane's standards, the film version of *I, the Jury* is overpunctuated. It is composed as a series of tableaux, where, despite Hammer's smash-and-grab antics, one static, dialogue-heavy scene follows another. There is much that impresses within these tableaux, but *I, the Jury*'s highly formalized jerk-and-pause pacing lacks the élan of *Kiss Me Deadly*, or perhaps it lacks its more celebrated partner's artistic pretensions.

It is not entirely clear why Victor Saville assigned Harry Essex to direct *I, the Jury*. This was Essex's first job as a director; he had previously worked exclusively as a scriptwriter, specializing in crime films. These were mostly middling productions, though a number have since found their supporters. Titles include *Boston Blackie and the Law* (1946), *Desperate* (1947), *Dragnet* (1947), *Bodyguard* (1948), *Undercover Girl* (1950), *The Killer That Stalked New York* (1950), *The Fat Man* (1951), *The Las Vegas Story* (1952), *Models, Inc.* (1952), *Kansas City Confidential* (1952), and *The 49th Man* (1953). There are no big hits here but plenty of solid programmers, certainly enough to suggest that Essex could turn in a reasonable adaptation of *I, the Jury* but nothing to suggest he would turn in an able job of directing. The film's star was equally lacking in experience. Biff Elliot was chosen to play Mike Hammer. *I, the Jury* was his film debut, though he had had a number of featured parts in television dramas. His costar, Peggy Castle, was also inexperienced. Saville was no doubt counting his pennies. The presence of Preston Foster as police captain Pat Chambers added a familiar face to the cast, as did Elisha Cook Jr. and John Qualen. John Alton's cinematography produced a strong visual connection with the crime films he made for Eagle-Lion, directed by Anthony Mann. Equally effective is Franz Waxman's score, particularly the jazz-inflected piano and double-bass passages that accompany Hammer on his nighttime prowls. Waxman had a good track record on crime films and a great track record on Hollywood films in general. His crime films included *Dark Passage* (1948), *Sorry, Wrong Number* (1948), *Night and the City* (1950), *Sunset Blvd.* (1950), *Dark City* (1950), and *He Ran All the Way* (1951).

Outside of this being a Spillane adaptation, an additional attraction and selling point was that the film had been shot in a 3-D process called Stereovision. Apart from first-run screenings, however, this process appears not to have been widely used in the film's exhibition, and the film did not make it to Britain in this format. Nevertheless, the format certainly left its mark on the film's structure. Discussing the low-budget horror movie *Creature from the Black Lagoon* (1954), for which Harry Essex crafted the screenplay, the film scholar

Kevin Heffernan has noted how the need to best utilize 3-D effects was responsible for the blocking of action in concentrated moments, so as to best exploit "hurling depth effects."[55] A good number of scenes in *I, the Jury* are constructed in just such a manner.

In his unpublished memoirs, written in 1974, Saville wrote that he had "deliberately set out to make a low-budget picture":

> United Artists were under new management. They had little product and their financial resources were limited. They were a little surprised to find I was financially able to guarantee completion of the films at the agreed budget. I had no intention of directing *I, The Jury*, but I was always at hand to take over if there were any signs of running over cost. I selected a young new actor to play Mike Hammer, one Biff Elliot. He was not unlike Mickey Spillane himself. He certainly had the appearance of the cigarette smoking, coffee drinking, raincoated private eye that Raymond Chandler drew so beautifully, but Biff was a little too green to pull it off, especially under the inexperienced direction I had provided for him.[56]

Saville may have intended only to make a low-budget programmer, but the film hit big with the public: "One thing I had guessed correctly, the publicity draw of Mickey Spillane. *I, The Jury* premiered at the large Chicago Theatre and took $90,000 in the first week—quite an achievement for a film budgeted at $375,000." Saville clearly held no artistic pretensions about *I, the Jury*; it was a project with which he sought to make money, and he stayed as true to his source material as the PCA and budget restrictions would allow. The next film in the series, *The Long Wait*, was a slightly different matter: "The audience reaction and the profitability of *I, The Jury* woke up my interest and I decided to direct the next one, *The Long Wait*, and to bring my friend, Lesser Samuels, to write the screenplay and act as producer. I secured Anthony Quinn to play Mike Hammer [Saville apparently misremembered that the character is actually called 'Johnny McBride']. It was his first solo starring role. What a good actor he is on every level. *The Long Wait* proved the best of the first two and I enjoyed directing it." The scene that Saville was particularly proud of is a visually abstract sequence. Venus (Peggy Castle) is being held hostage in a disused power plant; tightly bound and lying on the floor, she asks her captor if she might kiss Johnny McBride for the last time. McBride had tried to rescue Venus but ended up also bound. The action takes place within a large circular pool of light. With sadistic glee the hoodlum allows Venus, with her legs and arms still bound, to crawl painfully and slowly toward Johnny. Kicked into her path are obstacles that she has to squirm past. Saville recalled the scene in his memoirs: "A Russian born Art Director, Boris Leven, designed a violent struggle and an escapologist scene for Quinn plus the girl, a most attractive blonde, Peggie [*sic*] Castle. There were eighty-seven set-ups or different camera shots for the scene, which lasted but

18. Publicity photo for *The Long Wait* (1954). Escapology or sadism? In the foreground Venus (Peggy Castle) is bound at her wrists and ankles.

a very few minutes. I directed the scene matching the camera to the drawings, shot for shot, eighty seven of them in one day." The scene might amount to an act of escapology, and that is how it would have been sold to the PCA, but it is also one of the most startling depictions of sadism in an American PCA-era film, certainly the equal of any of the more celebrated S&M scenes in *Kiss Me Deadly*.

Leven had been the art director on such outstanding productions as *Shanghai Gesture* (1941), but aside from this his best work prior to *The Long Wait* was on the crime films *Criss Cross* (1950), *House by the River* (1950), *Quicksand* (1950), *The Prowler* (1951), and *Sudden Fear* (1952). Saville's selection of creative personnel is crucial to an understanding of the adaptations' distinctive styles. He chose writers, directors, actors, and art and musical directors that had an affinity with the crime genre, but with *The Long Wait* and *Kiss Me Deadly* he also looked for personnel that would bring something distinctive to the production and yet were affordable—filmmakers whose reputations were still in the making.

Saville had made his reputation in the prewar British film industry. Born in 1896, he entered the industry in 1916 as a salesman. By the early 1920s he had established a professional relationship with Michael Balcon as his producer, followed by a stint with Maurice Elvey. He made his directorial debut in 1927. At Gaumont-British, in the early 1930s, he again worked with Balcon, where, along with Alfred Hitchcock, he was one of the studio's most prized directors. At Gaumont he established the career of Jessie Matthews and worked on the studio's prestige productions. In the mid-to late-1930s he directed independent productions for Alexander Korda. At the outbreak of war he was in Hollywood, having returned to the role of producer and now working for MGM. At MGM he was also assigned to prestige productions, including *Goodbye Mr. Chips* (1939), *The Mortal Storm* (1940), and as director, among other films, *The Green Years* (1946) and *Kim* (1950).

The Spillane adaptations were something of an anomaly in his filmography, but, as he explained in his memoirs, he was looking for something to distract him after the death of his son. Having learned of the enormous sales figures for Spillane's novels, Saville "read several of the published books and they were all raw sex and violence, and violence for violence's sake. Nothing could be further removed from my previous work" (228). Saville bought the rights in perpetuity to four of Spillane's books:[57] "The Mickey Spillane films were unique in my picture making life, not because of their quality, but because I made more money for myself than any other picture finance I had dabbled in and yet my interest in making them had been to flex my muscles—to busy myself without emotional involvement" (230).

The Long Wait featured a new Spillane hero, Johnny McBride, an amnesiac who discovers he is wanted for the murder of a district attorney. His doctor explains he is suffering from "general amnesia," which means he is a "total blank." "You're not yourself," he is told. And so Johnny sets out on a voyage of self-discovery: "I've got to start looking for myself," he says. The figure of the amnesiac was a pulp fiction cliché when Spillane wrote the novel, and it was still a tired idea when the film was released.[58] Amnesiacs appeared in around 140 American films released between 1930 and 1955, and they featured as a key trope in the cycles of 1940s psychological melodramas and war veteran dramas: *Random Harvest* (1942), *Street of Chance* (1942), *Two-O'Clock Courage* (1945), *Spellbound* (1945), *Deadline at Dawn* (1946), *Somewhere in the Night* (1946), *Black Angel* (1946), *High Wall* (1948), *The Crooked Way* (1949), *Home of the Brave* (1949), *The Clay Pigeon* (1949), *Beware, My Lovely* (1952), and *The Big Frame* (1953). The amnesiac's journey in *The Long Wait* enabled encounters with the same gallery of lowlife grotesques and bottle blondes as found in *I, the Jury*, but it also enabled Saville to open out the world of the hero from the claustrophobic spaces of New York in the first film to the suburb of Lyncastle. In these more open, well-lit spaces McBride encounters four women, any one of whom could be his ex-girlfriend, Vera. She has the key to his lost identity and to his innocence or guilt in the murder of the district attorney. The problem is that Johnny cannot remember what she looks like, and when he finds a photograph of her, he also uncovers the information that, with plastic surgery, she has radically altered her features.

Saville shifts the emphasis away from Mike Hammer's bullying tactics and angry outbursts in *I, the Jury* to emphasize McBride's attractiveness to the female set. The key scenes turn on acts of seduction, where Johnny attempts to discover Vera behind the visage of Venus, Wendy, Carol, or Troy. The lovemaking involves an exaggerated fetishization of the women's hair, which is given some narrative credence by making the fact that Vera was a natural blonde the only clue to her identity. The film features a number of fistfights and assassination attempts, enough to keep things busy, but the combined effect of the scenes of bondage, sadism, and fetishism is to create an overwhelming aura of inconclusiveness and lack of attainment. McBride's fear that he will discover that he is indeed a murderer explains his fetishistic practice of disavowal and delay.

The first three Spillane adaptations each attach a particular sexual perversion to the hero's character traits: in *I, the Jury* Hammer is a sadist; in *The Long Wait* McBride is a fetishist; and in *Kiss Me Deadly* Hammer is a narcissist. The emphasis placed on these elements of sexual perversion plays havoc with a narrative system based on attempting to achieve equilibrium through heterosexual coupling. Narrative resolution is enacted with the destruction of the hero's enemies. The endings of *The Long Wait* and *Kiss Me Deadly*, which show their respective heroes in a clinch with a woman, are no more than a sop to narrative convention. In *Kiss Me Deadly*, for example, Hammer's narcissistic streak forbids his lovemaking to move beyond an initial kiss. Noting this foible in Spillane's hero, the British magazine *Picture Post* chided, "A special feature of the Hammer toughness is that he never makes love to the beauties who ache for his embrace. An upstanding American, he pets and runs."[59] Rather than a neat cause-and-effect chain, leading to containment and resolution with the formation of the couple, these films all operate on a principle of drag and jerk. As individual scenes, fostered by the heroes' perversions, drag into inconclusiveness and incoherence, completion endlessly forestalled by sadistic, fetishistic, or narcissistic acts, the filmmakers then jerk the narrative forward by shifting to a new scene.

In *I, the Jury* Hammer is hyperactive, acting autonomously, free from any carefully arranged cause-and-effect chain. The plot jerks forward as Hammer batters his way toward the final revelation of who killed his buddy. The denouement arrives not through any rationally pursued investigation but through the investigator's gut intuition and his ability to extract information from others by violent means. This is the same form of storytelling used by Spillane in his novels: narrative development occurs through jolts in the plotting that eventually lead to a heavily predetermined conclusion. *The Long Wait* is full of languorous, often tedious, scenes that drag as the hero, like a sleepwalker, moves with poor effect to uncover the truth about himself. By the time of *Kiss Me Deadly* Saville had learned some important lessons, and he and his cofilmmakers balanced the jerkiness of the pulp tableaux of *I, the Jury* with the dragged-out fetishism and sadism of *The Long Wait*—successfully combining the pulp movie kinetics of the former with the sadomasochistic leg-show of the latter. In France *Kiss Me Deadly* was called *In Fourth Gear*—suitably suggestive of the film's rapid velocity.

The opening sequence of *Kiss Me Deadly* is as well known as any in cinema history. The soundtrack is filled with the pantings of a woman, whom we see

Big Hit: His films, based on books, were epics of violence. Here, he acts out his favorite part.

the way.

Mickey, as he is known, is the dirtiest writer in the nation. He may even be the dirtiest writer of all time, in terms of writing for the sake of sex, violence and money. He admits he is out to make a buck and his candor is to be appreciated.

SINGS HYMNS

The curious part of all of this, is that he is a hypocrite who pretends to be a highly religious person. A second curious aspect is that book im-
(Continued on page 42)

MICKEY SPILLANE

ONE LONELY N

SIGNET BOOK

The New Mike Hammer Mystery Thriller by the Author of I, THE JURY

A SIGNET BOOK

25

19. Mickey Spillane shows actor Biff Elliot how to slap a woman in a publicity shot for *I, the Jury* that is here run in *Lowdown* magazine (Aug. 1955) but was much reproduced in lowbrow journals.

dressed only in a trench coat and lit by a single bright light as she runs down a highway. Caught in the glare of headlights, she forces the car driven by Mike Hammer off the road. As he tries to restart the failed motor, Christina Bailey slips into the passenger seat. On the radio Nat King Cole sings "I'd Rather Have the Blues." And then, as they drive off together, the film's credits scroll down the screen . . . backwards. This sequence, and subsequent scenes, including the capture and death of Christina, follows closely the events established by Spillane at the beginning of the novel. The differences are in the details, and it is on the film's details that the best commentators have focused.

J. P. Telotte has argued, for example, that "the film's first images immediately . . . undermine the expectations we draw from classical narrative." The uncontextualized and fragmented first views we are given of Christina, along with mismatched shots, "make us feel uneasy, even hesitate in our reading of this world." He continues: "For they jeopardize the continuity that classical editing usually enforces, and thus the film's reality illusion. What they subtly signal is that the ensuing narrative might not be playing by the normal rules, that it may well be out to depict a very different sort of world than we are used to seeing on film."[60] It is not clear from the shooting scripts whether the disruption of the film's illusion of reality was an intentional strategy on the part of the filmmakers, but Bezzerides did set out to enhance the viewer's experience of the film as being filled with kinetic energy. This was to be achieved through forcing an abstraction of the film's formal elements. The key word used in the screenplay is *swelling*, which is used to describe changes in both light and sound: the swelling of Christina's breathing after the sound of the engine has stalled, and the swelling of lights "to give the impression of great speed."[61] The fragmentation, discontinuities, and heightened soundtrack effects are not part of a Brechtian strategy of estrangement, which is what Telotte argued, nor are they strategies to deflect attention away from potentially censorable actions or images, as Maltby might argue; rather they are a way of providing the illusion of speed similar to that encountered on a whirligig or on a roller coaster—a dissembling of the senses.[62] This dissembling of the senses is in keeping with Spillane's writing and, importantly, with generic convention.

After stopping his car, Hammer, in the novel's opening sequence, appraises the dame's physical qualities: "wide-set eyes, large mouth, tawny hair that spilled onto her shoulders like melted butter." And then he recalls what has just happened:

> I remember her standing there in the road like something conjured up too quickly in a dream. A Viking. A damn-fool Viking dame with holes in her head.
>
> I kicked the stalled engine over, crawled through the gears and held tight to the wheel until my brain started working right. An accident you don't mind. Those you half-way expect when you're holding seventy on a mountain road. But you don't expect a Viking dame to jump out of the dark at you while you're coming around a turn. I opened the window all the way down and drank in some of the air.[63]

The oneiric, irrational qualities of the experience are matched to the thrill of driving at high speeds. Hammer considers her a "damn rape-happy dame," who thinks all guys are the same. Conversation between the couple is limited. "You'll get cold," he says after she opens her coat and invites him to "explore the curves and valleys that lay nestled in the shadows and moved with her breathing" (10). In the screenplay Bezzerides changed the point of view so that after they are safely past the police roadblock, it is Christina who does the appraising:

> I was just thinking how much you can tell about a person from such simple things. Your car for instance. . . . You have only one really lasting love. . . . You're one of those self-indulgent males who thinks about nothing but his clothes, his car, himself. Bet you do push-ups every morning just to keep your belly hard. . . . You're the kind of person who never gives in a relationship, who only takes. Woman! The Incomplete sex! And what is it that she needs to complete her? Why, man of course! What else! *Wonderful man!*

Hammer's dealings throughout the film lend credence to Christina's depiction of him as selfish, self-obsessed, and narcissistic. These are not traits that Spillane has ascribed to Hammer, but they are implicit in his creation nonetheless. In Spillane's fiction Hammer's characteristics are marked by a righteous, all-consuming anger at the failing of society to deal swiftly with those who threaten the masculine order of things. As vocalized by Bezzerides, Christina is exposing this side of him, explicitly confronting his misogyny.[64] In an earlier version of the screenplay Bezzerides has her speak directly to the anger that motivates Hammer: "I don't know what you do for a living, but whatever it is, I'll bet it's something nasty. But it pays awfully well. And you spend every cent of it on yourself. Right? It's all right. You can express your anger. I wouldn't want that steering wheel to snap off in your hands. . . . Please forgive me, if you can, for needling you. When I was very young, and afraid I wouldn't have a way with boys, an old woman told me to arouse any emotion, even anger, if I wanted to make a connection."[65] Subsequent versions of the script downplay the idea of Hammer as "something nasty," and replace it with a more amorphous criticism of the character as narcissistic, rather than just plain malicious, in order to explain his misogyny.

Bezzerides scripted a neat coda to Christina's little speech that did not make it to the final cut; it reads as if she were quoting from Simone de Beauvoir's *Second Sex*, which had been first published in English in 1953, two years prior to the release of *Kiss Me Deadly*: "If she is necessary, it is because he needs her. If she has beauty, it is because his is the eye of the beholder. Woman exists solely by the grace of man! Without him, she is as nothing. Only within his arms does she have substance."[66] In *The Big Kill* Hammer explains to a "tomato

20. Press ad for *Kiss Me Deadly*—"Boldest of All Spillane Scorchers!"—publicizing the film's leg show.

in a dress that was too tight a year ago" that he never has "dame trouble" because he is a "misanthropist":

> "I don't like people. I don't like any kind of people. When you get them together in a big lump they all get nasty and dirty and full of trouble. So I don't like people, including you. That's what a misanthropist is."
>
> "I could've sworn you was a nice feller," she said.
>
> "So could a lot of people. I'm not. Blow, sister."[67]

Bezzerides and Spillane agreed that Hammer was not a nice feller. Bezzerides, however, did not appear to agree that this was a positive trait. Dialogue and sequences in the screenplay, but cut from the film, make this clear. Reacting to Lilly Carver's question about what will happen to her if Mike leaves her alone in his apartment, Bezzerides described his reaction "as cold and impersonal, indicates he would sell his own mother, if the correct price were offered."[68] In the screenplay, when the FBI questions Hammer about the events that led up to the death of Christina, the agents' distaste for him and his profession is made even more overt than shown in the film:

> 2nd FBI officer: She [Velda, Hammer's assistant] makes out all right too. The only place she doesn't make out, is with him. Why is that, Mister Hammer?
>
> Mike registers real anger for the first time.
>
> 1st FBI officer: Careful you're hurting his feelings!
>
> 2nd officer: Perhaps you're right. Perhaps we're treading on dangerous ground. . . .
>
> 4th officer: Do you think he'd mind if I made a guess? It's obvious he means a good deal to her. She's very devoted. She loves him. But if he let her mean anything to him, he wouldn't be able to use her in his sordid profession. Would you Mister Hammer?[69]

In the film Hammer's exploitation of Velda is hardly latent, but this reading of his motivation, coming so close on the heels of Christina's deconstruction of his character, suggests a critique of Spillane's creation that fully justifies Chabrol's characterization of the source material as putrid and confirms Bezzerides's assertion that he had contempt for the material. This argument has even more resonance when the two scenes are linked to a major sequence that was scripted but not filmed. In this long Hitchcockian suspense scene Bezzerides fully reveals his conception of Hammer as a cynical and malevolent being. After being grilled by the FBI, Hammer returns to his apartment, but he has been tipped off that some heavies may be lying in wait: "A lanky boy, around eleven, is tossing a baseball up with one hand and catching it with the glove on the other, and whistling a tune in a jivey fashion." Hammer approaches the boy and, on the pretext of getting him to open doors, on account of his injured arm, offers the boy two-bits to accompany him up to his apartment. Before too long, the boy knows something is wrong with the arrangement:

> The long empty hall stretches beyond.
>
> The CAMERA MOVES from man to boy and back to man. First the boy gazes at Mike's face, sees him watching intently and with the trace of alarm. Then the boy turns to gaze into the hallway. The sight of the long, lonely hallway frightens him, and when he turns again to Mike, his face is no longer smiling but alarmed too.
>
> MIKE (firmly) go ahead . . .
>
> The boy hesitates, but Mike touches his shoulder almost sharply, and the boy goes ahead. Mike is a space behind him. The boy pauses before the elevator doors . . .
>
> MIKE (softly) Open the door. (fiercely, but quietly) Open it!
>
> CLOSE SHOT—MIKE AND BOY
>
> The boy gazes at Mike's intent, cruel face.[70]

The screenplay suggested that Hammer is not only prepared to sell his mother if the price is right, and to act, in all but name, as Velda's pimp, but that he is also prepared to sacrifice an eleven-year-old boy, if it means protecting his own skin. This is so far removed from Spillane's conception of Hammer, and so direct in its meaning, that I doubt Bezzerides ever imagined the scene would be shot, but it does give validity to critical readings that see the film as subverting the source material, even if it does not invalidate Richard Maltby's argument that ambivalence was a state desired by the filmmakers in order to avoid trouble with the censors. The two positions are not incompatible.

Before it can be co-opted as Brechtian, or as an art object, *Kiss Me Deadly* should be recognized as a genre movie, because insofar as it is self-reflexive or subversive, it is only so in terms of generic convention. Over and above any other intentions the filmmakers may have had, ascribed or otherwise, they were always mindful of their commercial obligations. This position does not deny *Kiss Me Deadly*'s amenability to different forms of interpretation, but given that it is susceptible to pluralistic readings it might, therefore, just as readily serve as a bop-prosody as a surreal poem. Such a twist would give back to the film its American specificity and relieve it of some of the imported European overlays. The logic behind such an interpretation is not based just in the film's formal (visual) rhythmic play between dissonance and consonance, suggestive of a jazzlike structure, but also in the way its soundtrack incorporates a host of musical styles and forms.

In considering the film's American specificity, particularly as it relates to musical passages, it becomes possible to see just how far removed the film version of Mike Hammer is from Spillane's conception, as well as how closely this issue is tied to topical concerns related to masculinity, class, and cultures of consumption. In its brazen play with the modern and the atavistic, with its violent mood swings through kinetic passages of intense violence, alternated with moments of languor and narcolepsy, proffering an investigation that is both eidetic and obscure, *Kiss Me Deadly* is like a pop standard, something familiar that is turned over, under, sideways, and down by a bebop combo playing hot and cool to an audience of hipsters and slumming tourists on South Central Avenue.

The panting, orgasmic, guttural breathing of Christina as she runs down the center of the highway opens the film, overlaid with the sound of automobiles flashing by and the militaristic charge of Frank DeVol's pounding musical track. When Hammer's car swerves to miss Christina, and eventually comes to a halt at the side of the road, we hear a pumping piano boogie pouring forth from the car's radio. Then the sultry tones of the female disk jockey announce the "fine new platter by Nat King Cole, 'I'd Rather Have the Blues.'" The new record continues to play under the sound of the car and Christina's sobbing, until Hammer clicks off the radio at the police roadblock. Cole's nocturne, contrasting with the piano boogie, tells the story of a lonesome man's nighttime walks along city streets; he is feeling mean and bought and would rather have the blues than what he's got. And what he has got is a woman who has him trapped in her web of deceit; a theme that neatly fits the concerns of the film. But with the reverse-rolling title credits and Christina's breathlessness, its slow cadence and quietly formed tale of entrapment seem at odds with the more strident elements of the setting.

One year later, and drawing from the same Hollywood-based music company's catalog, Capitol, the filmmakers could have used the more apposite Gene Vincent and His Blue Caps' debut 45 "Woman Love," which was coupled with "Be-Bop-A-Lula"—a doubleheader of orgiastic bumps and grinds that found a home in the hit parade but really belonged on a jukebox in a cathouse—or on Mike Hammer's radio. ("Be-Bop-A-Lula" eventually appeared in Frank Tashlin's *The Girl Can't Help It* and had a role at the tail end of Jack Smith's *Flaming Creatures*.)

The contrast, however, between the clamorous and the somnambulistic components is part of the film's uniqueness.

Coupled with "My One Sin (in Life)," "I'd Rather Have the Blues" peaked at number twenty-four on the *Billboard* charts; it was part of a run of hits that for Cole had begun in 1944, with "Straighten Up and Fly Right," and continued on through 1947 with "Nature Boy," which hit the number-one spot and stayed there for eight weeks. The orchestra on that recording had been arranged and conducted by Frank DeVol, the man responsible for *Kiss Me Deadly*'s music and fifteen other Aldrich soundtracks. Cole was the era's epoch-making crossover artist. After redefining the composition and sound of the jazz combo with the King Cole Trio (1937–51), he set off on a hit-making solo career that included stints in the movies and a television series. Cole entered into the domesticated white middle-class homes of America as no other African American had done before, presenting a nonthreatening and highly sophisticated image of the modern and debonair entertainer. A contemporary of Frank Sinatra and Dean Martin, Cole played to mass audiences, cutting tunes to suit all tastes. The Nat King Cole employed to sing DeVol's "I'd Rather Have the Blues" was not the troubadour of the *King Cole for Kids* album but the troubled, heartbroken drinker that was epitomized in his 1949 cover of Billy Strayhorn's "Lush Life," a tale of lonely cocktail hours, empty glasses, and full ashtrays.

The cocktail culture exemplified in Cole's more urbane performances suited the Mike Hammer of *Kiss Me Deadly*, while Vincent's "Woman Love" better fits Spillane's conception of his hero, who would never hang out in a cocktail club, killing time. Spillane's Hammer preferred drinking suds and smoking Luckies in some neighborhood tavern, where the only music comes out of the jukebox in the corner or the drunk at the end of the bar. The filmmakers put Hammer into the mid-1950s and into the period's bachelor culture, a world exemplified by *Playboy* magazine. Founded in 1953, *Playboy*, like its competitor *Esquire*, made the new movements in jazz central to its lifestyle concepts. *Playboy*'s editor, Hugh Hefner, described his idealized reader: "We like our apartment. We enjoy mixing up cocktails and an *hors d'oeuvre* or two, putting a little mood music on the phonograph and inviting in a female acquaintance for a quiet discussion on Picasso, Nietzsche, jazz, sex."[71] Spillane had found a home and his audience in the pocket-sized cheesecake and titillation pulps and men's adventure magazines that Parklane Pictures had used to such good effect in the promotion of the film adaptations. In the August 1955 edition of *Real: The Exciting Magazine for Men*, a photo spread presents "Mickey and His Mayhem Molls," featuring promotional stills of the female leads from *Kiss Me Deadly*. The reader is informed that a "cozy evening with Spillane's dames includes slippers, pipe—and pistol," while Hammer is described as the "first swinging shamus," who is "harassed by girls the way some guys are plagued by mosquitoes."[72] For readers of *Real*, Hammer may have been swinging, but *Playboy* ignored

Spillane: his proletarian stammering out of step with its advocacy of male consumption. Bachelor culture was avowedly misogynistic and antidomestic, just like Spillane and Hammer, but it was also, paradoxically, a principal means of bringing men into a (feminized) culture of consumption—the world of Ralph Meeker's Mike Hammer but not Spillane's Mike Hammer.

In a process that had begun before the war, but accelerated in the postwar years, jazz underwent a series of profound cultural shifts in its reception. No longer perceived primarily as a dance music, with roots deep in African American culture, its championing as an art form by small coteries of dedicated white fans, and the evident musical sophistication of its key purveyors, such as Duke Ellington, Dizzy Gillespie, Charlie Parker, Ornette Coleman, and Miles Davis, united to present jazz, at its best, as a music that equaled anything that had come from Europe but that in its emphasis on interpretation and improvisation was, indisputably, an American art form. Specialist journals, book series, radio programs, networks of fans, and concert circuits helped promulgate ideas and proselytize on behalf of the new music. New technologies, such as the hi-fi and $33^{1}/_{3}$ rpm twelve-inch phonograph records, introduced by Columbia in 1948, provided a platform for more extended musical pieces and served as a centerpiece for the bachelor pad.

The shifting of the sites of jazz's consumption, from the dives, taverns, and dance palaces to nightclubs, concert halls, and bachelor pads, brings in train a shift in jazz's articulation of a commonality. In his discussion of civil liberty and jazz in postwar crime movies, Sean McCann worked through the changing reception of jazz from Popular Front era of the 1930s, when jazz was conceived as the "heroic fulfillment of art's ability to transcend the class and racial divisions that marred American society," to the postwar bebop years, in which jazz was more directly the product and the representation of "the contradictions in our social life."[73]

Jazz in the postwar years, principally through bebop, but also in Ellington's new work, "points away from the Popular Front language of democratic fraternalism and toward the emphasis on individual virtuosity and personal freedom."[74] This process is exemplified in the idea of jazz as a component in a set of men's lifestyle choices determined in the context of a culture of consumption. By updating Mike Hammer, taking him out of the long hangover from the 1930s and World War II (Spillane's Hammer is a war veteran and is as much a child of the politics of the New Deal as he is a reaction to the cold war), the filmmakers define him in terms of his acts of consumption: the fast cars, smart clothes, his gimmick-laden apartment stocked with piles of magazines rather than shelves of books, and the women with whom he comes into contact, who are a product of Madison Avenue feeding into, and informing, bachelor fantasies—always available, always willing, always wanting: Playboy bunnies and Bond girls in waiting.

21. Frame grab from *Kiss Me Deadly*. The only white man in the room, Hammer listens to the blues in the Pigalle Club.

The one woman in *Kiss Me Deadly* who does not fit this criteria is the jazz singer played by Madi Comfort; she too sings "I'd Rather Have the Blues." The setting is the Pigalle Club, which offers a phony French exoticism for its homegrown divertissements. He is at the club because Velda has asked him to meet her there at two o'clock, but she does not show, and he drinks himself unconscious. The scene is filled with grief and remorse, or at least that is what Hammer appears to be acting out after he learns about the death of Nick, and the sad lament of the singer aids this appearance; but beyond the emotional masquerade, why put Hammer into this scene? Why have him appear as the only white man in a club otherwise exclusively black? Why make him a familiar with the singer and barman?

In an early version of the screenplay, the scene at the Pigalle opens with a shot on Eddie Yager, the boxing promoter,

> sitting with his back to a television set, which everyone else is facing, though we do not see the set itself. The SOUNDS of the brawl COME ACROSS, cheering crowds, the fierce thud of blows. Now the crowd roars, as some fine point in fisticuffs is achieved, and the Negro habitués of the café stir, excited. Eddie looks briefly, but turns away, vastly pained, with his face buried in his hands. Such a grief does he suffer. Now CAMERA PANS TO SHOW, past and beyond all others, that Mike Hammer is standing in the doorway. He crosses slowly toward Eddie. Now he is standing beside Eddie, who has his back to it, the better not to see the tragedy. Eddie gazes up.

As Hammer had predicted at the gym, the fighter takes a dive, and the audience in the bar are "shocked, aghast. They have not only lost a bet. Their faith in a soul has been abused. But Mike is cynically pleased." Eddie and Mike talk about the fight and the setup: "We sure made ourselves a bundle, didn't we Mike?" The two share a laugh, and then, as "Eddie threads his way through the innocent crowd, a sadness comes over Mike. He sits thinking of Nick." The scene emphasizes a key theme brought to the adaptation by Bezzerides of contemporary social affairs reduced to commercial transactions. Commerce marks Hammer's relationships, even with those who appear closest to him—Velda and Nick. Mike's eye is always on what's in it for him. The missing scene with Eddie would have underlined that even in a space often represented as being outside the machinations of capital, or at least only tangential to it, the black club, commerce is fundamental.

In the script the club's MC introduces the singer by first referencing the fallen fighter:

> "Oh man, he came in like a lion. But he went out like a lamb. And now Ladies and Gentlemen, a little dirge music suitable for the occasion. Miss Pearl Kelly will render a requiem to a dead gladiator. And that's Brother Dave Brown at the old eighty-eight. Belt it out, Pearl.
>
> CAMERA PANS to an extremely attractive young colored woman who stands beside the piano where Brown is pounding the keys. The woman begins to sing.
>
> Eddie and Mike talk about the fight and dive and bets. Eddie leaves and Mike talks to Art. Art is full of hip lingo, Mike asks him why do bartenders talk so much: "Us shakers flip the lip because it's a long street, stark and dark, way back here behind the bar, and everything is on the other side. Life, man, if you dig."

The implication is that Mike does not talk much, does not have anything to say, unless it can help get to the "great whatsit." Hammer's link to a jazz culture is just a pose, an empty gesture, and another lifestyle choice: something to be consumed. The black nightclub is just another space through which Hammer, in his new guise as a member of the bourgeoisie, is able to move effortlessly, untouched by, and unconcerned with, the Pigalle's underlying racial reality. In the film Pearl, at the end of the evening, is sitting at the bar when a messenger comes into the club to let Hammer know that Velda has been kidnapped. Slumped at the bar, Hammer is woken by the bartender. Hammer passes Pearl on his way out, and she tells him she is sorry about Nick, apparently reinforcing a shared grief. In the screenplay, however, there is no expression of empathy: "Singer: (anxiously) 'You said for me to wait for you, Mister Hammer . . . ' Mike touches her cheek, as he exits." The suggestion here is that their relationship is unequal—"*Mister* Hammer"—and exploitative; she does what he tells her.

Bezzerides's version of the black nightclub does not offer yet another representation of the black public space as an authentic alternative to white domesticity
and a feminized culture of consumption, à la Jack Kerouac's *On the Road* or
Norman Mailer's "White Negro." These works made explicit the hipster's expro-
priation of blackness as a marker of nonconformist cool, best exemplified by the
fulsome and romantic view of the black jazzman as a cultural and social outlaw.
In counterpoint Bezzerides suggested the Pigalle was as compromised and
corrupt as any of the social spaces Hammer moves through, all the while tacitly
underscoring Domarchi's Marxist explanation of the film's social critiques.

Further evidence of an intellectual engagement on the part of the filmmakers
with Spillane's pulp mentality is provided by the numerous references to
European high art that Bezzerides and Aldrich brought to the screenplay, none
of which appear in the source novel: Christina Bailey's rented apartment is lined
with paintings, African masks, and books, and her radio is permanently tuned
to a classical music station; Velda keeps in shape by practicing ballet routines;
Hammer's ultramodern apartment is decorated with art objects and abstract
paintings; and three key figures in Hammer's investigation are linked to high
culture: Dr. Soberin, with his overreaching allusions to Greek myth; Carmen
Trivaco, and his overblown operatic performance; and William Mist, the over-
weight owner of the "Modern Art Gallery." On a simple semantic level these
references to an elite culture strike a contrast with the film's pulp origins, a
clash displayed most violently when Hammer snaps in half one of Trivaco's rare
shellac phonograph recordings of Caruso. But they are also in keeping with
pulp's representation of high culture as a sign of effeminacy, duplicity, corruption, and villainy. As Raymond Durgnat has pointed out, the film is deeply
ambiguous about cultural status:

> The script is full of laboured anti-egghead detail. The culture-crammed
> flat is associated with the mental imbalance of Christina and Lily Carver;
> behind the arty weirdies loom the foreign spies. Christina is a scientist,
> intellectual and therefore unreliable. Classical music comes from these
> sinister foreign stations. The mysterious Mister Mist, director of the art
> gallery, hastily gulps down sleeping pills so as to escape Mike's grilling—
> the implications of cowardice, passivity, even death-wish and suicide,
> all allegedly characteristics of those masochistic intellectuals, aren't
> far away.[75]

By this account, the filmmakers are aligning themselves with neither high culture nor the barbarianism of Spillane but instead are in accord with generic
convention. Hammer's inability to "read" the high-cultural references, without
considerable effort on his part, suggests his middle-class credentials are little
more than half-formed aspirations, which are underpinned by his playboy values; he is a thug hiding behind a veneer of sophistication. High culture, however,

offers no more grounded values than those presented by the superficial bourgeois environment of Hammer's apartment. The effeminate, duplicitous, con-
cealing, and elitist nature of high culture is sensationally torn apart, Hammer's
acts of destruction displayed for the pleasure of those who feel excluded from a
world of education, civility, and privilege. In turn, the low-rent, working-class
spaces in the Bunker Hill district, which a number of the film's characters
inhabit, offer little in the way of a more authentic experience.

High culture, however, marks key points in Hammer's haphazard move
toward solving the riddle of the "great whatsit." The "great whatsit" is Velda's
name for the mystery object they are all pursuing. The art dealer compounds the
cryptic nature of the investigation by suggesting to Velda that the search is for a
work of art: there is a "new art in the world" and Soberin is starting a collection,
he tells her.[76] These gnomic pronouncements lead Hammer's investigation
back to a poem, "Remember Me," by Christina Rossetti, that he found in a book
by Christina Bailey's bed. The central clue to the mystery lies in a book of poems,
that in turn leads to the key to the "great whatsit," which is found in Christina
Bailey's stomach. In the process of helping to unravel the mystery, art is stripped
of its connotative value, most blatantly in Hammer's reading of Rossetti, where
the poem is reduced to a sign literally pointing to the morgue—the allusive or
allegorical potential of the poem is reduced to a raw corporeality. Poetry and
a dead woman in the morgue hold the answers to the film's mystery; they form
the shared space where art meets pulp.

If not paramount, Saville was, nevertheless, central to the process of bringing pulp and art together in *Kiss Me Deadly*. He guided closely all of the adaptations, and he was a hands-on producer: "There is little doubt that the creative
producer imposed his story ability and his good taste on a picture," he wrote in
his memoirs.[77] But with Spillane good taste is not a virtue; it is a vice, and this is
perhaps why mention of Saville's role in *Kiss Me Deadly* is roundly ignored, not
even mentioned in the director-producer's BFI profile, and even he had little to
say about the film, except that, like many, it left him confused:[78] "I produced
Kiss Me Deadly and Robert Aldrich directed it [Aldrich also received producer's
credit on the film]. This opus has become a cult film. There is hardly a film
society in Europe that has not asked me for a loan of the print. I cannot say
why, I never completely understood our finished screenplay and my confusion
was still there when we ran the completed film."[79]

A couple of years after the last of the adaptations, the desultory *My Gun Is
Quick*, Saville approached United Artists and proposed buying the rights to Ian
Fleming's *Dr. No*. "I thought the books would be a good follow up to the Spillane
pictures." The proposal was turned down: "The fact that the James Bond pictures,
a few years later, became a bonanza for United Artists is neither here nor there,
for I am quite sure I would not have made them as well as the producers of the
series—indeed, not in the same class. I could never have spent such large sums

of money on what, in my book, is such indifferent and characterless writing."[80] The overlap between the Hammer and Bond films has been noted, as have the similarities in Spillane's and Fleming's fiction. In a 1958 review of *Dr. No* for the *New Statesman*, Paul Johnson echoed Philip Wylie in his piece on Spillane for *Good Housekeeping*; Johnson wrote, "I have just finished what is, without doubt, the nastiest book I have ever read. . . . There are three basic ingredients . . . all unhealthy . . .: the sadism of a schoolboy bully, the mechanical, two-dimensional sex-longings of a frustrated adolescent, and the crude, snob-cravings of a sub-urban adult. . . . Mr Fleming has no literary skill, the construction of the book is chaotic, and entire situations are inserted, and then forgotten, in a haphazard manner."[81] Indifferent, mechanical writing, sensational attractions, incoherent plotting, and an appeal to the lower classes (or adolescent mentality)—the grounds on which the condemnation of pulp fictions took place had changed little, if at all, since concerns were raised in the 1920s about cheaply produced magazines, with formulaic stories, wrapped in lurid covers.

As it comes down to us today, as a part of the Library of Congress collection, *Kiss Me Deadly* has been used to turn a negative conception of pulp into a positive. The film was formed out of Spillane's pulp aesthetic, which was exploited by Saville and regulated by institutional censorship. While transforming the character of Hammer, Bezzerides and Aldrich respected the appeal of Spillane's fiction—its sensational and lurid aspects, and, in particular, the amphetamine whirl of Spillane's storytelling. But just as important to the lasting appeal of the film, as Maltby so rightly pointed out, has been the critical investment of cinephiles—French, British, and American—who made the film into a work of art. This mix of determining forces produced a marvelous example of a putrefied hard-boiled thriller, wracked with incoherence and senselessness, awash with moments of priceless giddiness, and marked with a superior clumsiness, a provocation to middle-class, middlebrow values—a cinematic and critical phantasmagoria. This is pulp art at its most convulsive and beautiful, made manifest through a series of critical interventions and appropriations, which, in their own way, were equally marvelous. *Kiss Me Deadly*: a world of small insanities.

4

American Primitive

Samuel Fuller's Pulp Politics

Frankly, My Next Pic Is All Action, Sex 'n' Violence.

–Samuel Fuller, *Variety* (October 28, 1959)

In the opening sequence of his 1971 novel, *144 Piccadilly*, Samuel Fuller sets the scene for his story of London's hippie and squatter culture. Strolling around the West End, an American film director encounters a group of young people breaking into an unoccupied four-story Georgian mansion located at the "ritzy junction of Park Lane and Piccadilly": "No one else was observing them. They seemed identical to the gypsies I had met in Paris, tolerated in San Francisco, avoided in Los Angeles. And whether they gorged on Yoga, swamis, gurus, intellectual masturbation against the square wind, boo or chug-a-lug, their freaked-out Bedouin menagerie always gave me the ring-a-ding to flush them down a sewer and clamp the lid tight."[1] The protagonist's journalistic instincts overcome his feeling of revulsion, and he joins the merry band of hippy squatters in their adventures. He calls himself "Charley," not his real name, and keeps his occupation secret from the hippies: "I could have told them I make movies; that seventeen of my feature films had just been shown at the Edinburgh Film Festival; that they are going to be shown again at the National Theatre by the British Film Institute" (12). Instead, he lies and tells them he is on vacation. By the end of the novel Charley has helped fight off skinhead attacks, slept with two of the hippie chicks, and taken, against his will, a hit of heroin administered by Lover Boy, leader of the Hell's Angels.

The novel was published in Britain in 1972 by the New English Library and was promoted as part of its series of pulp youth culture novels, featuring skinheads, suedeheads, hippies, glam rockers, bikers, boot boys, and the like. Although *144 Piccadilly* was not a commissioned novel in the series, the many sex scenes, the gratuitous violence, and the drug use made for a good fit, nonetheless.[2] It was Fuller's sixth novel, and he was to publish another half-dozen books before his death in 1997.[3] In typical Fuller style, he claimed that *144 Piccadilly* was a "fictional re-creation of a factual incident with fictive characters."[4] The jacket blurb described the author as a "well-known . . . film director and producer." Whether Fuller would have been known to the series' principal readership of teenagers is doubtful, but for cinephiles familiar with Fuller's films the collapsing of the boundary between the novel's fictional protagonist and the identity of the author is intriguing.

In 1969 Fuller's films did play at the Edinburgh International Film Festival (EIFF) and at the National Film Theatre in London, the first of many major retrospectives he was to enjoy. Like Fuller, the book's protagonist smokes big cigars, is a proud war veteran, and speaks in a manner best suited for dictation rather than conversation:

> I punctured a hole in my cigar with the end of a wooden match stick and, puffing slowly, enjoyed the clear Castro I couldn't get back home. . . . "We have laws back home too, but it doesn't mean a damn thing unless it's used the way *they* want to use it—not the way *you* interpret it."
>
> He evidently liked the ring of my words, judging from the way his dark blue eyes brightened. "That's radical talk."
>
> I can't stomach radicals or bunions. I'm telling you facts."[5]

Rat-a-tat-tat goes the dialogue, punctuated, one might imagine, by the stabbing motion of his cigar. With Fuller truth transcends politics, and facts are what he knows to be true. And the truth is that there was indeed a squat at 144 Piccadilly in 1969, though it was an Edwardian mansion, not Georgian, on Hyde Park Corner. But this misidentification of the building was the least of Fuller's falsifications. Writing in the countercultural journal *Oz*, in November 1972, one of the squatters at 144, Phil Cohen, alias Dr. John, puts the boot into Fuller's distortions and fantasies:

> This is the book of the film Sam Fuller never made. . . . It is written from the viewpoint of a first person author/narrator, candid camera style. But judging from the content the nearest Uncle Sam got to 144 was a few drinks with Hells angels [*sic*], and the clipping file of the worlds [*sic*] gutter press. This device does however give him the chance to give full vent to his political prejudices; a right wing populist view of the world, with a strong dose of sexism and racism to back it up. The tone is alternatively moralistic and cynical; one minute our hero is giving a 16 year old girl "fatherly" advice about going back home to mummy and daddy, the next he is writing like this:
>
> "Suddenly a girl screamed. Two long haired bearded youths had ripped off her clothes. When I trailed Robert through the squatters toward the scream we came upon them urinating on the panic stricken girl. The two maniacs were dragged off. Their false beards fell. Their long haired wigs fell. They were bald youths.

NEW ENGLISH LIBRARY

144
PICCADILLY

SAMUEL FULLER

A shocking novel of today's
intolerance and savagery

22. Cover of Samuel Fuller's *144 Piccadilly*, the 1973 New English Library edition.

"SKINHEADS" shouted Peter.

As you can see, the book is amazingly funny, just because it is so incredibly dishonest.[6]

Cohen's evaluation of Fuller's book as "obnoxious," particularly in its contradictory moral and exploitative address, allied to a reactionary political stance, can brook little argument; Fuller wrote pulp. His films, though, are objects of extraordinary contestation, valorized as examples of pure cinema at one extreme and condemned as violent, sadistic, lurid trash at the other. Out of this contradictory conception of Fuller arises the question of whether he was sui generis or an *objet trouvé*—an artist with a unique and original vision or a blank canvas, no more than the sum of the ideas of critics who wrote their own names across his films? This chapter examines Fuller's critical reception by popular film reviewers, film censors, and cinephiles.

In his focus on life's losers, the dispossessed, and the outlawed, Fuller showed no interest in dramas that promoted conspicuous consumption or in characters who had aspirations that extended beyond their immediate survival or momentary gratification. In an age of abundance, his supporters claim, he mounted a rearguard action against consumerism, yet Fuller also held up a belief in his country and in the system of free enterprise that he accepted without question. The contradiction implied in his finding fault with the system and his unyielding support for the foundation on which that system was built—his critique *and* championing of the United States—is the basis on which Fuller is fashioned as an American primitive.

In validating Fuller as a critic of middle-class culture, a number of his supporters have constructed him as a "primitive," that is, someone who appears to exist outside of the corrupting influence of commercial imperatives and bourgeois mores. But positioning him as a primitive also meant that Fuller's work had to be explained; he could not be relied upon to comment authoritatively on his own work; that function needed a trained and insightful critic. Fuller's intelligence, his erudition, lay in his skills as a filmmaker; it was expressed through his films, not outside of them. The talented critic needed to demonstrate the ability to discriminate not only between Fuller and middling American film productions but also between Fuller and other pulpsters. The combined consequence of the critical work on Fuller in the late 1960s and early 1970s may have made him into a more reputable filmmaker, but this was not the effect his apologists were working for; quite the opposite. Fuller's lack of respectability, his low reputation, was what they were drawn to. The brash, crude, sensationalist elements of his films were crucial in helping to funnel an insolent rebuke to a critical orthodoxy that shunned the brutish aspects of a pulp sensibility as keenly overwrought as Fuller's.

Key to my analysis of Fuller is an understanding that his work draws on the rich resource of popular culture, most notably tabloid news reporting, crime photographs, cartoons and comic strips, scandal magazines, and pulp fiction. He had an intimate knowledge of these forms of sensational mass communication. The historian of the *New York Graphic*, where Fuller worked, described the twenty-year-old reporter as someone "known to more subway nickel changers, guards, firemen, pimps, cops, whores, bookies and bootleggers than perhaps any other reporter in the big town. They were calling him by his first name."[7] His experience as a crime reporter meant that he knew the value of an illustrated story to his editors and readers. This training gave him the ability to encapsulate ideas in concentrated form, through combination of text and image. The *Graphic* was a tabloid that specialized in the day's sensational and lurid stories, which notoriously used composite photographs, recreations of scenes, for illustrations.[8] Though his stock in trade was journalism, Fuller was also writing pulp fiction, both novels and short stories, during his prewar years in New York and San Diego.

His service as a foot soldier during World War II and his career as a reporter have received much comment in the criticism of his work, and, indeed, these experiences formed the basis for a number of his films and novels. My analysis, however, concentrates on how his films used the techniques, traits, and formulas found in the long tradition of pulp and sensational media, with which Fuller was fully conversant. I am less interested in retracing the autobiographical overlap between the director and his subjects than I am in the means he used to tell his stories. Like the newspaper editor in his novel *The Dark Page*, Fuller found his drama in the quotidian and the sensational, the everyday event made remarkable. On his way to work at the *Comet* the editor reflects on what lay ahead and "looked forward eagerly to a new day of horror, terror and thrills."[9] Fuller reveled in the ambiguity and contradiction he found in the everyday, when other pulpsters, Spillane among them, found only the certainty of absolutes.

Coupled with my analysis of his films is an inquiry into why Fuller has been singled out for such sustained critical validation. As with *Kiss Me Deadly*, a good deal of this criticism is concerned with exploring a surreal current that runs throughout his films. I argue that this surrealism is a side effect of the sensational materials with which Fuller worked, which are similar to those found in the Fantomas stories. Fantomas and Fuller's fiction engaged with the world through provocation, arousing middle-class ire; in particular, they provoked through a lack of regard for the conventions of the well-made story and traditions of good taste. Fuller's films are wracked by inconsistency, incoherence, and a disregard for character motivation based on accepted notions of realism. In their place, Fuller explains character action in terms that are hardly ever subtle, usually base in nature, and crude in effect. His films are indeed violent, lurid, and vulgar; and they are bold, declamatory, and often shrill. The value afforded to the combined effect of his sensational presentation of ideas, characters, and stories is the ground on which Fuller's reputation as a filmmaker of standing is contested.

In his analysis of "dissident" filmmakers and novelists working in the 1950s with popular forms and fictions, David Cochran produced a summary of Fuller's appeal for critics who affect a nonconformist stance toward mainstream culture: "Fuller's work resists the trappings of midcult and transcends the genres in which he worked. His films refuse to obey established formulas or offer easily digestible morals. They constantly flaunt expectations and resist closure. Within the heart of mass-culture, Fuller launched an all-out assault on the easy assurances and palliatives of the dominant cultural sensibilities."[10] Whatever the truth in this conception of Fuller, it is not readily apparent from the films themselves that his westerns, gangster films, or war movies transcend generic constraints, that they resist formulaic platitudes and conventions, or that they undercut ready-made assumptions and remain open-ended; in sum, it is not readily apparent that he practiced a form of cultural dissent. An extraordinary amount of effort has gone into producing a critical validation of Fuller, and it has done this in the face of popular and expert criticism that dismissed and condemned the films, often on the grounds that they were sensational, formulaic, and tedious, that they were, in effect, as debased—indeed, if not more so—as any other example of popular culture.

The initial wave of American reviews for *Shock Corridor* exemplify the general practice of vilifying Fuller's filmmaking and the ridiculing of his cinephiliac apologists. *Variety* considered the film a "tasteless, tedious quagmire of shock and sensation"; *Cue* magazine agreed it was "swamped by a predilection for tossing shocking features . . . for the sake of shock." The *Los Angeles Times* feared for the "spectator-listener [who] is assailed by so much sound and fury that he emerges after 101 minutes feeling groggy and, I am afraid, largely unconvinced." *Film Quarterly* considered it "one of the most preposterous and tasteless films of all time." And, the *New York Herald Tribune* warned that it "hasn't got the decency to qualify as a lower B-level film. It's coated with sexual jargon, psychiatric and political palaver and pathetic photographic effects . . . but nothing can hide the film's infintile [*sic*] pretensions and drooling preoccupations."[11]

Writing in *Film Quarterly*, Robert G. Dickson sardonically noted in his review that Fuller was "currently the subject of much fatheaded adulation in France and England" and that, no doubt, *Shock Corridor* would soon be "hailed, by the *Cahiers/Movie* mob, as 'Fuller's Testament' or 'A Masterpiece—symptomatic of our age,'" when, "in fact," it is "a cheap, nasty, lurid melodrama with artistic pretensions."[12] Discussing *The Naked Kiss*, made the following year, the *Cosmopolitan* reviewer wrote: "If it is true that the French New Wave of film-makers dotes on Fuller's underdone cinematics (they are said to consider his *Shock Corridor* an American classic), then all one can say is that fifty million Frenchmen can be wrong. The words *low budget* would upgrade this low-budget melodrama."[13]

The popular critics were not inclined to engage with Fuller's pulp aesthetic, nor were the censors inclined to see it as anything but shock and sensation, a callow exercise in sexploitation. In Britain *Shock Corridor* and *The Naked Kiss* were not available for public screenings until 1970, when the Greater London Council granted them "X" certificates, which meant that they could only be shown if no child under the age of eighteen was present. Outside of London the films could still not be seen, and as late as October 1968 the British Board of Film Censors had confirmed its initial decisions in 1963 and 1964 not to grant certificates. The censors thought *Shock Corridor* was a "thoroughly objectionable picture that could not be made acceptable by cuts."[14] What the censors apparently found so unpleasant was the misrepresentation of a mental hospital and its staff, "which could cause grave concern to people who have friends and relatives with mental illness." This worry was coupled with the belief that it is "thoroughly irresponsible to suggest that a sane person could secure admission to a mental hospital by putting on an act and convincing qualified medical men that he is mentally disturbed, and equally irresponsible to suggest that residence as an inmate of a mental hospital could make a sane person insane. Furthermore we feel that the film would have a bad, and possibly dangerous, effect on viewers with any degree of mental disturbance."[15]

If this was not enough in itself, there were also "incidents which would be completely unacceptable for normal censorship reasons."[16] These incidents were the open discussion of incest; the motive for the murder, which was that an attendant had been having sex with an inmate; that a male inmate thought himself impotent *and* pregnant; the ward full of nymphomaniacs; the general level of violence, but particularly the electric shock treatment; the nightmare when Johnny imagines he has been struck by lightning; and the fight between him and Wilkes, the murderer. In sum, the censors thought the film was "full of raving lunatics, nightmares, violence," and an "undercurrent of sex." By the end of the film, Johnny, the investigating journalist, has himself become insane. His case was "hopeless," wrote the censor, and "so is this film. *Shock Corridor* shocked us." The censor's concluding remarks recommend that the film be seen by other censors, because "it is, in its way, a connoisseur's item and, though at times boring, worth any censor seeing."[17]

What could the censor have meant by "connoisseur's item"? Did he mean for connoisseurs of censorship, or connoisseurs of pornography, or connoisseurs of film art? Certainly the film brought forth a reaction that was not at all commonplace, the decision to refuse a certificate based not so much on the elements of sex and violence, which could be excised, but on a rather contrived set of concerns over the film's representation of madness and mental institutions; did the censors really think that the film might have a negative effect on people suffering from mental illness? Did it really matter that the film's representation of mental health professionals was inaccurate or irresponsible? What did matter was that the representation of mental health was cast in such lurid and exploitative terms. The censor began his report by calling the film "sensational,"

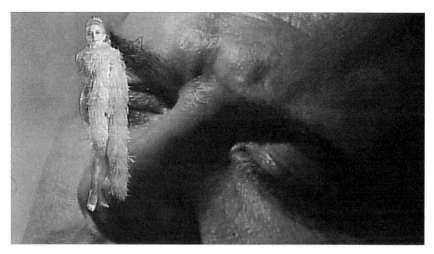

23. Frame grab from *Shock Corridor* (1963). Cathy, the coy stripper, superimposed on the face of investigative journalist and boyfriend, Johnny.

and it is, I think, the film's excessive emphasis on shock and sensation that so upset the sensibilities of the British censors.

And American publicity for the film only confirmed its pulp pedigree; marketing materials promised that the film would open "the door to sights you've never seen before!" And gave "case histories" of the film's protagonists:

Case History 1—Rachel G.

19 years old, unmarried. Outwardly a completely normal personality. However, subject is uncontrollably promiscuous, continually seeking the company of men to an abnormal degree. Has no sense of moral values. Diagnosis: Sex psychotic.

Case History 2—John B.

Brilliant newspaper reporter, bachelor. Suffers hallucinations that his stripteaser sweetheart is his sister. Goes into frenzy at any romantic advances she may make. Yet has attacked men who attempt affairs with her. Diagnosis: Erotic dementia.

Case History 3—Cathy R.

Young, intelligent, beautiful. Claims she is a stripteaser only because of the higher monetary returns than other professions. Her torchy performances however, reveal her avid reaction to the excitement of male audiences. Diagnosis: manic sensualist.

These are some of the shocking people you'll meet in *Shock Corridor*.

Diagnosis: sensational sexploitation picture.

This tastelessness, the meaningless shock and sensation, the lack of conviction, the pretension, and the juvenile concerns, all of which so appalled the

American reviewers and British censors, delighted cinephiles. The filmmaker and critic Bertrand Tavernier wrote in his introduction to the 1965 French translation of *Shock Corridor*'s screenplay that "dramatic rules are trodden underfoot. Syntax is manhandled. From the height of his camera, Fuller thunders, howls, insults, rages, calms down to achieve a scene of prodigious tenderness, and then goes off again, not hesitating to go too far, to break the traditional rhythm. It always pleases me to see this director ranked among the good technicians, he who systematically takes a stand contrary to that of the good workman, who mistreats the cutting process, who moves the camera against all the rules."[18]

Why should this aesthetic resonate so strongly with cinephiles? For Tavernier it clearly is the potential to use Fuller to upset those with cultivated sensibilities and less discerning critical faculties than he and his fellow filmmakers and critics have developed. But the answer might also lie, as the American film critic Ronnie Scheib has suggested, in the way Fuller's aesthetic reflected on contemporary culture more generally: "Disconnected, fragmented images of violence, solipsism, exploitation, discussions of racism, bigotry, war, atomic apocalypse and local murders—how better to describe a TV news broadcast in 1963—or *Shock Corridor*. But what TV homogenizes, deadens, disconnects radically and connects trivially, Fuller electrifies, forcing his audience to confront the impossible juxtaposition of absolutes, of consciousnesses that cannot, yet do, share the same frame, and the multiplicity of absent syntaxes which could articulate their coexistence and their consecutivity."[19] Fuller's audience, however, is not "forced" to confront any of this; it chooses to, or it does not even recognize the confrontation, as the case may be. Certainly, the film reviewers and censors did not confront *Shock Corridor* as if it were a complex object of study, but the best of Fuller's critics did ask difficult questions of his films.

The first significant essay on Fuller was by Luc Moullet in the March 1959 edition of *Cahiers du cinéma*. In the essay "Sam Fuller: In Marlowe's Footsteps," Moullet made his case for the director in terms very similar to those made by Tavernier and Scheib, and his ideas would be echoed in other important critiques of the filmmaker. Moullet understood Fuller to be "Faustian in principle and Promethean in fact."[20] It was the filmmaker's attempt to reconcile the desire to put oneself at the center of the universe, whatever the cost, with the opposing communal desire to rebuff authority, which, Moullet argued, formed part of Fuller's identity. However, unlike other American filmmakers that work on this opposition, Fuller refused to resolve the conflict by the artificial "intervention of outside influences" (154). The dark heart of Fuller's work, Moullet suggested, is that he reveals the resolution of the opposing needs of the individual and the community to be impossible even as he continues to search for such a synthesis.

The identification of this thematic tension at the heart of Fuller's art allowed Moullet to reject the notion that Fuller is little more than a figure of crude reactionary impulses: "Could Fuller really be the fascist, the right-wing extremist who was denounced not so long ago in the Communist press? I don't think so" (147). The reason Moullet is able to reject this position is that he also rejects a conventional way of explaining a film's politics. When critics examine only the surface qualities of Fuller's film, culled from story, character, dialogue, and theme, they are reading Fuller's films as if they were a bourgeois text. Moullet argued that "we have a strong aversion to would-be philosophers who get into making films in spite of what film is, and who just repeat in cinema the discoveries of the other arts. . . . If you have something to say, say it, write it, preach it if you like, but don't come bothering us with it" (145). Fuller, he contended, dealt with what film is: camera movement and editing—its mise-en-scène. Beyond identifying the theme of Fuller's work, Moullet's signal importance in Fuller scholarship is in recognizing the filmmaker's extraordinary formal achievements. Evidence of Fuller's politics cannot be found simply in the story, which would only confirm him as a reactionary, but must instead, he argued, be discovered in the elements that are exclusive to the medium of film. Moullet selected Fuller for validation because he is first and foremost a *film*maker. Over and above everything else, Fuller's films foreground their filmic specificity. Only when this is conceded is it possible to recognize Fuller as a major filmmaker.

In Fuller's films ambiguity exists not in the story, which often employed a relativist stance with regard to political and moral questions, but between the story and its form; *how* the story is told is what is important in Moullet's thesis. It is the film's formal elements that call into question the otherwise reactionary worldview posited in the story. On this basis Moullet made his grand claim that "morality is a question of tracking shots" (148). This much-noted pronouncement has the effect of pulling the reader's attention away from Fuller's putative support for a reactionary political line, and instead focuses on his mastery of the cinematic medium, where *the* truth can be found. Camera movements in Fuller's films, according to Moullet, are gratuitous. The "emotive power of the movement" is what organizes the scene; and it is not dependent upon "dramatic composition" (148). That is, Fuller's aesthetic is based on incessant progression that is often unmotivated and appears spontaneous and improvised. His films' form and design are autonomous, unchained from realist conventions of story, character, and theme. Through Fuller, Moullet turns upside down the terms on which an understanding of film aesthetics has traditionally been conceived. If Moullet's provocative and contrary working method seem somewhat arbitrary and irrational, then we might use in his defense the same argument he makes in defense of Fuller: "there is a grain of madness in him," and only madmen can break with the chains of tradition, particularly the shackles of "realism" (149).

Fuller's cinema is a world in revolt with the established order of things; where "rotters become saints" (146). Moullet wrote that in "Fuller we see everything that other directors deliberately excise from their films: disorder, filth, the unexplainable, the stubbly chin, and a kind of fascinating ugliness in a man's face" (149). The short fat man is representative of Fuller's true hero, because man "belongs to the order of the earth, and he must resemble it, in all the harshness of its beauty" (149). The link to the earth is compounded by Fuller's obsession with showing feet, particularly in movement. The link to an earthiness, to the director's tellurian concerns, is furthered by Moullet's claim that Fuller is an "instinctual" and "spontaneous" director: "Fuller is an amateur; he is lazy, agreed. But his film expresses amateurism and laziness: and that is already a lot." It is enough for Fuller "just to be himself at every moment. . . . His rough sketches take us by surprise and are more powerful, more revealing than a fine piece of construction." Behind them is the "force of the instantaneous and of the unfinished" (152–53). Fuller is a "primitive," Moullet states, but the critic qualifies this description by adding that Fuller is an "intelligent primitive" (149). The paradox is important; Fuller is both erudite *and* instinctive.

In his seminal book of auteurist hagiography, *The American Cinema* (1968), Andrew Sarris wrote of Fuller that he came from "somewhere on the far side of paradise." Sarris's conception of the director was as an "authentic American primitive whose works have to be seen to be understood. Seen, not heard or synopsized."[21] In calling Fuller a primitive, and in drawing the reader's attention to the filmic elements on which his cinema is built, Sarris is clearly echoing Moullet. The idea of Fuller as a "primitive" has come to fix his image, just as surely as the director's gnostic pronouncement, in Jean-Luc Godard's *Pierrot le fou*, that "a film is like a battleground—love, hate, action, violence, death. In one word—emotion," has been overworked as a ready-made description for his elemental cinema.

It should be recalled that Fuller's appearance in Godard's film comes toward the middle of a languorous sequence where the putative hero, played by Jean-Paul Belmondo, listlessly eavesdrops on groups of partygoers describing the latest wonders of material culture. In between the ad-speak for antiperspirant—"It's easy to feel fresh. Soap washes, cologne refreshes, perfume perfumes . . ."—the merits of the new Alfa-Romeo or Oldsmobile 88, hairspray, and lingerie, Fuller introduces himself: "I'm an American director, my name is Samuel Fuller. I'm here to make a picture in Paris called *Flower of Evil*." Against the moribund scenario of the mouthing of empty truths and hollow advertising copy, Fuller sounds like the only sane man left alive. Love, hate, action, violence, and death are precisely what is missing from this vision of an emotionless bourgeois hell. In a world of middling ambition, mundane concerns, and crass commercial imperatives, all figured by an overwhelming sense of ennui and mediocrity, Fuller's pronouncement appears to carry a shocking truth. But, beyond offering a small litany of nouns that suggest base elements of human nature, a primitive wellspring of emotions, is he in fact saying very much at all?

Is it unfair to ask Fuller to speak his cinema? Perhaps it has to be seen, not described, as Sarris recommended. Like Godard, Sarris clearly values Fuller as some kind of riposte to middle-class complacency and solipsism. In the entry on Fuller in his dictionary of American filmmakers, Sarris compares *China Gate* with Joseph Mankiewicz's adaptation of Graham Greene's *The Quiet American*; the latter's film is "anecdotal, microcosmic, symbolic. With Fuller, the distinction between the personal plot and its political context evaporates with the first leggy sprawl of Angie Dickinson." Sarris concluded that it "is time the cinema followed the other arts in honoring its primitives. Fuller belongs to the cinema, and not to literature and sociology."[22]

In the spirit of Sarris's call, and again in keeping with Moullet's thesis, George Lipsitz claimed Fuller as a New York intellectual—not because Fuller revealed a mastery of "abstract standards of refinement and performances" but because his vision of urban experience challenged "the preoccupation of traditional intellectuals by privileging human interaction and inter-subjectivity."[23] Reading across the critical literature on Fuller, Lipsitz located three key frames of analysis: the representation of the crises in American popular mythology, the challenge posed to the unrealistic glamour of Hollywood conventions, and, in counterpoint, the purveying of shock realism. Integrating these three frames, Lipsitz argued, "Fuller's artistic choices flow naturally from his politics. His uneasiness about the oppressions of modernist rationality lead him to value interruption, incongruity, and difference." This is particularly evident in his rejection of the "allure of grand narratives that account for everything but the lives of ordinary people like ourselves." Furthermore, rather "than rubbing our noses in the dirt of everyday life, Fuller seeks to make us suspicious of the 'prettiness' of Hollywood and Madison Avenue images that dominate our lives and to rediscover the unconventional beauty that we might find all around us" (193–94). Lipsitz's argument that Fuller confronts the specious attractions of commercial culture complements the use Godard made of Fuller in *Pierrot le fou* and, like so much of the critical work on the director, confirms the conception of him as a caustic response to the blandishments of cultures of consumption.

This conception of Fuller is clearly related to Moullet's understanding of the director as a primitive artist, whose insights into the human condition are uncorrupted by a refined existence, education, and a cleaving to tradition. Moullet is working within a countertradition of the intellectual and artistic fascination with primitive art and cultures. As the art historian Jack Flam has noted, "When we speak of Primitivism, we refer not only to artists' use of formal ideas from the works of so-called Primitive cultures, but also to a complex network of attitudes about the processes, meanings, and functions of art, and about culture itself." Key to this is the idea that primitivism acts "as a force in regenerating modern Western culture."[24] The "discovery," however, of a primitive aesthetic in traditional African woodcarving is not the same as its "discovery" in a phonographic recording of a rural blues performance from the 1930s or in an expensive motion picture production. The technological and industrial determinants on the blues and on the movie would suggest that the critic has to ignore some rather stark truths if he or she is to position the performer or director as a "primitive."[25]

During the 1920s and 1930s, in Paris, the New York dancer Josephine Baker and the New Orleans jazz clarinetist Sidney Bechet had been remade in the likeness of primitives, albeit a primitivism that comes from the United States, not Africa, or at least not directly. Minus the racial caste, Moullet molded Fuller into a similar form. These American artists are primitive insomuch as they offer a corrective to an overdetermined European sensibility that is governed by the restraint of tradition, cultivation, erudition, refinement, and, above all, good taste. As such, the Americans are "primitives" because they are free from tradition, spontaneous, given to improvising, self-taught ("amateur" in Moullet's construction), lacking in self-consciousness, and unafraid to embrace the physical and sensational. But as Americans, and unlike Africans, they are also modern; they belong to the moment, and they are products of an entertainment industry—the greatest the world has known. The "American primitive," then, is an oxymoron: someone who sits outside of the modern *yet* is a representative and product of a highly modernized culture. This construction was particularly attractive to European cinephiles.

Looking back on the debates within film culture, in which he was deeply embroiled as the 1960s moved into the 1970s, David Will noted that disputes were often defined by the politics of the left and the right, or, to be more precise in the case of the latter, an Oxbridge elitism. Nevertheless, among these warring cinephiles a consensus formed around Fuller as a totem. According to Will the various factions had a "common desire to act as *interpreters* of American popular culture," whether as "quasi surrealists" marveling at the bizarre excesses of Hollywood or as Marxists trying to come to terms with proletarian taste. In doing so they attempted to "colonise the colonisers," to explain to Americans what "their cultural products were really about, to act as civilised interpreters of the savages." The factions also shared an antiliberalism, and the "valorisation of Fuller represented the triumph of the anti-liberal position and scandalised the mainstream bourgeoisie." In sum: "The *excesses* of 'Fuller Films'—their violence, the caricatures, their florid, 'senseless' camera movements and tension ridden sequence shots were to fuel the quasi-surrealist demands, the anti-liberal requirements and the (albeit conflicting) need for 'primitive' texts that were required by auteurists of both the left and right in 1969."[26] Whether from the perspective of the right or the left, the film's politics needed to be dealt with if Fuller was to be considered a paragon of a new film culture. As such, Fuller can be seen as a symptom of a wider concern with the politics of film among progressive critics, who were asking the question, How can you love the attractions of commercial cinema and at the same time hate the repressive forces of capitalism that produced those films? Fuller's films suggested ways of living with that contradiction.

Fuller's critical ascent began in France but only took off when he was championed by a new generation of British critics.[27] Initially this move was led by the critics at *Movie*, notably V. F. Perkins, and by Peter Wollen in the guise of "Lee Russell" writing for the *New Left Review*.[28] In 1969 David Will and Lynda Myles helped mount the retrospective at the EIFF, an event Fuller believed was key to his later renown: "I would say that I owe the festival anything that is in connection with making a dollar or being 'bankable.'"[29]

As part of his review of British film culture since the late 1960s, Will wrote that the festival "arrived as an institution of oppositional culture in 1969. The index of that arrival and oppositionality was the retrospective devoted to 'Samuel Fuller: The Complete Works.'"[30] During the 1970s the EIFF radically challenged the accepted idea of a film festival as no more than a showcase for new releases and a benign cultural event designed to foster tourism and investment. Against the grain, the festival gave a platform to film theory, experimental film, new European and world cinema, maverick filmmakers, and American exploitation movies. The paradox of an established organization working as an instrument of resistance toward the dominant culture, and using the films of a lowbrow American filmmaker as their first and most effective tool, underscored not only the history of the EIFF during the 1970s but also a significant strand within film studies generally.[31]

That strand would form the bedrock of the Education Department at the BFI, discussed in chapter 1, which would make its reputation of oppositionality by championing maverick American directors, such as Hawks, Siegel, Mann, Fuller, and Boetticher. These were filmmakers who appeared to espouse conservative values, which were certainly at odds with the left-leaning sentiments of the British cinephiles clustered around the British Film Institute and the Society for Education in Film and Television. While validating these filmmakers, however, each of whom produced films with decidedly masculine appeal, the film educationalists rejected liberal filmmakers such as Kramer, Wyler, and Kazan. The mavericks, they argued, were the true radicals. The liberal filmmakers *conformed* to a notion of consensus politics, producing socially responsible films, couched within the tradition of the well-made film that confirmed a certain smug self-righteousness. Moreover, Kramer et al. were overly respectful of older art forms, theater and literature, in particular, whereas Hawks, Fuller, and the others displayed a vitality that belonged to film alone, and, whatever the filmmaker's personal politics, they were more democratic than the liberal filmmakers because they did not show any deference to an artistic hierarchy in their desire to make a movie move and to tell a story through the medium of film. They also made films about men doing things and being very good at what they do, which clearly appealed to the critics' own sense of masculinity. Writing under the byline Lee Russell, Wollen, in a 1964 piece on Hawks, wrote, "His ideology is primitive and anachronistic. For Hawks the highest human emotion is the camaraderie of the exclusive, self-sufficient, all male group." Even as Wollen recognized the limits of the appeal—"a faked up ethic, born from freakish and stunting social conditions"—he was not prepared to fully resist its seductive masculinist enchantment.[32] Fuller's similar masculine ethos was equally seductive.

Under the spell of this ethos Wollen joined forces with Myles and Will in organizing the Fuller retrospective and in producing a provocation aimed squarely at the critical establishment. In this spirit of revolt the organizers introduced Fuller to festivalgoers with an aggressive verve: "This retrospective is designed to give the first fully comprehensive showing of his works in Britain, and is intended to demonstrate unequivocally that Fuller is one of the major film directors to have emerged from America since the war. There is no need to substantiate this claim. Fuller's vindication lies in his films, which are obligatory viewing for anyone who claims to have an interest in the cinema."[33] The organizers were putting on a show of bravado; the unequivocal claim that Fuller was an important film director, and that his films were obligatory viewing, was made in the face of what they knew would be disbelief on the part of the old guard of festival patrons and cynical film fans. The high valuation given to Fuller's films by the organizers was as heartfelt as it was provocative. The imprimatur placed on him by being showcased at such a prestigious event had the effect of drawing a heavily demarcated line in the sand. In 1969 the festival, as a purveyor of middlebrow film fare, came to an end.

Tied into the EIFF retrospective was the first book-length publication on the director, which featured seventeen short essays on individual films, an interview, and a biography.[34] In the same year, *Screen* published two lengthy articles on Fuller, one of which would become a key chapter in Colin McArthur's *Underworld USA* (1972), which took its title from a Fuller crime drama.[35] In the following year the house publication of the Cambridge Film Society, *Cinema*, itself a sponsor of the retrospective at Edinburgh, ran an interview with Fuller conducted at the festival and a lengthy review of the EIFF book. The journal had already featured a substantial piece on Fuller by Peter Wollen in its 1968 inaugural issue.[36] In 1970 *Film, the Magazine of the British Federation of Film Societies* got in on the act with "The World of Samuel Fuller"; the *Brighton Film Review* ran its own "Sam Fuller Special!"; and Phil Hardy's small book, *Samuel Fuller*, was published.[37] A year later, the third British book on Fuller, this one by Nicholas Garnham, was published.[38] By any means of accounting, this was an extraordinary body of work produced around a film director about whom, Wollen had said in his introduction to the EIFF book, "almost nothing of value has been written." He could little have imagined the deluge that was to follow.

Among the first of the British critics to engage with Fuller was V. F. Perkins in the second issue of *Movie*.[39] Perkins considered Fuller to be a "sensationalist" whose movies were akin to "illustrated lectures." Following Moullet, he celebrated Fuller's use of the camera, particularly its ability to surprise and shock, and, like many critics to come, he noted that Fuller's "art is built on contradiction."[40] Working through political contradictions they found in his work became the dominant activity of British critics who engaged with Fuller.[41] Perkins presented a particularly astute reading: "It is necessary to emphasise the film on its most obvious level partly because Fuller is often, and too glibly, characterized as a simple fascist; but mainly because not to do so would be to rob *Underworld USA* of its peculiar force. Fuller is not an 'underground' director whose films actually *do* the opposite of what they overtly *say*. His ambiguity is such that he makes opposites co-exist. Thus he celebrates democracy at the same time, and with as complete a sincerity, as he celebrates the most violent individualism."[42] Through his observation on the coexistence of opposites, Perkins pinpoints why critics have been able to find complexity in Fuller's films, while others have found them to be overly simplistic. Perkins puts the onus on the critic to be astute enough to identify and understand the potential for contradiction in Fuller's films. The critic has to put in the spadework; the films will not simply give up their treasures for the taking. In this construction the critic's ability to discriminate is valued as much as the film or filmmaker that allows him or her to practice the art of criticism.

In late 1963 Wollen had submitted a short overview and critique of the director's work to the *New Left Review*. He put forward the idea that Fuller's contradictory critique *and* celebration of the idea of America was at odds with the period's prevailing liberal sentiments. He wrote that the director had confronted the contradictions raised by American history. "He has not shirked those contradictions but has sought to dissolve them in an extreme statement of romantic nationalism."[43] His point was ably echoed by Raymond Durgnat in his critique of *China Gate*: "Fuller is ambivalent with furious energies as Godard with cool despairs. Like Losey and Kazan, his American dynamism is networked through European intricacies. Fuller is one of the great American moralists. Lia–Lucky Legs incarnates America's internal race problem. 'I'm a little of everything and a lot of nothing,' she says, like the younger brother in *Shadows*. Fourteen years before the fact, Fuller has the Detroit riots in his heart. His hysterias and brutalities are those of Civil War."[44] Although they did not use the description, Wollen and his peers understood Fuller to be an American heretic, someone who challenged the doctrine of Americanism in order that the *ideal* might be more readily realized. Allegiance and treachery to the United States is what Wollen considered to be Fuller's principal theme.[45] If Fuller was a placard-carrying heretic, marching up and down Main Street USA with his merry band of outsiders in tow—prostitutes, pickpockets, turncoats, infiltrators, commie

24. Publicity still for *Pickup on South Street* (1953). Skip McCoy (Richard Widmark) dips into Candy's (Jean Peters) purse.

baiters, stool pigeons, mercenaries, madmen, and other assorted gutter life—then the British film critics, who so loudly declared their interest in this American lowbrow-intellectual, libertarian-commie hater, and racist defender of civil rights, were performing their own parade of revolt. Their professed admiration for Fuller amounted to no less than a major assault on the established critical order, which understood American cinema to be a crass commercialized medium of little aesthetic value generally and believed that the formulaic low-budget movies Fuller traded in were no more than sewer-bound ephemera aimed at the lowest common denominator—pulp for the proletariat.

The critical consensus among cinephiles was that Fuller's characters were suspended between worlds, particularly in their contradictory relationship with the United States. They are extreme loyalists, yet the country they champion, and often die for, sees them as outsiders. None better represents this than the character Moe (Thelma Ritter) in *Pickup on South Street*, a stool pigeon who dies rather then give information to a commie. Moe is busy "making a living," so she can afford to die. She has been saving her money to buy her own grave in Long Island, fretting all the while about getting a commoner's burial in potter's field—"It would kill me," she says. What she wants is a private plot, and she has one picked out—"You got to be screened before you can be put away there, that's how exclusive it is." In death, through an act of individuation—she wants a *private* plot, not a commoner's grave—Moe seeks respectability. Yet despite this patently absurd and certainly self-centered ambition, Moe is absolutely committed to the community of the USA through her hatred of communism: an idea for which she is willing to make the ultimate sacrifice.

Moe's outsider role is fixed in terms of her class, age, sex, and dubious occupation, but she is wholly American. In other films Fuller turns to racial others as representatives of loyal Americans. The Nisei sergeant and the black medic in *The Steel Helmet*, who in anyone else's war film would have met early though no doubt heroic deaths, are here ranked among the survivors. Against the accusation that they are oppressed in their own country, they mount a defense that is based on gut intuition rather than rational argument. What is the use of explaining things, the Nisei responds to his communist inquisitor, who wants to know how he can fight for the United States when his parents were interned during the war. "You could never understand," is the best the Nisei can muster as an argument. These examples typify Fuller's politics, which appear to be based on the logic of melodrama—a world constructed out of clear-cut notions of right and wrong, good and bad—a Manichean worldview. Moullet, however, argued that Fuller could not be considered Manichean because he offered too many conflicting points of view. The Nisei and the Moe are too unstable, too filled with contradictions to function as fixed points in a Manichean scheme of things.

To see how Fuller slips outside of the idea that he holds an essentialist's conception of the world, he is worth comparing to Spillane. In a 1973 interview, conducted by novelist Angela Carter for the British soft-core magazine *Men Only*, Spillane is asked how he defined *good*. "That's easy enough," he replies. "You've got an issue—which is the right side of the issue? And which is the wrong side? A murderer is strictly on the wrong side of the issue. When a man is running down a killer, the line is right there. It's black and white. I don't pull the greys. I never have."[46] Moullet would argue that there are considerable areas of gray in Fuller's films, which pull the blacks and whites into question: Spillane's world is fixed; Fuller's is fluid.

A critic at the *Los Angeles Times*, reviewing, upon its initial release, one of Fuller's pictures, was clearly unable to see the difference: "HARD-BOILED FILM STRESSES REALISM—Samuel Fuller, who wrote the screenplay and directed *Pickup on South Street*, follows the Mickey Spillane school in his exposition of sex and sadism. . . . Brutality at times reaches the point where audiences snicker instead of being horrified. Beauteous Jean Peters is the recipient of nine-tenths of the violence. . . . The boys, Widmark and Richard Kiley as a Commie agent, take turns beating her up."[47] For this film reviewer there is no ambiguity or contradictory position articulated in the film. For the cinephile champions of Fuller, reading contradiction and ambiguity into his work was at the heart of their critical strategies. Fuller's films, they argued, unsettle the absolutes of a Manichean worldview that are held on to and espoused by Spillane.

Discussing what makes for a good pop song, Greil Marcus, like Fuller's apologists, latched onto works that carry "surprise, shock, ambiguity, contingency, or a hundred other things, each with a faraway sense of the absolute." This he opposed to the bad object, "one that subverts any possibility of an apprehension of the absolute . . . that disables the person whose life it enters into living less intensely." Marcus's definition of a "bad object" is a fair approximation of how Spillane's work is generally received and understood by his critics. On one hand, confronting the contradictions that life throws up is what makes us alive, Marcus argued, and, echoing Fuller in Godard's film, "produces rage, desire, hate, and love, and real art brings all those things to life." On the other hand, art that "quiets or buries those cultural instincts can't survive the human faculty— it falls apart. But as it does, it humiliates whoever carries it."[48] Though Fuller and Spillane work with similar material, and often deploy similar techniques, Spillane's fiction does not allow for ambiguity or uncertainty, does not invite the reader to question its existence. Fuller's films do precisely the opposite, and the consistency of critical work on Fuller is evidence to support such a position, but is it tenable?

Writing in 1969 about *Hell and High Water*, David Will made the apparently extraordinary claim that "the movie is not so much a violent anti-Communist tract as a tract about violent anti-Communism."[49] In debating this conclusion, the critic Paul Joannides thought Will's acts of critical transformation were palpable nonsense, a gross misreading of *Hell and High Water*, which he understood to clearly and categorically equate communists with the nonhuman.[50] In his critique Joannides could have found support for his position in an essay by Gérard Gozlan, who was writing for *Positif* in 1962. Gozlan thought that the theory of ambiguity, proffered by the critics at the rival journal *Cahiers du cinéma*, floundered when it came to Fuller, particularly when it came to *Hell and High Water*.[51]

Will is not alone among Anglo-American critics in turning things on their head when it comes to Fuller, and though his example may be extreme, it is also somewhat familiar. The New York critic J. Hoberman managed a similar act of

25. Publicity photo for *Hell and High Water*. Under a red light Capt. Adam Jones (Richard Widmark) makes love to the scientist Denise Montel (Bella Darvi), tenderly stroking her bruised face.

transformation in coming to grips with the director's politics. Hoberman believed Fuller's films espoused a social progressivism so that the "neurotic loners or loudmouthed members of the lumpen proletariat . . . test society's official pieties."[52] If Hoberman's reading seems at odds with the reactionary red-baiting found in so many of his films, then the excessive nature of that polemic, which is what Will was also arguing, "pushes McCarthy-style anti-Communism to the far side of parody."[53] In one neat critical stroke, then, these two critics have transformed Fuller from a reactionary into a progressive—he was not supporting the forces of reaction but parodying them; it is not a violent anticommunist tract but is about violent anticommunism. These readings of Fuller are entirely in line with a critical consensus that has emerged since Moullet's seminal essay.

Despite the weight of critical support for Fuller, Joannides's argument cannot be entirely dismissed. A more balanced critical position was hardly possible, however, in the hothouse atmosphere of debates on film theory and criticism in the 1960s and 1970s. Discussing Fuller's *Pickup on South Street* alongside cold war propaganda movies, such as *I Was a Communist for the FBI* and *My Son John*, Michael Rogin, writing in the less politically charged mid-1980s, managed to contain both sides of the argument. He maintained that this "right-wing, antiliberal B movie" is the only "genuine work of art among the films which promote the cold war" but that Fuller's politics were deplorable.[54] This was because Fuller had "succeeded in making politics into aesthetics" (31). Unlike the other films in the cycle that equate communism with crime, Fuller, according to Rogin, makes crime the alternative to communism (and bureaucracy in general, here embodied by the FBI). In bringing this distinction to our attention, Rogin clarifies the contradictions inherent in Fuller's films, revealing how this oxymoronic "anarchofascism" is able to both support the state and proclaim an antibureaucratic stance:

> Other anti-Communist films claim to defend the American individual. But they do so by marrying him to supportive, entrapping institutions— motherhood, mass society, and the state. These institutions, which the filmmakers can neither believe in nor resist, spread a fog through cold war cinema. By contrast Fuller finds a place to stand with an impious, violent, antibureaucratic Red-baiting. There is nothing attractive about such politics. *Pickup on South Street* harks back to a nineteenth-century predatory individualism, moved from the frontier to the city and placed openly outside the law, in which property is acquired through theft. That individualism, always masked in political discourse by appeals to civilization, produced the very world from which Fuller was alienated. (33)

According to Rogin, Fuller represented an authentic American voice but one that had been buried by cold war pieties. Much of the better criticism on Fuller—Moullet, Sarris, Lipsitz, Wollen, Perkins, Hoberman, and Durgnat—is in explicit or tacit agreement with Rogin. They also agree, as Rogin wrote, that "Fuller invented characters with rough edges and style, whose gestures and dialogue contrast to the mass-produced figures of other cold war movies" (33). But they cannot be seen to agree with Rogin on Fuller's frontier politics; to do so would have been to concede too much ground to his detractors and to have unsettled their own left-wing sensibilities. Better to have Samuel Fuller "American Heretic" than Samuel Fuller "Populist Demagogue."

But for some critics it was also desirable to simply move debate away from politics altogether. Discussing cinephilia's intense preoccupation with Hollywood films between Pearl Harbor and the Bay of Pigs, the film theorist Paul Willemen argued that the love of cinema from this period became "strictly a space for the play of desire, asocial, irresponsible":

> That the phenomenon of cinephilia should have arisen first in France is largely due to the still active residues of surrealism in post-war French culture. Like the surrealist's attitude to cinema, cinephilia was founded on a theory of the sublime moment, the breathtaking fragment which suddenly and momentarily bore witness to the presence and force of desire in the midst of appallingly routinised and oppressive conditions of

production. In such moments, cinema suddenly revealed itself to be founded on a desiring-looking, a mise en scene not of stories but of a sexualized look. The script was shown to be merely a device to sustain that look, to motivate the parade of images incarnating desire itself. Which is why cinephilia (and surrealism) shies away from the "quality" film and its respectably literary pretenses deflecting attention from the sheer pleasure of looking.[55]

Though they are often anything but low-budget (the 20th Century–Fox films in particular have excellent production values), Fuller's movies are clearly not "quality," certainly have no literary pretenses, are shot through with breathtaking fragments framed within formulaic routine stories, and the sexualized look is so often overly dwelt upon that it takes on a fetishistic and often sadistic form.

In Fuller's pulp narratives, topicality, or the everyday, the known and the recognizable, play off against the exaggerated, the sensational, the unknown, and the unfamiliar. Discussing true crime magazines that appealed to the "public fascination with police procedures even as they recognized that the police themselves were of little visual interest," Will Straw has noted: "In their place we find enlarged fingers pointing accusingly at suspects, spider webs trapping villainous women and the martini bubbles in which a swindler's victims are imagined. These graphic images represent leaps into extravagant visual metaphor at odds with the standardized police imagery or plodding accounts of detective work that follow them. True crime magazines nourished the sense that crime took place in worlds more vivid and fantastic than our own, worlds of heightened expressivity and dream-like juxtaposition."[56] The heightened expressivity and dreamlike juxtaposition is formed out of a world that is instantly recognizable to its consumer, but as much as it may have matched any lived experience, it was a world made familiar primarily through genre convention. Fuller's films are formed in this world, and like Fantomas, true crime magazines, and *Kiss Me Deadly*, his movies overflow the mold in which they were made and therefore become amenable to surrealist readings.

There is much to support a surrealist reading of Fuller's films; not least, there is a heavy emphasis on subjectivity that runs throughout his oeuvre, which often takes on an oneiric coloring. His debut film as director, *I Shot Jesse James* (Lippert, 1949), is a story of *l' amour fou* between Jesse and his assassin. The film begins as a bank robbery is under way. Cutting between tight close-ups on the faces of James and his confederates, the bank tellers, and a foot inching toward an alarm bell, the scene builds in tension until the inevitable release in the sounding of the alarm and an explosion of gunfire. In an interview given to a French film journal in 1963, Fuller responded to the question of why he used so many close-ups: "eighty per cent of my film consisted of faces." This was later mistranslated by some British critics, who claimed that as much as "80 percent of the film was shot in close-up." In *The American Cinema* Sarris contended the film was "constructed almost entirely of close-ups of an impressive intensity the cinema has not experienced since Dreyer's *The Passion of Joan of Arc*."[57] Key scenes use a sequence of close-ups, but they do not dominate the film's visual scheme any more than the rather frequent use of montages of newspaper headlines determine the film's narration.

What Fuller was trying to emphasize in the interview was how close-ups of protagonists' faces allowed him to intimate an intense subjectivity; the close proximity of a character to the camera is used to suggest a privileged access to his or her thoughts and emotions, which are, we understand from the context, in turmoil. The emphasis on the subjective is carried forth from the first-person declaration of the title, *I Shot Jesse James*, into the stylized visualization of the lead character's interiority. The tumultuous psychic state in which Bob Ford finds himself, before and after the assassination, is underpinned not through a voice-over, which is the usual way to carry this kind of subjectivity (a technique Fuller gives full-reign in his fourth film, *Fixed Bayonets!*), but by having the actor, John Ireland, who plays Ford, deliver his lines in a hushed monotone, as if he were speaking to himself, and not just responding to the person he is ostensibly in conversation with.

Explaining the film to his French interviewer, Fuller noted, "I wasn't at all interested in the action. None of my films is, for me at least, an action film, even though there is action in all of them." Fuller saw things this way: "Maybe people understand my films in a different way, and if I were to tell them the stories completely as I conceived them, it is possible that they wouldn't accept them. Look, I don't want to deceive the public. I'd rather satisfy them. That's why I put action in my films, so that the action can carry the message and so the public doesn't get the idea that I'm trying to deliver a sermon or a lecture."[58] The desire to tell an abstract story of a man who kills the thing he loves, the need to respect generic convention and audience expectation, gave the film its particular tension. Fuller finds himself locked in a conflict between dramatizing as simply as possible Jesse James's assassination and finding a visual and aural schema to show the emotional turmoil felt by the assassin. Despite his belief that he found an acceptable balance, Fuller, in fact, puts such a strong emphasis on representing Ford's subjectivity that it continually threatens to overwhelm the film. The highly constructed eidetic moments that call forth an oneiric ambience punctuate the film in a heavy-handed manner, creating a false memory in Sarris and others of the film's use of close-ups. The overemphasized representations of subjectivity in the film appeal to an audience already tuned in to popular film's surrealistic potential. These critics may not have been the audience Fuller had in mind when he made his films, but they were an attentive audience, nonetheless.

Fuller's films are peppered with hallucinatory moments where disjuncture, brought about by the absurd or the irrational, disturbs the commonplace, producing those sublime moments desired by cinephiles and surrealists alike. In *House of Bamboo* (1955) the head of a gang of racketeers executes his second-in-command when he believes he has betrayed the mob to the police. Death comes quickly to the defenseless man as he is taking a bath. With water pouring out of the bullet holes in the tub, the gangster talks to the corpse about loyalty and leadership and how he is always right. To make his point, the gangster holds back the dead man's head so as to get his undivided attention. In *China Gate* a dead man safely crash-lands an airplane, his eyes having been held open by a comrade. In the same film a man apologizes for taking too long to die, and a Hungarian mercenary has a recurring nightmare of killing a Soviet soldier. The nightmare is visualized by having him attack the fantasy figure, only to wake and discover he had tried to kill the character played by Nat King Cole. In the opening of *The Steel Helmet* a G.I.'s helmet with a bullet hole is shown in close-up beneath the rolling credits; as the text "written, produced and directed by Samuel Fuller" peels away, the helmet rises up and reveals two eyes staring out from under its rim. As the camera pulls back and up, we see an American soldier, with his arms tied behind his back, crawl up a low embankment. He pushes himself, turtle-fashion, between the dead bodies of his comrades, who have also had their hands bound. In a series of exchanges between the soldier and a young South Korean boy, we discover that he is a sergeant, the only survivor from a platoon of infantrymen who had been captured and executed by North Korean communists. He got lucky when a bullet entered his helmet and, rather than killing him, spun freely around inside.

But is Sergeant Zack (Gene Evans) alive, or is he a dead man walking? He shows few human emotions or desires but simply responds to the needs of the moment. His reaction to being helped by the boy is to offer him the butt of an old chewed cigar. He barely makes eye contact or conversation, giving terse orders instead, seeing to a leg wound, and reeling off the name of a rifle and the kind of ammunition he needs. The sergeant's words are blocks against emotion, a stop against the welling of sentimentality. The film's core dramatic tension is between depicting the mundane practicalities of staying alive and a felt need to give in to sentiment and emotion that will show your humanity but that also puts you in peril. The sergeant does not pause over his dead comrades, and he tells the boy, whom he names Short Round, to take PeeWee Johnson's boots. He knew the men when they were alive, at least well enough to know their names, but their passing seems not to have touched him. All Johnson represents now is a good pair of boots. As the sergeant will say later to a naive lieutenant who sends a soldier to collect the dog tags from the body of an unknown American, "A dead man's nothing but a corpse. Nobody cares who he is now." In this case the body turns out to be booby-trapped; sentiment had made the lieutenant

26. Lobby card for *House of Bamboo* (1955).

27. Frame grab from *The Steel Helmet* (1951) title sequence. The eyes belong to Sgt. Zack (Gene Evans).

send a man to his death. After a soldier is killed in *Fixed Bayonets!* there is the utterance of a common mantra: "Strip him of everything we can use, roll him in a blanket, bury him, and mark it." The sergeant in *The Steel Helmet* does not give himself the cold comfort of even this small ritual. During the climactic bombardment of the Buddhist temple, the sergeant is again taken for dead. Only three out of the platoon appear to have survived, and as they sit among the rubble and dead bodies, rather than mourn their comrades, each in turn announces that he is hungry. "First we'll eat, and then we'll bury them," intones Sergeant Tanaka dryly.

Toward the end of *The Steel Helmet* the sergeant recalls the words of an officer who, as they struggled to get off the beach during the Normandy landings, described his men as "those who are dead and those who are about to die." *The Steel Helmet*, like its companion piece *Fixed Bayonets!*, is a haunted film—haunted as much by the living as by the dead. Fuller's characters live half-lives in these films. The dead walk among the living, and it is hard to tell them apart. *Fixed Bayonets!* begins with a general ordering a rearguard action to cover the army's retreat; a forty-eight-man platoon must be sacrificed to save the lives of the division. As the division pulls back, half the platoon watches, a tightly composed group of men in white overalls framed against the high banks of snow-covered hills—white on white. On the soundtrack a male chorus sings "On the Banks of the Wabash, Far Away," a maudlin tune, sung over a vaguely militaristic arrangement. The song is sunk so deep in the mix that we have to strain to hear the words. The grouping of the soldiers into a tight bunch set apart from the division, and the audience's knowledge that not many, if any, of these men will survive the coming action, suggest that they are already dead; they simply have not yet been killed.

The attrition of combat, the marking of the dead, pushes the story to its end and to the discovery that the corporal (Richard Basehart) does have the brains, and the guts, to lead what is left of the platoon to safety. Although he has been fearful of taking command, and has done all he could to keep his superiors alive, even crossing a minefield, he has no choice but to embrace what he most fears. The scene in which he is forced to take command begins with a young soldier digging a bullet from his own thigh with a bayonet. The sound of the blade scrapping against bone or lead accompanies a 360-degree pan, taking in all the faces of the men grouped together in the cave that offers uncertain refuge from the enemy. With the return of the camera to the soldier operating on himself, and the successful excavation of the bullet, the sergeant prophesies his own death. Following the ricochet of an enemy bullet inside the cave that strikes the sergeant in the chest, the corporal works feverishly to keep him alive. Against his work, and wishes, the sergeant, in an emotionless voice, tells the corporal that he now has the command because, "I'm dead." He says this in a dramatically underplayed manner: "Remember what I told you," he continues; "killing is

28. Frame grab from *Fixed Bayonets!* (1951). Sgt. Rock (Gene Evans), center, has been killed by a ricochet. His men barely register his death.

a business; it will be much easier from now on. Just like spitting." Soldiers kill, that is their reason for being, and in the process they get killed. The sergeant's last words are, "I told you, I'm dead." But has he ever been truly alive?

While the excessive emphasis on character subjectivity, eidetic moments, and the breakdown between realism and fantasy are open to surrealist readings, these are also traits that characterize contemporary comic book narrative strategies. The war stories in the EC comic books *Frontline Combat* (1951–54) and *Two-Fisted Tales* (1950–55) show little interest in the broad panoramic history of whatever conflict they are depicting, nor are they particularly concerned with the heroics of conflict, of superhuman endeavor, that would become the mainstay of DC's Sgt. Rock or Marvel's Sgt. Fury comic books. But like Fuller's choice of protagonists, the EC war comics told the stories of the marginal and the nondescript who could give a new spin to otherwise overworked tales. In this manner the legend of the Alamo is told from the point of view of a Mexican infantryman who forms part of the firing squad organized to execute the five Texican survivors of the siege. In "Custer's Last Stand" a lowly cavalryman gives a running commentary on the "peacock" Custer, whose vanity leads to their destruction. "Rubble," the tale of a Korean peasant building a house, is concluded when the newly completed home is blown apart by a single artillery blast.

"Hungnam!," the story of the mass evacuation of troops from the port of Hungnam, is told from the viewpoint of a dog.

All these stories sit among the many that recount the deeds of the enlisted man; sometimes he might be a hero, but mostly he is just trying to survive.[59] Like Fuller's films, these stories are highly ambivalent in their attitude toward war; they take pleasure in the technology and comradeship but offer tireless condemnation of the wanton loss of life and the dehumanization of otherwise perfectly ordinary people on both sides of a conflict. This refusal of the allure of grand narratives and the focus on the commonality was a signal trait in Lipsitz's definition of Fuller as an intellectual, as someone who worked against the grain of the dominant ideology, but I think it is also fair to say that the story, character types, and mode of address Fuller used in his films were shared with other artists, such as those who worked at EC comics and who similarly spoke for and to a proletarian audience. These stories addressed their readers as individuals, and unlike the combat films made during and immediately after World War II, the stories make no appeal to a collective sensibility, to a shared, yet abstract, common goal.[60] Instead these stories are about the effects wider political events have on individuals.

Along with the work of his colleagues at EC, Jack Davis, Wally Wood, John Severin, and Will Elder, Harvey Kurtzman's comic strips for *Two-Fisted Tales* and *Frontline Combat* are the perfect visual and narrative complement to Fuller's hyped-up war films—filled with close-ups of lantern-jawed G.I.s with six-day beards and grizzled, gnarly sergeants with a lifetime of combat experience and no life outside of the army. The characters are motivated by unreflexive emotional drives and belief systems: greed, hate, fear, lust, duty, fidelity, and loyalty. There is a marked absence of psychological complexity; in its stead are stories that resonate at an elemental level, such as the 1952 story "MUD!": "'April showers bring May flowers!' . . . a cute little ditty for children! But when April came to Korea in 1951, the April showers did not bring flowers! Instead, April brought brown, wet, slippery, oozing . . . sucking . . . MUD!" Jack Davis fleshed out this Kurtzman yarn with his illustrations of G.I.s trudging along mud roads and through muddy fields in the pouring rain, before eventually mounting an attack up a muddy hill. Trench coats and backpacks hang heavy, sodden by the rain, and boots are mud-caked: "Ah, yes. . . . The mud stopped the powerful trucks, the roaring tanks . . . but one thing the mud couldn't stop . . . never has stopped and never will stop! That most remarkable weapon of all wars, past and present . . . a pair of strong legs with a man and a rifle on top. . . . That queen of the battle, the infantryman!" Kurtzman and Davis share with Fuller an interest in depicting the travails of the infantryman, locked together with a group of ill-assorted fellows who share the same fears and desires, suffer the same deprivations, and join in the same work—walking mostly. As Moullet has remarked, Fuller loved to show infantrymen's boots and feet. The most memorable scene

29. Title page for "Mud!" in *Two-Fisted Tales* (Jan.–Feb. 1952).

in his catalog of tellurian sequences is in *Fixed Bayonets!*; the G.I.s are warming each other's feet in a cave, and their squirming toes look like a barrelful of anemic eels. Each soldier slowly withdraws his feet so Sergeant Rock can find out whose foot he is holding and pounding, only to discover it is his own, the cold and the damp having denied him any sensation.

Like Fuller, Kurtzman and Davis keep the compositions tight, moving between close-ups of individuals in small panels to wide panels that hold a small group of men closely bunched together. Shifting between individual subjectivity and the uniformity of the group, both claustrophobic and intimate, Davis and Kurtzman make the situation compelling by emphasizing the imminent presence of death, followed by the explosion of action—close-quarter combat with the enemy. Broad panoramic views, visual and contextual, are disregarded. Prior to the attack on the muddy hill, conflict had been between the men and the elements, mud and rain, and the mutual hatred between a sergeant and a private, expressed only via sullen or angry looks and thought bubbles. But when the sergeant and the private work together to knock out a pillbox, they overcome their animosity toward each other and reroute their hatred toward the common enemy: "War is funny that way! In the face of danger, men unite, and enemies become friends! It was April in Korea! A platoon of men filed up a hill to occupy the high ground! It had stopped raining! The clouds parted, and up above the steaming ground, the sun was shinning brightly!" This is the kind of paradox Fuller reveled in—"In the face of danger, men unite, and enemies become friends!"—the coward who becomes a hero (*Fixed Bayonets!*), the outlaw who works for the law (*Pickup on South Street* and *Underworld USA*), the altruistic mercenary (*Hell and High Water*), the man who kills the thing he loves (*I Shot Jesse James*), the maternal prostitute (*The Naked Kiss*), or any of the characters in *Shock Corridor*: the coy stripper, the racist Negro, the childlike atomic scientist, the caring guard who is a rapist and murderer, the impotent-pregnant man, and so forth. It is a story type that plays well within the spatial limits of the comic book format, or the eighty-or-so minutes allotted to Fuller's movies.

Fuller also shared with the EC artists and writers a distaste for character psychology, even as they searched for ways to represent subjectivity and interiority. They depended on the character types of melodrama, on stock characters whose motivations were elemental and who acted out of clearly defined fears and desires. Of all the revered postwar American filmmakers, Fuller and Don Siegel are perhaps the only ones who do not stand in thrall to Sigmund Freud. The position the character Cathy takes in *Shock Corridor* could hold true for Fuller himself. To a psychiatrist, a newspaper editor, and her journalist boyfriend, Johnny, she explains: "Mark Twain didn't psychoanalyze Huck Finn or Tom Sawyer. Dickens didn't put Oliver Twist on the couch because he was hungry. Good copy comes out of the people, Johnny, not out of a lot of explanatory medical terms. You're in a hopped-up, show-off stage. Get off it. Don't be Moses leading your lunatics to the Pulitzer Prize. I get sick at the thought of you playing games with your mind and riding that crazy horse." *Shock Corridor*'s use of a psychiatrist is to help authenticate the performance of sexual perversion by a journalist so he can work undercover at an insane asylum and thereby solve a murder mystery. The psychiatrist carries little if any weight in explaining the intricacies of motivation, not least because motivation is made utterly transparent. Furthermore, the premise of the story and investigation is ludicrous because it is never established why the solving of this murder is of any importance whatsoever beyond the stated overambitions of Johnny: "Honey, even if I don't crack the case, my experience alone can mean a book, a play, a movie sale. Every man wants to get to the top in his profession. Mine is winning the Pulitzer Prize. And if this story doesn't win me one nothing ever will."[61] There may be an award for this kind of storytelling, but it would not be the Pulitzer, not unless it has a category for pulp fiction.

The pulp aesthetic Fuller worked with encouraged the use of startling images through the production of disjuncture and disruption, like the linked images in *Underworld USA* of a child killed while riding her bike and plucked turkeys pulled from a sack. The little girl is struck down by an automobile driven by an assassin, a horrendous scene of cold-blooded murder, which is immediately followed by a character waving two very large turkeys about by their necks; the juxtaposition of infanticide and swinging poultry is both horrible and hilarious. Disruption and disjunction also describe crime-scene photographs; the photography historian Luc Sante notes, "We know we are looking at an image of radical disjunction before we are consciously aware of its narrative content. But then crime retails death, or at best loss, so that even before spectators with no personal stake in the matter it is charged. It is surrealism with a knife."[62] But this is sensationalism, as much as it is surrealism, and in its appeal to sensation it also connects to wider currents within an industrial culture.

In his essay on Fuller, the photographer Weegee, and the comic strip artist Chester Gould, J. Hoberman argued that artists of this stripe "developed an esthetic of shock, raw sensation and immediate impact, a prole expressionism of violent contrasts and blunt, 'vulgar' stylization. At once cynical and sentimental, this mode fed on incongruity, mordant humor and the iconography of the street." They represented what Hoberman called the "tabloid school": "The work of the tabloid school is brutal in both form and content, as assaulting as the cities which gave it substance and the subways where it was digested. Literary fellow travelers might have once included pulp writers like Dashiell Hammett or Horace McCoy. But the tabloid has always been half devoted to images, and the purist exponents of Abstract Sensationalism worked in visual media: B-movie director Samuel Fuller, *Dick Tracy*'s cartoonist Chester Gould, the press photographer Weegee."[63] By calling Fuller an "abstract sensationalist," Hoberman draws an alliance between high and low culture; at one point he likens *The Steel Helmet* to a "Korean war film that suggests *Waiting for Godot* rewritten by Mickey Spillane" (30). The suggestion is that the high modernism of Beckett coupled with the low popularism of Spillane humanizes Fuller or at least compromises the essentialist traits found in pulp forms. Another line of critical thought, however, is that the comparison between Fuller and high modernists, such as Beckett, is a facade, the purpose of which is to make Fuller respectable.

In 1970 Paul Joannides argued that Fuller "suffers a false and pompous systemization, designed to elevate him to the top floor of critical attention. Analysis purporting to be solid and sober is generally stolid and inaccurate. Fuller's real virtues, those of the gutter as well [as] of the gut, are not observed. Fuller is crude, clumsy and prejudiced; he also has a strongly integrationist vision of American society, even if allied to a (perhaps decreasing) fanatical anti-communism. Above all he possesses an extremist visual courage and dynamism, which few other directors ever approach."[64]

Joannides matched Fuller's virtues with his sins, without diminishing the fact that the films have critical value and interest. *Hell and High Water* (1954) wears its anticommunism on its sleeve, with the enemy portrayed as a cartoon mix of Yellow Peril and Red Menace, which might explain why it has been given less critical coverage than almost any other film Fuller directed—the Fuller hagiographer Nicholas Garnham found it "almost unwatchable."[65] It is, however, an outstanding example of Fuller's filmmaking: sensational, violent, garish, explosive, colorful, packed with thrills and spills, heaving with adventure and intrigue, and all glued together with an agitated sexual undertow that constantly threatens to overwhelm the story. It was the fourth film in a row to take the threat of communism as its subject, and to work this through established formulaic stories. *The Steel Helmet* and *Fixed Bayonets!* are war films set in Korea, *Pickup on South Street* is a contemporary crime story set in New York, and *Hell and High Water* is an adventure tale about scientists and mercenaries set in the world of international espionage. The film begins with a Technicolor and CinemaScope image of a nuclear explosion, accompanied by a voice-over explaining that the film we are about to see is the story of that event. The film then moves location from Paris (partly shot outside the offices of the *International Herald Tribune*, calling to mind Godard's *Breathless*), to London, Berlin, Rome, New York, and Tokyo. In Japan a group of Free World scientists, businessmen, and statesmen have gathered to pool their expertise and to act, without political interference, against communist forces that are believed to be building a nuclear base on an island somewhere between Japan and the Arctic Circle.

To carry out their mission, the consortium have overhauled a World War II Japanese submarine and employed the talents of ex-U.S. Navy submarine commander Adam Jones (Richard Widmark). For fifty thousand dollars Jones will ensure the safe passage and return of Professor Montel and his beautiful assistant, Professor Denise Gerard (Bella Darvi). Their job is to obtain evidence of the communist plot, which can then be used to galvanize the governments of the Free World into confronting communist aggression. The film is chock-full of spectacular special effects: submarines engaging in combat with one another above and below the waves, the electric flash of hydrogen being burnt off inside the sub, a gas depot being blown sky-high, the shooting down of a B-29 bomber, and the subsequent nuclear explosion are coupled with moments of action between the mercenaries and communist soldiers, a trapped hand and severed thumb, fistfights, and the brutal murder of a sailor with a monkey wrench, lots of comedy, some song ("Don't Fence Me In"), and the sexual attraction and distraction of Professor Gerard. Against the combined onslaught of these divertissements there is little time to ponder the absurdity of the film's basic premise of individual action ensuring the survival of the Free World.

Hell and High Water offered a story line drawn from men's adventure magazines, a virtual recreation of the cover illustration of the 1954 issue of Sir! A Magazine for Males with its strip headline, "Can the H-Bomb Stop Sex?," that runs over an image of a man clasping a women to his chest as behind them, in lurid red, a mushroom cloud forms. In his illustrated history of men's postwar adventure magazines, Adam Parfrey writes, "With a nearly rabid patriotism pitched to a war vet readership, men's adventure magazines increased their circulation during the height of those uneasy days known as the Cold War. The magazines themselves helped disseminate Cold War code words, issuing anxiety, paranoia, Red Threat, and Yellow Peril every month, though it did so in many issues with a Terry Southern sort of satirical exaggeration."[66] The reference to the writer Terry Southern links his screenplay for Kubrick's Dr. Strangelove with the excesses of the pulps. But the men's magazines were not in the business of satire; they were in the business of selling sensation. These magazines acknowledged the concerns of the day, such as the perceived threat of the feminization of public culture through conspicuous consumption, against which the fantasy worlds offered to readers were always positioned in stark contrast. The promise they offered was that an enervating domestic suburban environment might be held in check through the consumption of a mass-produced magazine offering stories set in exotic locations, or in World War II, or in cold war battle zones. The contradiction of escaping consumer (feminine) culture through an act of consumption—buying a magazine—would not be dwelt upon.

Neither would the broader meaning of the magazines' obsession with sexual proclivities be a cause for self-reflection. In the display of women in various states of undress, an overt appeal to heterosexual desire is made, but this normative address is qualified by the dual emphasis on homosexuality. Cover copy promises to deliver insight on a variety of social taboos: "What are your homosexual tendencies?," "The queer ring that rocked NY," "How to tell if your girlfriend is a lesbian," "Is lesbianism a cure for frigidity?," and "I was a homosexual."[67] This obsession with reporting on "deviant" sexual practices is without doubt a symptom of the overvaluing of male bonding, set against the threat of female control and domination. The confusion and dissembling around sexual

30. Cover of *Sir!* magazine (Oct. 1954): "Can the H-Bomb Stop Sex?"

identities spirals into acts of sadism, the depiction of which was as much a
mainstay of the magazines as it was of Mickey Spillane's fiction or as it is of
Fuller's films. For examples in Fuller's work recall Richard Widmark's character
Skip McCoy coldcocking the prostitute Candy (Jean Peters) in *Pickup on
South Street*, yet again rifling through her purse, before bringing her back to
consciousness by pouring beer over her (given the way the scene is shot he

might as well be urinating). He then makes rough love by rubbing her bruised face; the shot is framed by ropes and a gently swaying large steel hook. Fuller and his producer, Darryl Zanuck, thought the scene effective enough in its charged violent eroticism that they basically replayed it in CinemaScope and Technicolor in *Hell and High Water*. And again, like Spillane and the men's magazines, Fuller extolled the "virtues" of the prostitute (or stripper) in *Pickup on South Street*, *China Gate*, *Underworld USA*, *Shock Corridor*, and *The Naked Kiss* (which also replayed the image of the hero erotically rubbing the bruised face of the heroine).[68]

Fuller's films were salty potboilers, aimed foursquare at the habitués of the Times Square fleapits. To attract this audience, like the men's adventure magazines, Fuller had to make the quotidian extraordinary. Like in Michael Dennings's interpretation of the attractions of dime novels for a working-class urban readership, Fuller had to produce an interruption in the flow of things and, as if in a fantasy, thereby transform familiar landscapes and characters.[69] Though somewhat unreflexive on the link between story formula and life experience, Fuller was keenly aware of the fact of the matter, as is evident in the way he talked about the link between his films and his own biography. He had fought in North Africa and in Europe; he had lived the life of an infantryman; he knew what war was like; and he used that knowledge in his films. In the early 1960s he offered his six commandments of the war film; they all emphasize his intimate knowledge of soldiering, played off against the clichés of genre conventions:

1. Don't stop the fight when someone is hit. If a guy is killed, carry on. What else can you do?
2. Never allow a dying G.I. to bring out his wallet to look at his fiancée's photograph. That never happens.
3. Let your soldiers be dirty, tired and unshaven. Men at the front don't shave.
4. Don't have girls in war films—no flash backs of women waiting at home for their men to return. If you can't show a man's character without showing what he's like at home, cut him out of the script.
5. Don't let the actors make too much of it. 80 percent of actors in war films are no good. They don't want to be soldiers, they just want to show off.
6. Put your actors into training for a while as if they were ordinary recruits and don't pamper them.[70]

In a letter dated June 1946 to Lewis Milestone, the director of *All Quiet on the Western Front* (1930) and *A Walk in the Sun* (1946), Fuller, an aspiring director and novice scriptwriter, saluted the deft touches and moments of truth in the former and condemned what he thought were serial picture and comic strip adventure characterizations in the latter. Soldiers, he wrote, "worry about wet toilet paper, wet weapons, wet ammunition. There is no melodramatic bickering. Some day the people will get a chance to see what actually takes place, and believe me, Mr. Milestone, the McCoy is far more dramatic than what you put together in *Walk*."[71] For Fuller the drama is in actuality, but this does not presume a documentary approach to his filmmaking, though he may well use documentary conventions (or, in the case of *Verboten!*, incorporate numerous lengthy montage sequences constructed of newsreel footage). Fuller is looking for the truth he finds in the sensational and the marvelous, which exists, paradoxically, in the quotidian, or at least in the life of the soldier, mercenary, prostitute, pickpocket, or other ne'er-do-wells and lowlifes that he chooses to dramatize.

Fuller described his background in newspapers and film in a short piece first published in 1974 and noted that he drew inspiration for his stories from a "Hellbox"—an imaginary container that held sensational stories he collected when he had been employed as a reporter. These included:

> Covering an execution . . . Told by a man who hacked his family to death with a meat cleaver on a Hudson River barge that he was sorry if he hurt them . . . Listening to a leaper's sex problem on a 30-foot ledge before he squashed a luckless passerby like a gnat . . . Phoning blow by blow from a Harlem cigar store during a race riot . . . Using Sunday editions as bedsheets and blankets duding the rods with Depression displaced persons . . . Taking footbaths with hoboes in troughs of condemned milk . . .[72]

Fuller's list of examples runs for a whole page and finishes with "Sketching whores in San Francisco while covering the General Strike as soldiers shot strikers in front of the Ferry Building . . ." The sensational, produced through its striking contrast, is a mainstay of Fuller's cinema. It is built to bridge the lack in any consideration of the "why" behind the story's incidents, which is always secondary to the story's intended shock impact.

China Gate (1957) opens with newsreel footage of the war in Indochina; a sententious voice-over gives a potted history of French colonial rule and warns that Vietnam is the last holdout against communist control of the region. This hyped-up propaganda turns to melodrama when the narrator announces that all animals have been eaten, except one. Cut away from the newsreel images to a shot of a small boy hiding a puppy in his tunic. Next shot shows an old Asian man, who, upon seeing what the boy has hidden, immediately draws his knife. Running throughout Fuller's oeuvre are interruptions, disjunctions, or disruptions of the everyday. If the melodrama obscures the facts of the cold war, it is of little consequence to Fuller because he does not reflect on the bigger picture. His idea of the truth is making sure he gets the facts right, and facts are what he can verify himself through his own experience. The cold war in Fuller's films is abstract, made into a more tangible form by viewing it through the lens of melodrama—a young boy and his dog and a hungry old man. If this is absurd to those with a more refined or knowledgeable grasp of geopolitics, then so be it. Fuller's understanding of the truth resides in the details of the everyday: in uniforms, weaponry, in the beard on a man's face, in how he smokes a cigar or drinks a beer. In this he is like the readers of men's magazines, who also found the truth in the details, in facts and not in complex explanations. Evidence for this is found in the letter pages of the magazines. Readers wrote to complain not of the evident lack of plausibility in the stories but about details.

Discussing his time as a writer of pulp for men's adventure magazines, the author of *The Godfather*, Mario Puzo, responded to a question about whether he ever met his readers: "Naw. But I got letters, the magazine got letters. They would correct factual details, which was very funny, 'cause the whole piece was usually made up. . . . I wrote 'A Bridge Too Far,' that story of the Arnhem invasion. After you got through reading *my* story, you thought the Allies won the battle, not the Germans."[73] Puzo received letters telling him he had got the airborne division wrong but none doubting his version of history.

In a 1929 article for the *New Republic* Alvin Barclay discussed the lack of firsthand experience of the worlds pulp authors wrote about: "And air stories are the meat of gentlemen who never reached an altitude to which an elevator could not take them. Sometimes, therefore, a slip occurs—as when a villain in one yarn made a parachute leap at an altitude of fifty feet. Such mistakes are the delight of the readers. The wise editor lets one or two get by occasionally because it gives the public such joy to write in to the office correcting the error."[74] This same concern with facts and detail can be found in the letters pages of EC Comics' *Two-Fisted Tales*, though, as the editors were quick to point out, their writers and artists did have firsthand knowledge of war: "Dear Editors, Your stories are really lethal! However, I cannot understand how your artists (their work is excellent!) could have made the mistake of drawing Navy F9F Panthers as ground support planes for the army in your story ENEMY CONTACT! Gerry McLaughlin, Springfield, Vt."[75] Similarly, Mickey Spillane often complained about the Saville adaptations of his fiction, not because they necessarily challenged his worldview, or paid too little fidelity to the original story lines, but because the films got the details wrong, such as giving Hammer a .38 instead of a .45 or having the detective pick up a perfectly formed bullet after it had hit a brick wall.[76]

Facts appear verifiable; they can be tested against experience. In the sphere of pulp fiction facts are valued above abstract and complex notions. Abstraction and complexity are suggestive of an elitist, intellectual, and effeminate conception of how things work. The proletarian and masculine certainty of worlds explained in terms of facts is, to some extent, a view held on to by Fuller, but as he clings to these absolutes, he is faced by a contrary pull that brings them into question. The best of his filmed dramas occupy that space between these antinomies. What keeps Fuller's work grounded within a pulp sensibility is that the tension is always worked out in terms of its effects on human sensibilities and people's capacity to live with the contradictions inherent in the world they experience. For Fuller, and for pulp, this is dramatized in the contradictory portrayal of the everyday as sensational. This is how, I think, Fuller understood his art.

At the start of *Fixed Bayonets!* a jeep carrying American G.I.s hurtles down a snow-covered track. As the vehicle comes broadside to the camera, it is hit by a mortar shell. On the side of the burning jeep in large white letters is written "MARTA." Marta, or Martha, was Samuel Fuller's first wife. What his wife thought of this unique *billet-doux* is not recorded, but eight years later she filed for divorce, citing mental cruelty, telling the judge that her husband was "completely possessed by his work."[77] Like a graffiti artist, Fuller left his tag on whatever he touched, whether it was getting an actor to deliver his lines in the same staccato voice as himself (Cliff Robertson in *Underworld USA*), putting a snapshot of himself on a stripper's mirror (*Shock Corridor*), having a character read one of his novels (*The Naked Kiss* and *The Big Red One*), and in just about all of his films he would have the toughest character smoke cigars, put in references to the 1st Infantry Division (in which he had served), or include a character called Griff. While leaving his tag on his films, he also left a trail of news items in the trade press, all of which effortlessly ballyhooed his films, past, present, and future, and made sure he was never less than visible, even when he was just going about the everyday business of making films.

During the early months of 1957 the *Hollywood Reporter* carried weekly items on Fuller and his films. These news squibs might ostensibly be about the promotion of a movie, but they also acted as self-promotion, like this one from January 18: "Fuller to Pentagon for Big Red One Huddles . . . Producer-director-writer Samuel Fuller who will produce 'The Big Red One' under Globe Enterprises indie banner following completion of his current 'China Gate' leaves for Washington next month for conferences with the Pentagon top brass regarding the filming of the saga of the infantry division during World War II. Shooting on 'China Gate' is making fast progress and the picture was given an April release by 20th-Fox."[78] Or a news item would emphasize some wild promotion line, such as, "Fuller Plans 'China Gate' Preem for Chiang Kai-Shek."[79] He would also lay out his production plans: "Fuller Adds 20th Production, Expands Slate to Six Films—'Woman with a Whip' to 20th, 'Big Red 7' RKO Commitment and 'The Iron Kiss' and 'Cain and Abel.'"[80] Even the coverage of his work in another journal could become the excuse for pushing a news story: "Sammy Fuller Spotlighted. Under the title of 'Phenomenon of the Movie Makers' writer-director-producer Samuel Fuller is the subject of an eight-page layout in the April issue of *Wisdom Magazine*."[81] And on it rolled through February and March: "Samuel Fuller

Plans 'China Gate' Tour—A Key-City Personal Junket."[82] "Fuller Rolls Next for 20th—'Woman with a Whip.'"[83] "Fuller to Exploit 'China Gate' At Exhib. Conclaves."[84] "Fuller Signs Robert Dix for 'Woman with a Whip.'"[85] When Fuller's career as a filmmaker faltered in the 1960s, he turned his attention away from the trade press and toward the critical journals, whether it was sending Andrew Sarris at *Film Culture* production stills of *The Naked Kiss* or writing "What Is a Film?" for *Cinema*, both in 1964.[86]

He also appeared in other filmmakers' movies, playing either himself or someone like him. Outside of his appearance in Godard's *Pierrot le fou*, he had cameos in Moullet's *Brigitte et Brigitte* (1966)—when he is interviewed by a student researching a term paper, the student declares, "Mr. Fuller, you are the world's greatest director!" In Dennis Hopper's *The Last Movie* (1971) he plays a pistol-waving director of a western—"Show me some balls when you die!" Wim Wenders cast him in four of his films, beginning with *The American Friend* (1977), followed by *Hammett* (1982), *The State of Things* (1982), and *The End of Violence* (1997). He had a role in the Finnish director Aki Kaurismaki's *La Vie de bohème* (1992) and another in Mika Kaurismaki's movie *Helsinki Napoli All Night Long*. Mika also directed the feature-length documentary *Tigero: A Film That Was Never Made* (1994), in which the director Jim Jarmusch travels with Fuller on a journey into South America. Jarmusch also appeared, alongside a host of other filmmakers, all testifying to Fuller's genius, in the BFI-sponsored documentary *The Typewriter, the Rifle & the Movie Camera* (1996).

All of these appearances in art-house movies and documentaries contributed enormously to Fuller's standing as a filmmaker of repute, but his appearance in the New World production from 1973, *The Young Nurses*, part of the cycle of sexploitation films made under Roger Corman's patronage, which feature professional women in various states of undress and partaking in thrilling adventures, should not be forgotten, because it represented his other face—his pulp half. Fuller plays Doc Haskell, a seemingly benign old man, but he is in fact a drug peddler, who turns on the film's heroine and tries to kill her. In the act of sticking her with a syringe, he is knocked over and falls onto his own needle. He dies with the syringe stuck in his neck—his death a form of poetic pulp justice.

Of the four screen credits he has for appearances in Wenders's movies, it is his role as Joe Corby in *The State of Things* (1982) that is the most memorable. Corby is a veteran cinematographer, working with a small European film crew on location in Portugal. They are midway into shooting a low-budget science fiction movie when they run out of film stock and money. Their American backer has gone missing, and Fuller's character kills time by dispensing sage advice to the young crew, alongside such aphorisms as "Life is in color, but black and white is more realistic." It is his function, however, as a figurative intermediary between European art cinema and American commercial cinema that is particularly significant. The film's division between Europe (art) and America (money) is simple, obvious, and clichéd, but Fuller's presence—a figure lauded by European art-house directors but dismissed by others as a pulp filmmaker—complicates things. His act of mediation muddies and confuses the divide and confounds the boundaries that separate art and commerce. In the critical ruminations on his work he had been made to play this role many times before.

5

Authenticating Pulp

Jim Thompson Adaptations and Neo-noir

> Jim Thompson had made him nervous when they were working together
> on *The Killing*, a big guy in a dirty old raincoat, a terrific writer but a little
> too hard-boiled for Stanley's taste. He'd turn up for work carrying a
> bottle in a brown paper bag, but saying nothing about it–it was just there
> on the desk with no apology or comment–not at all interested in putting
> Stanley at ease except to offer him the bag, which Stanley declined,
> making no gestures whatever to any part of the Hollywood process,
> except maybe toward the money.
>
> –Michael Herr, *Kubrick*

Jim Thompson made his living in the 1950s writing paperback originals for the
New York publishers Lion, Gold Medal, and Signet. He wrote crime stories in the
tradition of James M. Cain's *The Postman Always Rings Twice*, overheated tales of
sex and murder, or, as Thompson wrote, "through thick and thin: the true story
of a man's fight against high odds and low women."[1] Like his contemporary
Mickey Spillane, he wrote fast, but, unlike Spillane, he was also prolific. Driven by
the period's unprecedented demand for paperback books, Thompson crafted his
novels to meet the heavy turnover called for by his publishers. The first filmmakers to use his talent were independents Stanley Kubrick and James B. Harris,
who had sought his help in turning a heist novel into a screenplay for *The Killing*
(1956). Thompson worked again with the two filmmakers on *Paths of Glory* (1957)
and then had no more film work until his novel *The Getaway* was filmed by Sam
Peckinpah in 1972. Though the movie was a box-office success, it did not lead to
other adaptations of his novels or to more than a couple of reprints. In 1975
Thompson made a cameo appearance in *Farewell, My Lovely*, and in the following
year, Burt Kennedy turned the novel *The Killer Inside Me* into a film, which
promptly sunk without a trace. When Thompson died, in 1977, none of his
twenty-nine novels were in print in either the United States or Britain.

Following two French adaptations of his novels in 1979 and 1981, and a series of American and British reprints in the early to mid-1980s, the Thompson estate received considerable attention from American filmmakers.[2] Three adaptations of his 1950s pulp novels were given cinema releases during the 1990–91 season—*The Kill Off*, *After Dark, My Sweet*, and *The Grifters*—while three others were reported to be in preproduction.[3] The *Los Angeles Times* announced that Thompson was "the hottest writer in Hollywood," and beneath the headline "Thompson Mania" *Variety* reported that Hollywood's "obsession with nihilist novelist Jim Thompson is a classic case of publishing meeting showbiz 'synergy.'"[4] The hype around the novelist reached such heights that the film critic Richard Corliss noted Thompson was "suddenly in danger of becoming that most fashionable of renovation projects, the overrated underrated writer."[5] How, then, did this once-all-but-forgotten writer gain such critical and cinematic currency?[6]

The trajectory that leads Thompson from obscurity to hypervisibility can be traced through the journalistic and scholarly reception that accompanied the re-presentation of his work in the specialized book markets, aimed at fans of hard-boiled pulp fiction. *Time*, *Newsweek*, *Vanity Fair*, the *New York Review of Books*, *Film Comment*, the *New York Times Book Review*, the *New Republic*, *Rolling Stone*, *The Nation*, and *American Film* all published reviews and articles on Thompson in the 1980s, and all showed a remarkable willingness to participate in his lionization.[7]

The cover blurb on the first reprint of *The Killer Inside Me* (Gold Medal, 1965) announced the novel was an "Underground Classic" and used quotes from Kubrick ("Probably the most chilling and believable first-person story of a criminally warped mind I have ever encountered"), George Milburn in the *New York Times* ("Jim Thompson is the best suspense writer going, bar none"), and R. V. Cassell in *Book Week* ("*The Killer Inside Me* is exactly what French enthusiasts for existential American violence were looking for in the works of Dashiell Hammett, Horace McCoy and Raymond Chandler. None of these men ever wrote a book within miles of Thompson's"). Versions of Kubrick's, Milburn's, and Cassell's copy have appeared on subsequent editions of Thompson's novels, which, post-1989, shared space with Stephen King's testimony: "My favorite crime novelist—often imitated but never duplicated—is Jim Thompson."[8] The taglines emphasized the generic nature of Thompson's fiction but also his originality, alongside his cult or underground status. Of particular note is the link made between a European avant-garde, "existential" sensibility and Thompson. The emphasis on the French fervor for American pulp would provide the ground on which Thompson's rediscovery was rooted. These elements were all revisited in the 1980s criticism that circulated around the republication of his novels.

The taglines suggested Thompson had his supporters well before his rediscovery, but academic criticism of his fiction before the 1980s was limited to an essay by R. V. Cassell in a collection on hard-boiled writers. Cassell anticipated the critics and scholars who were eager to develop the idea of Thompson as an "American Original."[9] Thompson had garnered some limited support among the critical fraternity prior to his death. The critic and author Anthony Boucher regularly reviewed Thompson's novels for the *New York Review of Books*, and, as Thompson's biographer Robert Polito noted, he did so in terms that also anticipated Thompson's critical reclamation.[10] But if what the critics had to say about Thompson in the 1980s lacked originality, the depth and breadth of the coverage given to him in this period was something altogether new.

Crucial to Thompson's critical exhumation was the publication in 1981 of Geoffrey O'Brien's *Hardboiled America: The Lurid Years of Paperbacks*.[11] This study offered connoisseurs of noir the knowledge necessary to build a personal library that extended beyond the overfamiliar figures of Hammett, Chandler, and Cain. O'Brien's book not only acted as a guide to pulp fiction for fans of film noir, but it also aided enterprising publishers in their bid to exploit this fan market. In a surprisingly short time publishers, predominantly small independents, reissued many of the titles that had been critically validated by O'Brien. Works by previously obscure, or all but forgotten, authors such as W. R. Burnett, David Goodis, Horace McCoy, Cornell Woolrich, Charles Willeford, and, most significantly, Jim Thompson were by 1983 readily available in bookstores on both sides of the Atlantic.[12]

Though he devoted fewer than five hundred words to Thompson, O'Brien's description of his oeuvre had the effect of promoting him above and beyond all other pulp authors: "Thompson could certainly not be accused of offering much by the way of public enlightenment. It is probably the persistent nastiness of his books that accounts for his status as Most Neglected Hardboiled Writer. . . . Thompson's preferred subject is not the righteous bully but rather the cool, calm, and collected psychopath who is the most charming fellow in the world until he decides it would be appropriate to kill you."[13]

It was not, however, simply Thompson's "persistent nastiness" that appealed to his new readers (*that* could be found in abundance elsewhere) so much as the view that his novels bridged the gap between lowbrow popular fiction and highbrow avant-garde literature. Reviewing *Savage Night* in the 1950s, Boucher stated that the book had been "written with vigor and bite, but sheering off from realism into a peculiar surrealist ending of sheer Guignol horror. Odd that a mass-consumption paperback should contain the most experimental writing I've seen in a suspense novel of late."[14] As Polito suggested, Thompson did not seek to transcend the hard-boiled tradition as an "important writer might be expected to do." Instead, he "detonated the clichés" of the tradition he inherited, and this is partly why filmmakers and critics singled out Thompson, rather than, say, the more formulaic Woolrich.

As the novelist Lawrence Block wrote, "Thompson's characters are holdup men and small-time grifters, corrupt lawmen, punch drunk fighters, escaped lunatics. They lead horrible lives."[15] Finding in Thompson's characters the raw material of a modernist dramaturgy, Cassell equated them with those of Conrad and Sartre. In an introduction to the original 1954 edition of *A Hell of a Woman* George Milburn wrote, "There will be those who see in *A Hell of a Woman* traces of James Joyce's *Ulysses* and of William Faulkner's *Sanctuary*."[16] Similarly, David Thomson evoked the ghosts of Nabokov and Faulkner, while Luc Sante wrote, "In literary-historical terms he is something of a missing link, the strand that ties together Celine and Dostoyevsky and Faulkner and James M. Cain and George Bataille and Edward Anderson (*Thieves like Us*). If he never existed, someone, maybe the French, would have to invent him."[17] In the Black Lizard editions of Thompson's novels Geoffrey O'Brien's afterword carried the title "Jim Thompson—Dimestore Dostoyevsky," a reworking, perhaps, of Lewis Milestone's description (following the publication of *The Postman Always Rings Twice* in 1934) of James M. Cain as an "American Dostoyevsky."[18] The references to the most celebrated European chronicler of low life, as with the name checking of high modernists, claimed cultural capital for Thompson that his status as a writer of pulp appeared to preclude. Cassell, however, counterclaimed that the paperback status of Thompson's novels did not hinder the author's modernist agenda: "what I would like to declare is that in Thompson's hands, the mode of the paperback original, husks and all, turns out to be excellently suited to the objectives of the novel of ideas."[19] The mass-produced pulp novel, Cassell argued, is more appropriate than the elitist hardback for echoing the voice of the democratic American Everyman, or the lowlifes that Thompson documents, producing a distinctly American form of avant-garde art.

Cassell's conception of a vernacular modernism parallels the idea of film noir as understood by James Naremore, who wrote, "Film noir occupies a liminal space somewhere between Europe and America, between high modernism and the 'blood melodrama,' and between low-budget crime movies and art cinema."[20] Erudite commentators on pulp and noir now view selected examples of what were once little more than ephemeral instances of commercial literature and film, produced for mass consumption, as an eruption of modernism from within the world of the popular.[21] This is distinct from a modernist intervention *into* the realm of the popular, which is practiced, for example, by pop artists who signify an often knowing, camp, or ironic detachment from the object that has been rendered.[22] Before it is anything else, Thompson's fiction is an object of mass culture. His ability to construct that fiction as subject, in the modernist sense, takes place out of view. In this version Thompson must tunnel away, like one of Manny Farber's termites practicing his dissident critique of culture and society in secret until discovered by a more discerning audience.[23]

Key to the validation of Thompson as a pulp, pop, or vernacular modernist, above and beyond his contemporary pulp fictioneers, is the overt play in his fiction with narrative and character fragmentation. Unreliable narrators appear throughout his work, and they are often revealed to be suffering from some extreme form of schizophrenia. In *Savage Night* the tubercular Charles Bigger is literally and figuratively wasting away from the opening page to the last, where he has been sliced into pieces: "You can do that, split yourself up into two parts. It's easier than you'd think. Where it gets tough is when you try to get the parts back together again."[24] Bigger narrates his story from beyond the grave, a fairly common occurrence in Thompson's fiction. *A Hell of a Woman* also ends with the narrator split into two, with alternate lines of text given over to the competing subjectivities. After several brutal murders, *The Killer Inside Me* similarly finishes with a bifurcated subject, here diagnosing himself as suffering from "dementia praecox. Schizophrenia, paranoid type. Acute, recurrent, advanced."[25] Through his manipulation of all those with whom he engages, the first-person narrator in *Nothing More Than Murder* appears to have a cool control over the flow of events. Things begin to unravel at such a pace, however, that the only way the narrator can explain what has happened is to make a reference to an encounter he once had with avant-garde poetry:

> One time, years ago, I sat in on one of Elizabeth's literary club meetings when they were discussing some lady poet. This poetry, this stuff this lady wrote, wasn't like real poetry. It wasn't like anything, in fact it was just a lot of words strung together about God knows what all, and they'd say the same things over and over.
>
> Well, though, it seemed like the stuff did make sense, once you understood what this lady was trying to do. She was writing about everything all at one time. She was writing about one thing, of course, more than the others, but she was throwing in everything that was connected with it: and she didn't pretend to know what was most important. She just laid it out for you and you took your choice.[26]

The narrator decides that if he is to tell his story, then he will have to follow the lead given by the poet. This is not a unique self-reflexive moment in Thompson's fiction; his work is rife with allusions to modernist writing and techniques. Echoing Polito's interpretation of Thompson's pop modernist aesthetic, Sean McCann argued that this compact between high modernism and pulp makes a "mockery of literary distinctions" and that Thompson used modernist techniques not to display his protagonist's learning but rather his disorientation. His mix of the high and low, as McCann argued, suggested not an "egalitarian national spirit, but the disappearance of meaningful perspective."[27]

Early in *Nothing More Than Murder* the narrator turns again to his wife's literary club to help him explain things. He recalls a visit from an author, "a big gawky guy named Thomas or Thompson," who turns up drunk, and spends most of his time talking about how people are always trying to get him to give them free books. "He said that sarcasm was wasted on such people and that the homicide laws ought to be amended to take care of them" (67). This further act of self-reflexivity, the author's placing of himself within the fiction, is a common trope in Thompson's work and is usually, as here, cast as a form of self-loathing. Thompson's conception of himself is as a failure, in particular, someone who is incapable of finding a means to support and nurture an intellectual and artistic response to life's vicissitudes. The suppression of creative and intellectual outlets for Thompson's protagonists is, more often than not, the cause of their sadistic and psychotic tendencies. McCann writes, "The calculation, the brutality, the perverse fatefulness, and above all the loneliness depicted again and again by his novels all depend for their effect on the *frisson* we may experience when we discover that sympathy is really manipulation, that protestations of disinterest conceal selfish calculation, that all people are predatory, and, most importantly, that as a consequence, public action is pointless."[28] McCann's critique of Thompson's fiction is particularly astute in his framing and explaining of the shift the work underwent from the 1930s novels, which were grounded in a New Deal–engendered philosophy of commonality and belief in a public realm, to the postwar paperback fiction, with its explicit emphasis on the despoiling of that vision of communal responsibility.

Thompson's political sympathies were formed in the Depression years and in his association with the Popular Front. This accounts for his interest in outsiders and outlaws, in life's losers, in people on the margins of society. In his production of a gallery of lowlifes he shares much with Samuel Fuller, but, unlike Fuller's work, Thompson's is marked by the betrayal and despoiling of individual agency allied to communal interests. Thompson's outsiders are not offered as an alternative to a corrupt mainstream but as an index of failure and as an example of the impossibility of succeeding in the face of an aggressive inhuman capitalism, an idea neatly encapsulated in a line of dialogue from *The Killer Inside Me*: "If we all had all we wanted to eat, we'd crap too much. We'd have inflation in the toilet paper industry."[29]

Like his modernist play with form and character subjectivity, his novels' proletarian roots remain untouched by Hollywood adaptations, but they were crucial aspects in his critical validation in the 1980s. The modernist allusions and proletarian subjects in Thompson's fiction were the indicators of his originality that distinguished his novels from those of his peers.[30] Thompson offered the thrills and sensations of reading trashy pulp, combined with the intellectual stimulation provided by his experiments with modernist techniques, which existed alongside a social awareness of capitalism's ability to incapacitate, to literally and figuratively emasculate the common man. In the context of the Reaganomics of the 1980s this latter point had clear resonance with his new, young-adult readers.

Thompson managed at least one act of transcendence (albeit one empowered by critics writing in the 1980s and 1990s): he was able to move beyond the cultural and social context in which his novels were produced. Polito writes,

"The nods to hard-boiled conventions do not so much toughen Thompson's novels as humanize them—they're all we have to hang on to in the downdraft. Everything else is a wasted, sucking nihilism that's as unsparing as the most lacerating rock 'n' roll—the Velvet Underground's 'Sister Ray,' say, or the Sex Pistols' 'Bodies'—and as final as a snuff film."[31] Polito's analogy with the Velvet Underground and the Sex Pistols is apposite because Thompson's fictions appealed primarily to a new hip readership weaned on the negationist rhetoric of punk.[32] Summed up in the following extract from an unfinished novel, Thompson foreshadows punk's rotten view on life:

> "Things're not as they seem."
> "Nothing? Nothing is ever as it seems?"
> "Only—hic!—only if it stinks. If it stinks then that's the way it is. Livin'
> proof of it . . ."[33]

This analogy between Thompson and punk does not carry over to other pulp writers, such as Woolrich or Goodis, who by comparison seem hopelessly tied to the past. Polito's location of Thompson, within a popular negationist tradition, connected the writer to those cultural movements that have (thus far) been exempted from critiques of commercial co-optation. This is in line with Michael Herr's description of Thompson as someone who made no gestures to Hollywood when he met with Kubrick.[34] The artist appearing to operate outside of capitalist imperatives is imbued with an aura of authenticity that is, as we will see, crucial to the 1980s reception of the novels of Jim Thompson. Before that could happen, Thompson's work needed to come back into public circulation.

O'Brien concluded his short appraisal of Thompson by calling for an "enterprising publisher . . . to resurrect some of his prolific output."[35] The floodgates soon opened. In addition to the compendium of four of his novels published in the Black Box Thriller series by the British company Zomba Books (1983), from 1984 the American company Black Lizard/Creative Arts published another thirteen of Thompson's twenty-nine novels. Mystery Press (an independent publisher acquired by Time-Warner in 1989) added a further seven titles in 1988, including a new collection of short stories.[36] With the backing of Time-Warner, Mystery Press had the clout to ensure that Thompson's books received even wider and more penetrating distribution. From 1988 Corgi books gave his work an equivalent profile in Britain, publishing eight titles in all. In 1986 Donald I. Fine published two hardback collections of six of the novels, and a hardback edition of the short stories collection. Coinciding with the vogue for film adaptations of his novels, Vintage Books, a division of Random House, bought Black Lizard and the rights to Thompson's work in 1990. Vintage would eventually republish the majority of his fiction.

This highly visible publishing activity precipitated Hollywood's cycle of Thompson adaptations and testifies to a more widespread reclamation by

Hollywood of pulp writers for what it explicitly marketed as "neo-noir" productions. Behind the simple neo-noir classification, however, lay a complex history of the consumption of pulp novels, the critical status of pulp writers, and their relationship to discourses of film categorization. The explicit conjunction of film noir and pulp fiction in the marketing and consumption of neo-noir forms the first part of this history.

From the initial popularization of the category "film noir" by the French critics Raymond Borde and Etienne Chaumeton, in *Panorama du film noir américain* in 1955, the centrality of the films' sources in some of the period's most celebrated crime novels has been noted.[37] For the book's preface the authors invited the editor of *Série noire*, Marcel Duhamel, to pen a few thoughts. Duhamel noted that 75 percent of the 250 or so crime novels thus far published in the series had been filmed, a percentage he applauded, given that "good books and good film noirs keep very close to current events and constitute an excellent testimony of our times."[38] (Nine of Thompson's novels had been included in *Série noire* between 1950 and 1968; if Thompson had no public profile in his home country in these years, he, nevertheless, had readers in France.)[39] Duhamel concluded that we should "read masses of noir novels and see film noirs in abundance" (xxv). Multitudes would concur.

The critical reception and validation of Thompson's novels ran parallel to, and would become intimately linked with, the popularization of film noir. Since the mid-1980s Thompson has increasingly been used to represent a noir sensibility. In a typical review of *The Hot Spot* (1990), an adaptation of Charles Williams's 1950s pulp novel *Hell Hath No Fury* directed by Dennis Hopper, the film is described as a "rock hard film noir. . . . This is a sweaty, really dirty movie. There's a Jim Thompson pulp tinge to the script."[40] As this review suggested, there was something akin to a consensus on the meaning of noir and Thompson's relationship to that category in the early 1990s. To a degree this was a kinship that had been formed by collectors of pulp fiction and film noir.

The French film scholar Marc Vernet wrote, "As an object or corpus of films, film noir does not belong to the history of cinema. . . . Film noir is a *collector's idea* that, for the moment, can only be found in books."[41] The critical and commercial association of Thompson and film noir developed out of a fan base whose acts of consumption were defined in large part by a collector's sensibility—the apparently endless retrieval and cataloging of film and book titles. "Who," Vernet asked rhetorically, "has seen and studied all the films listed by Silver & Ward" in their encyclopedia of film noir?[42] In his book *Somewhere in the Night* Nicholas Christopher made a claim to just such a heroic feat and confirmed Vernet's observation that "there is always an unknown film to be added to the list."[43] Christopher announced that he had "viewed all 317 titles in the *Film Noir Encyclopedia* . . . as well as about fifty other films I would classify as films noirs which are not included in that compendium."[44] The mystery writer

Arthur Lyons has fashioned a whole book, *Death on the Cheap: The Lost B Movies of Film Noir!*, based on this concept, and he adds more than a hundred new titles to the canon. Academics such as James Naremore are equally guilty of playing this game: "I also nominate neglected titles as film noirs, or at least question their absence in previous writings."[45] As a game, film noir is open to anyone with an interest in what Vernet has called Hollywood's "middling productions."[46] "This is the scenario," writes Paul Duncan in his pocket guide to film noir: "you are sitting down with a copy of the TV listings, trying to work out whether or not to record a film on video. Is it, or is it not a Film Noir? A decision has to be made."[47] Indeed.

As a "collector's idea" noir is not just found *in* books; it is also manifest in the acquisition *of* books.[48] The desire to collect films under the rubric "film noir," however defined, is carried over to the films' source novels. With the establishment of something like an agreed-on corpus of film noir, the process of cataloging and republishing books, either connected to that corpus through adaptation or by some other loose understanding of generic resemblance, began in earnest.

As Steve Neale has noted, using even the most inclusive list of film noir, the number of films so identified represent a little less than 5 percent of Hollywood's output between 1941 and 1958.[49] So despite the ever-growing number of films listed as noirs, the category is also marked in terms of the relative scarcity of examples. "For the collection or hoard," as the folklorist and cultural critic Robert Cantwell has written, is "at once treasury, armory, sanctum, and shrine," which has as "its own context an absence or vacuum; the hoard is an index of scarcity, vulnerability, exile, and isolation."[50] Like Duncan's noir fan searching through the TV listings, O'Brien perfectly displayed this collector's sensibility when he noted that the devotee of America's lowbrow literary past had actively to search out elusive titles: "Naturally, the lack of availability made them all the more tantalizing."[51]

The vulnerability of film noir as a category, and the anxiety on the part of the collector/critic when his or her "treasury" or "sanctum" comes under attack, is manifest in Alain Silver's symptomatic rebuke of Vernet's essay in which the French academic accused Emperor Noir of being naked. Vernet wrote, "Complacent repetition is more or less general, rare being those who venture to say that *film noir* has no clothes, [who] have the courage to cry out in the desert that the classical list of criteria defining *film noir* is totally heterogeneous and without any foundation but a rhetorical one."[52] Silver counterclaimed that "Vernet's revisionism is like any of the neo-Freudian, semiological, historical, structural, socio-cultural, and/or auteurist assaults of the past." Vernet's work, however, is none of these things. In the face of academic criticism Silver's anxiety leads him to defend his position on the basis of "evidence" provided by the films themselves: "In order to see the subject of film noir as it is, one need look no farther than the films."[53] But this solipsistic return to the films as primary evidence of noir's existence is precisely what, according to Vernet, occludes a fundamental understanding of noir as a critical construct. For Vernet, Silver's noir collection is empty of meaning, except as the collector defines it, whose critical turn is inevitably toward a definition constituted on the films he has already listed.

For its part noir has worked as a bulwark against irony and camp completely submerging classic Hollywood. Ironic detachment is not part of the noir fan's critical armament. The noir film is received in terms of its apparent face value—appreciated for its aesthetic beauty, philosophical integrity, and authentic view of American mores. According to Vernet noir comes down to us through the decades as an "object of beauty, one of the last remaining to us in this domain." It is conceived as such for a number of reasons, among them because Bogart and Bacall are found there, because it is made to fit so "neatly" into a decade (1945–55), and because "Americans made it and then the French invented it."[54] Noir, however, remains an object of beauty only if the beholder restricts his or her view. To contemplate the actual conditions of the films' production and initial reception, as do Vernet and Neale, reveals noir to be no more than a cinephile's fetish that exists only to mask an absence.

Is film noir, then, little more than the fulfillment of critics' wishes and imaginings—a subject in search of an object? Neale has argued that as a "single phenomenon, noir never existed" and as such it is an utterly incoherent critical object.[55] If this is true, and film noir is no more than a rhetorical construct that does not even identify a genre, style, narrative, or even a production cycle, to what then does "neo-noir" refer? And what of the "noir" films made after 1955, which sit outside of the last golden age of studio productions and are marked by an ironic or camp sensibility? Are they, too, a cinephile's fantasy? As with the beginning and end of "classical" film noir, there is no consensus regarding the first occurrence of postclassical noir as a distinct cycle of film production. Was it as early as the first years of the 1960s, as Nicholas Christopher has suggested, and, more specifically, immediately following the assassination of President John F. Kennedy, a suitably dark phase in America's history?[56] Leighton Grist considered it to have begun slightly later, with *Harper* (1966), which, he argued, is the "most generally accepted starting point for modern film noir."[57] Edward Gallafent, however, argued that the starting point was in the mid-1970s, when films such as *Chinatown*, *The Long Goodbye*, and *Farewell, My Lovely* "explicitly signalled themselves to their audience as contemporary films noirs."[58] Foster Hirsch, though, contended that noir did not conclude its project in 1958 with the release of *Touch of Evil* but continued to linger in the margins: a "shadowy presence in the negative space surrounding genres of the moment; and that from 1959 to 1966, there were some choice thrillers that began the work of reinventing noir for the 'post-noir' era."[59]

Neale wrote, "However, and somewhat ironically, if in [Elizabeth] Cowie's words noir is a 'fantasy,' or if an attachment to the term can in Naremore's words mark 'a nostalgia for something that never existed,' the phenomenon of neo-noir—itself vehicle for this fantasy—is much more real, not only as a phenomenon but also as a genre."[60] As an idea, neo-noir followed in the wake of the widespread acceptance among consumers (critics, academics, filmmakers, and filmgoers) of film noir as a form of categorization but which, as Naremore noted, is nevertheless a "kind of mythology": "noir is almost entirely a creation of postmodern culture—a belated reading of classic Hollywood that was popularized by cinéastes of the French New Wave, appropriated by reviewers, academics, and filmmakers, and then recycled on television."[61] The process of disseminating the idea of film noir began in the mid-to-late 1960s and reached maturity around the time of the publication of Silver and Ward's encyclopedic *Film Noir* (1979).[62] Noir's critical maturation was signaled, as Rick Altman has suggested, by the shift from "full noun-plus-adjective expression" (film noir) to the "neologistic use of 'noir,'" which he believes occurred during the mid-to-late 1970s.[63]

This same period is also marked by a homage to the classic detective film of the 1940s, involving adaptations of Raymond Chandler's *Little Sister* (filmed as *Marlowe* [1969]), *The Long Goodbye* (1973), *Farewell, My Lovely* (1975), and *The Big Sleep* (1978); Polanski's *Chinatown* (1974); *The Black Bird* (1975), which featured George Segal as Sam Spade Jr. (Hammett's *The Dain Curse* had been turned into a television miniseries in 1978); and the detective parody *The Late Show* (1977).[64] This cycle was complemented by detective films with contemporary settings from across the 1970s, which, in one way or another, commented on their predecessors, such as Alan J. Pakula's *Klute* (1971), Coppola's *The Conversation* (1974), Arthur Penn's *Night Moves* (1975), and Ivan Passer's *Cutter's Way* (1981). These two cycles of films also linked back to their 1960s precursors, such as *Harper* (1966), starring Paul Newman and adapted from Ross Macdonald's *The Moving Target*; *Tony Rome* (1967) and its sequel of the following year, *Lady in Cement*, both starring Frank Sinatra (the latter film, in all but name, a remake of *The Big Sleep*); and *A Lovely Way to Die* (1968), with Kirk Douglas.

Discussing this cycle, Lawrence Alloway wrote:

Does the private eye match the style and folklore of the 1960s? Frank Tashlin explained that he did not care for the "basic idea" of his Jerry Lewis movie *It's Only Money*, "Here we are in 1962 doing private eyes." His caustic comment seems inaccurate in the light of several attempts to revive the form. . . . *Harper* ends inconclusively with the hero's moral problem tossed away, and the Sinatra films, set in Miami, though solidly made, have a period look like those 'Scope films of the mid-1950s when the camera was mobile, both on a crane and on location in sunny places.

The more permissive sexual code (admitting lesbians and navels, for instance) updates the films mildly, like a five degree lift in a Cadillac's tail fins, but there is no sense now of the narrative conviction and emotional identification that the early private-eye films could simultaneously assume and create.[65]

Noting several ways that aesthetic conventions become systematically exposed as mere conventions, Robert B. Ray suggests the following as one of them: "When a commercial art form, trapped by apparent need to repeat successful formulae, repeats them so often and so obviously that the audience begins to recognize how much of what once seemed 'real' is actually convention. This mechanism of exposure, the development of camp responses, arose in the 1960s and 1970s, at the tail end of Hollywood's genre period. It was unlikely to work during the studio years when Hollywood was intent on *developing* the genres, which still remained relatively fresh."[66] The late 1960s, and after, was marked, according to Ray, by a "schizophrenic alternation between a developing irony and a reactionary nostalgia" (261), which is clearly seen in the period's detective films. The development of an ironic and critically savvy viewer was fostered, in part, by television, "a nearly identical twin whose features revealed the hidden flaws in the familiar one" (265). The revival of classic films on television, juxtaposed with news broadcasts, offered an implicit critique of the myths promulgated by Hollywood, Ray argued, producing a greater knowledge of movie convention and a "growing sense of American cinema's dense intertextuality" (266). This, coupled with the spread of "serious film criticism," gave the "movie audience ample occasion to develop an incipiently ironic posture toward Hollywood's traditional thematic paradigm" (266).

The early 1980s film cycle that included *Body Heat* (1981), *Hammett* (1982), *Dead Men Don't Wear Plaid* (1982), *The Postman Always Rings Twice* (1981), *Union City* (1980), and *Blood Simple* (1984) continued to pay homage to the classic noirs and were either influenced by or based on novels by Cain, Hammett, and Woolrich. Fredric Jameson has offered a particularly pointed critique of these films in general, and *Body Heat* in particular, as symptoms of a "society that has become incapable of dealing with time and history."[67] If the previous cycles had been marked by redundant or overly familiar conventions that appeared anachronistic within a contemporary setting, then *Body Heat* and its companion films were at best simply recycling the past in the form of parody and pastiche.

While critics discussed the films in this cycle through their knowledge of noir, encouraged and informed by the publication of such widely disseminated texts as E. Ann Kaplan's *Women in Film Noir* (1978), Silver and Ward's encyclopedia, and Foster Hirsch's *Dark Side of the Screen* (1981), it was not until 1990 that the industry began to explicitly market movies as "film noir" or, to be more accurate, in the case of *The Hot Spot*, as "FILM NOIR LIKE YOU'VE NEVER SEEN."

The Hot Spot was part of a much-remarked-upon cycle of films exhibited during the 1990–91 season that focused on the trio of movies adapted from Jim Thompson stories, alongside adaptations of other crime novels (Chester Himes's *A Rage in Harlem*, Charles Willeford's *Miami Blues*, Barry Gifford's *Wild at Heart*, David Goodis's *Street of No Return*), related films based on original screenplays, such as the *Chinatown* sequel, *The Two Jakes*, and remakes of 1950s noirs *Narrow Margin* (1952) and *Desperate Hours* (1955).[68]

The mid-1970s cycle was defined, in large part, by adaptations of Raymond Chandler's novels and the figure of the private eye, which offered a clear link to classic film noir.[69] The early 1980s cycle continued this process of adapting novels filmed during the 1940s, but the emphasis shifted away from the private eye to adaptations of James M. Cain's novels and character types derived from his work. This is significant because neo-noirs produced during the 1990s, as exemplified by John Dahl's films (*Kill Me Again* [1989], *Red Rock West* [1992], and *The Last Seduction* [1994]), do not revisit the mean streets patrolled by detectives Spade and Marlowe but rather concern themselves with the Cain-like topoi of "desire and transgression." "Cain's tales," as Frank Krutnik has suggested, "replay the scenario of men who invest all in the gamble of sex, in pursuit of the thrill of transgression."[70] They are character types for whom it appears, as Joyce Carol Oates wrote, "the world extends no further than the radius of one's desire": "Cain's parable, which is perhaps America's parable, may be something like this: . . . Giving oneself to anyone, even temporarily, will result in entrapment and death; the violence lovers do to one another is no more than a reflection of the proposed violence society holds back to keep the individual passions in check."[71]

This would work equally well to describe the male protagonist of *The Hot Spot*, whom Hopper characterized as "an amoral drifter led around by his sex,"[72] or any of the male leads in the Thompson adaptations. Krutnik's and Oates's concise definitions of Cain's work can be effortlessly, and transparently, used to elucidate the concerns of the neo-noirs that followed the early 1980s cycle.[73] But this would obscure the fact that Cain's currency had diminished, primarily because his work too strongly signified its historical roots in the 1930s and classic Hollywood cinema and was less well matched to the contemporary concerns of the 1980s than was Thompson's fiction. Certainly, Jim Thompson has superseded Cain as an eminently marketable property. Yet, when the first revival of interest in Cain's work occurred in the late 1970s and early 1980s (evident from the film and television adaptations of his stories, in the publication of a monumental biography, scholarly studies, and the republication of six of his novels by Vintage Books in 1978–79), Thompson's fiction was virtually invisible.

At the same time that the Cain cycle was being played out on American screens, however, French film adaptations of Thompson's *A Hell of a Woman*

(1979) and *Pop. 1280* (1981) were released in Europe. In homage to the esteemed Gallimard crime series, Alain Corneau renamed his adaptation of *A Hell of a Woman* as *Série noire*, a move designed to recognize the privileged place Thompson held in the series—*Pop. 1280* had been selected as the series' thousandth title. The title change from *A Hell of a Woman* to *Série noire* also suggested the film should be seen, first and foremost, as part of the French engagement with selected aspects of American popular culture.

The adaptation was a joint effort between Corneau and the avant-garde writer Georges Perec—who had previously written a novel composed without using the letter *e* and another novel in which *e* was the only vowel used. Though Perec enjoyed the puzzles set by such self-imposed constraints, little of this formalism is apparent in his screenplay, which cleaved to both the broad plot outline of Thompson's story and much of the detail. Nevertheless, Perec and Corneau amplified Thompson's use of adage and aphorism in the dialogue they gave his characters, so as to suggest the hollowness of their lives. According to Perec's biographer, the screenwriters used a "language almost entirely constructed from clichés, quotations, and set phrases, and every phrase uttered is repeated elsewhere in the film."[74]

Like many of Thompson's tales, *A Hell of a Woman* is told from the point of view of a first-person narrator who, the reader soon comes to understand, is clearly psychotic. Across all the adaptations, the search for filmic equivalents to suggest the disturbed subjective state of Thompson's protagonists is a core creative affair. Corneau maintained a blank, anonymous, formal and stylistic approach and used the actor Patrick Dewaere's skill to evoke, with great

31. Frame grab from *Série noire* (1979) title sequence. Poupart (Patrick Dewaere) in iconic trench coat.

subtlety, a man caught between irreconcilable forces, a man who aspires to take control of things, to impose order on chaos, but who only creates more disorder and eventually loses all power over events.

The film opens on a wasteland surrounded by indistinct industrial buildings and overhung by a colorless sky. A lone character, played by Dewaere, dressed in a trench coat, plays out cops and robbers with himself, shadowboxes, and then dances, accompanied by an invisible partner, to the tinny sound emitted from a small cheap cassette player of Duke Ellington and Juan Tizol's "Moonlight Fiesta."[75] Dewaere's movements suggest a grace that might transcend the awful drabness of his surroundings, but he nevertheless remains firmly rooted in the mire. The Ellington tune is the only American music heard on the soundtrack; what follows are a number of utterly mundane European pop songs. These songs are the aural equivalent of Formica, summed up by Boney M's "Rivers of Babylon," which plays on the radio that Mona (Marie Trintignant) is listening to when she is sold for sex. For the price of a quilted housecoat Mona is pimped by her aunt to the door-to-door salesman, Frank Poupart (Dewaere). Standing naked in front of Poupart, Mona is presented without erotic charge—a helpless, emotionally blunted, child-woman. Her bedroom, the house, and its immediate surroundings are as drab as the wasteland to which Poupart continually returns.

Poupart lives with his wife in furnished accommodation; the apartment is a tip. Clothes and unwashed dishes are everywhere; the bath is full of slime-covered cold water; the bed is unmade. An argument ensues, and Poupart knocks his wife into the bath. She says nothing about him hitting her; just mildly complains that he has ruined her last pair of tights, and then, as a matter of fact, she says she is leaving him. Later, Poupart imposes order on the rooms; everything is neat, tidy, and clean. But if his domestic life now appears regimented, his working life remains in disarray. He is caught fixing the books and skimming the top off payments from his customers. He is jailed but released when Mona pays what he owes; she has taken the money from her aunt, who has a million francs stashed away. With the girl's help Poupart steals the money. He kills the aunt and uses a dumb lunk called Tikides as a patsy. Poupart shoots Tikides with the aunt's automatic pistol, and Mona is left to tell the police what happened. Her story is that Tikides tried to rob her aunt, who shot him and then promptly fell down the stairs and, unfortunately, broke her neck. Amazingly, the police believe the story.

Back at home, Poupart's wife has returned and caught sight of the money. She wants to know where it came from; an argument ensues. Just before he strangles her, she tells him she is pregnant. Having figured out that Poupart was involved in the murder of the aunt, his boss appears and demands the money. With only a rudimentary struggle, Poupart gives up the cash. With three murders on his hands, and no reward, he leaves the apartment with his empty salesman's case. Mona meets him on the street; the money is in the case, he lies, and tells her there is nothing to be afraid of anymore—spinning her around in his arms as if she were a child. The camera pulls back from the couple, and the film ends.

Sexual intrigue and violence in this film are as woebegone as the rain and sleet, which form the perpetual environment in which these characters exist. Relationships and emotions are as cheap, common, and exploitative as the shoddy goods Poupart hawks from door to door; cheap gimcracks and folderol designed to catch the eye of those without the wherewithal to buy from stores. These characters operate on the bottom rung of economic exchange between people, summed up by the figure of the pimping aunt.

Dewaere's performance is mesmerizing; against the blank exteriors presented by the mise-en-scène and the supporting cast, he seems to be the only man alive. He ricochets between moments of cool control and complete mental disorder, screaming and shouting, ramming his head against his cruddy car, endlessly conversing with himself, trying, in his own mind, to do the right thing by Mona. He is always trying to get ahead but always falling behind.

The Parisian industrial suburban location used in *Série noire*, which does not even have the limited romanticism of the postindustrial Mancunian sites used in contemporaneous Joy Division photo shoots, is at first sight in marked contrast to the West African location and the formal interests of Bertrand Tavernier's adaptation of *Pop. 1280*, released as *Coup de torchon* (*Clean Slate*). Thompson's American story is transferred to a French colony and set on the eve of war with Germany, in July 1938. The film is marked by bright sunshine and pastels and is shot by a highly mobile camera, but, once past the location's unfamiliarity, it soon becomes apparent that the social world of Bourkassa is as quotidian as that found in any industrial suburb in France, or small town in the American South. Furthermore, the tone of the story, carried by an underlying cynicism about the human condition, is consistent with *Série noire*.

A priest reattaches the figure of the crucified Christ to a new wooden cross, but termites will eat this crucifix, as they have eaten the previous two. In this sun-baked land all is corrupt and rotten: sport is taking potshots at corpses floating down the river; the village is undergoing one of its regular bouts of dysentery; the chief of police lives in an apartment that overlooks a stinking latrine; bribery is rife, adultery endemic, and casual racism pervasive. Even the work of the new schoolteacher is besmirched, when she is cynically told that owing to her classes the little black children will now be able to read their father's name on a French war memorial.

Philippe Noiret plays Lucien Cordier, the chief of police, a man who believes he is best doing his job by "overlooking" infractions of the law, if that means he is able, at least on his terms, to keep the peace. In doing his job properly, as he sees it, he must accept daily humiliation yet act as if this is of no consequence. Not the least of these assaults against his dignity is the behavior of the town's

32. Publicity photo for *Coup de torchon* (1981). Lucien (Philippe Noiret) and Rose (Isabelle Huppert).

two pimps, who use him as the butt of their jokes, and his wife's infidelity with Nono. This man is supposed to be Lucien's wife's brother, yet he bares not the slightest resemblance to her—a point that at least one character feels the need to remark upon. But as Lucien says, "Better the blind man who pisses out the window, than the joker who told him it was the urinal."

Things, however, begin to unravel: Lucien kills the two pimps, implicates his superior in their deaths, murders his lover's husband, and then shoots a young black man who foolishly brings the body of the dead husband back to his house. He also stage-manages the shooting of his wife and Nono. With six deaths on his hands this paragon of small-town self-effacement has announced that he is Jesus Christ trying to save the innocent, but there are no innocents to be found. All crimes, he believes, are collective. "Anyway," he says at the end, "I've been dead for such a long time."

The film opens with a young African boy hunched down on the dusty ground, caught on camera as if he were the subject of an ethnographic film. As we watch the boy being watched by Lucien, the moon moves in front of the sun; with the eclipse the world darkens. Before running back toward town, Lucien starts a fire, a feeble attempt to bring light into the darkness. The film, though, is neither a documentary nor a supernatural thriller; rather, it is the story of a trickster, who, even though he is delusional, reveals the hypocrisy, cupidity, and lies of others. As the relocating of the time and place of Thompson's original story to colonial Africa on the eve of war suggests, Tavernier has taken a tale of native American fascism and reworked it for a European sensibility. Like *Série noire* it is a film of extraordinary achievements.

Beyond the shared epistemological journey that the highly flawed protagonists undertake in these two films, the films also share, between themselves and the Thompson originals, an exquisitely refined sense of black comedy. Much of this occurs not just in intricately woven barbs at the absurdity of life, or in a surreal delight in juxtaposition and disjunction, but it also takes place at the level of a coarse, vulgar, comedy, which can quite literally turn into toilet humor. The stench from the outside lavatory in *Coup de torchon* becomes intolerable to Lucien, who saws through the clapboard floor above the latrine's pit. His act of wanton vandalism ensures that when the mayor, in his crisp white suit, arrives for his regular morning ablution, he plummets into shit packed head-high. In a willingness to give credence to Thompson's cynical, misanthropic worldview, laced through with a mordant humor, the French filmmakers tackle aspects of Thompson's work that remain barely touched in American adaptations.

Validation by the French, however, does not necessarily ordain a similar recognition in the States, as Luc Sante has noted:

> There is a peculiar purgatory of esteem reserved for those American artists who have been lionized in Europe while enduring neglect at home. The obligatory jokes about Jerry Lewis aside, the history of this ambiguity stretches back to Poe and forward to such disparate figures as Nicholas Ray, David Goodis, Sidney Bechet, Samuel Fuller, Memphis Slim, Jim Thompson, Joseph Losey, and the Art Ensemble of Chicago. These writers, musicians, and filmmakers failed to be prophets in their own country, were recognized too late or too little, in part because they worked the side of the street deemed "popular" (although not sufficiently popular), ever a focus of American cultural insecurities.[76]

In figurative or literal exile in Europe, Thompson and his compatriots offered a view of America that Europeans found particularly beguiling. In his introduction to the British compendium of Thompson's novels published in 1983, Nick Kimberley took pleasure in the vernacular American aspects of Thompson's work. These aspects he characterized as low, lurid, and brutal, but, like so many others when reading and looking at American pulp, he found a surrealist's delight in the "maudit aspects" of the writing, a marvelous compact of European and American cultures.

Corneau had originally planned to film *Pop. 1280* and had traveled to the States in 1975 to work with Thompson on a screenplay. In his mind's eye he imagined making the film in America with a cast drawn from the principal actors used in Sam Peckinpah's *The Wild Bunch*.[77] Polito notes that Thompson produced a "passable screenplay . . . but he never resolved the puzzle of translating Nick Corey's inward menace into filmic images, and the dialogue slumped under the freight of his speeches. Corneau eventually pronounced the project 'infeasible.' "[78]

Peckinpah and Thompson had already been linked through the 1972 production of the author's 1959 novel *The Getaway*; the film was a poor translation of Thompson but a fine heist movie, a Steve McQueen vehicle, produced by his company, and designed to appeal to the audience that had made *Bullitt* (1968) one of the biggest hits of the star's career. Polito considered *The Getaway* to be Thompson's "most subversive fiction because it so completely masks itself as a routine caper."[79] The greater part of the novel is the story of an outlaw couple that specializes in bank robbery, who after the initial heist, followed by the inevitable double-cross, head out cross-country with their pursuers hot on their tail. This is the story that McQueen bought; he did not buy the "subversive" part, or at least he did not care to film that part. According to Polito, the final chapters of the novel "exploded a theme park of crime fiction motifs" that show the outlaw couple escaping over the border into . . . Hell, or, as it is called by Thompson, 'El Rey.' "[80] The end chapters are a symbol-heavy set of allegorical passages that equate capitalism with cannibalism and show the protagonists twice buried alive, once in a dung heap.

Peckinpah's oeuvre could serve as well as Fuller's or Thompson's as a form of pulp that in some quarters has been received as transcending its base material. In a 1972 interview in *Playboy* magazine Peckinpah was confronted with the accusation that he was anti-intellectual; he countered that he was in fact an "intellectual that embodies his intellect in action," which is as good a description as we are likely to find of any of the pulp filmmakers and authors discussed in this book.[81] Peckinpah, and the then-novice scriptwriter Walter Hill, fashioned a fast-moving, thrill-packed action movie from Thompson's novel, which shifts effortlessly among tense scenes relieved by explosive, violent, climaxes. The film opens with a languorous sequence that begins with close-ups of grazing deer, which are revealed to be penned behind the high-wire fence of a state prison. The idea of contained nature is carried over into a montage that shows Doc McCoy (Steve McQueen) being turned down for parole, and his mounting frustration at being confined. The montage carries a sexual charge, which is formed out of inserts of intimate moments shared between McCoy and his wife, Carol (Ali McGraw), that break into shots of McCoy trying to deal with the daily grind of prison life. The rhythm of his time in jail is ratcheted up to a fever pitch by the deadening sound of mechanical cotton looms; the noise of the factory shop comes to dominate the sequence. The montage ends with McCoy's early release from prison, which follows his wife's meeting with the gangster Beynon (Ben Johnson).

Near the end of the movie, Doc and Carol hide out from the police in an industrial waste container that is emptied, with the couple still inside, into a garbage truck, its hydraulic system threatening to crush them before they are deposited, along with the rubbish, onto wasteland. The projected image of desolation, of the couple fallen to wrack and ruin, however, is muted by the sentimentalism of Quincy Jones's soundtrack (which features the harmonica playing of Toots Thielemans, reprising the musical role he had on the soundtrack for the 1969 hit *Midnight Cowboy*) and the film's ending. The McCoys head off into "the sunset" and into Mexico, reunited, and once again in love with one another. As with the ending of *Pickup on South Street*, the formation of the couple legitimates the outlaw heroes, having them twice conform to convention—narrative and social.[82] This is the polar opposite of Thompson's ending of the novel, which has the pair conspiring to kill one another.

The opening is a fevered, rhythmic montage that jumps backward and forward in time, setting, character, and plot with economy and storytelling verve. The wasteland sequence is a backhanded comment on Thompson's ending, but it shucks all the political overtones and uses the location merely to add an overwrought symbolic poignancy to the dissolution faced by the loveless couple. Politics are not entirely absent from the film, which uses uniformed military personnel in almost all of the street scenes and public spaces, giving the impression of a nation at war. At one point McCoy is shown reading a newspaper with a headline about the war in Laos and a downed helicopter gunship. As he reads, McCoy is shot in the face by a young black boy with a water pistol.

33. Publicity photo for *The Getaway* (1972). In an image straight out of Spillane, Doc McCoy (Steve McQueen) slaps Carol (Ali MacGraw).

The boy is wearing a military cap that sports a Black Power button; he is described in the screenplay, no doubt with intended irony, as a "Black Panther."[83] The film is ripe with such topical references to a country uneasy with itself.

The loss of Thompson's ending and the shift in tone, particularly the sentimentalism, are often attributed to McQueen's desire to produce a conventional thriller, but apart from the Jerry Fielding soundtrack being dumped, which Peckinpah resented, it is not clear how complicit the director was in the orchestration of these changes.[84] Hill's shooting script, dated February 23, 1972, however, offered an alternative ending, with McCoy and Carol across the border in Mexico, riding in a Greyhound bus: out of shot a voice shouts "Hey!" McCoy and Carol look back. "The Black Panther is leaning over the seat, his empty fist cocked up like a pistol." He grins, and then pulls the imaginary trigger: "Bang!" "Doc and Carol look at him. FREEZE FRAME. FADE OUT. THE END."

If this ending was shot, and had been retained, it would have made for a finale that was more in keeping with Peckinpah's work.[85] The alternative ending would have helped to undercut some of the film's sentimentalism and its conventional happy ending, but it would still not have been faithful to Thompson's pessimistic vision. Closer by far to the author's view of human relationships is the ménage à trois consisting of McCoy's fellow bank robber, the psychopathic Rudy; the veterinarian, who tends to his wound; and his gum-chewing wife. The threesome are a horribly perverted image of a "family," an overripe version of the grotesquery that runs through Thompson's fiction but one also redolent of Peckinpah's casual misogyny.

Playboy regularly reviewed Peckinpah's movies and even gave *Bring Me the Head of Alfredo Garcia* rare coverage via a nude photo-shoot of the film's star Isela Vega.[86] Peckinpah's philosophy, particularly when it came to sexual politics, made the magazine something of his natural home, and the magazine's readers no doubt formed a significant part of his core audience. His view of women expressed in the interview as "cunts" and "whores," out for whatever they can get from a man, and his highly romanticized notion of relationships with prostitutes—"Of all the whores I've been with . . . I've failed to end up in some kind of warm personal relationship with only about ten percent"—is carried over into most of his films, which for all their perceived artistic merits might just as readily be characterized as the equivalent of men's magazine fantasies.

In 1977, along with the directors Roger Vadim, Federico Fellini, Michelangelo Antonioni, Jerry Schatzberg, Gordon Parks, Richard Brooks, and Louis Malle, Peckinpah was invited by *Playboy* to picture his sexual fantasy.[87] Of the eight, only Fellini and Peckinpah were given double-page spreads. Fellini's fantasy featured two priests flying a kite; at the end of the line a naked goddess hovers above them. Peckinpah's fantasy is a little more earthbound. He recalled his days as a marine, seventeen years of age, stationed in Canton, China.

He witnessed an "Oriental beauty" entering the quarters of his commanding officer; later the young marine dreamed she lay with him in his bunk. His whimsy, as he succinctly put it, is the Dragon Lady—a femme fatale from the long-running newspaper serial *Terry and the Pirates* (1934–46).[88] Peckinpah's fantasy is drawn wholesale from the pulps, as are the stunted, immature relationships in his films between his male heroes and their concubines.

The American paperback tie-in trailed the story of *The Getaway* as "the bloodiest cross-country run since *Bonnie & Clyde* . . . . The most breathtaking chase since *The French Connection*."[89] The film was sold as a star vehicle for McQueen and as a genre picture, which was how it was originally received. On the part of the filmmakers there was no reaching out toward the modernist eruptions that Thompson's critics had found in his fiction. The same was also true of Burt Kennedy's *The Killer Inside Me*. This adaptation has been described by Polito as a "car wreck of a film," which is hard to argue with if you approach the movie as an admirer of Thompson's work.[90] If, however, the film is seen as part of the rural crime cycle that ran through the late 1960s and into the 1970s, it is not without some redeeming features. The cycle included *Cool Hand Luke* (1967), with Paul Newman; Don Siegel's *Coogan's Bluff* (1968) and *Charley Varrick* (1973); the Elmore Leonard adaptations *The Big Bounce* (1969) and *The Moonshine Wars* (1970); and *Mr. Majestik* (1974), with Charles Bronson; as well as mob and heist movies with midwestern settings, such as *Prime Cut* (1972), with Lee Marvin; and *The Outfit* (1973), with Robert Duval (a chase movie that bears a strong resemblance to *The Getaway*); and *Thunderbolt and Lightfoot* (1974), with Clint Eastwood.[91] But, it was *Walking Tall* (1973), starring Joe Don Baker as sheriff Buford Pusser, a significant box-office success, that, undoubtedly, led to the acquisition of Thompson's novel.

The Killer Inside Me has a first-rate cast of second-string stars: Stacey Keach, Susan Tyrrell, Don Stroud, Charles McGraw, John Carradine, Keenan Wynn, Royal Dano, and John Denner. The cast form the core circle of familiars that populate the small mining town policed by Keach's sheriff, Lou Ford, who pitches himself as everybody's friend. Ford, though, is a schizophrenic with psychotic tendencies, which are served up to the audience like Freud on a two-dollar plate. As a child, Ford had witnessed his mother having sex with his father and, when caught watching, had been beaten by his father. As a consequence, Ford has incestuous fantasies of making love to his mother. As his psychotic side becomes dominant, Ford disappears into shadows, and his house takes on a gothic appearance. The film shifts from being a crime story to a horror movie, the generic conventions helping to make the strange familiar rather than, as Thompson does at his best, making the familiar strange.

Working against convention and the strictures of genre was a motivation behind a number of the Thompson adaptations in the late 1980s and early 1990s. *The Kill Off*'s director, Maggie Greenwald, considered that the interest in

Thompson's writing grew out of dissatisfaction with the unreality of early 1980s soap operas, such as *Dynasty*, and other forms of empty and meaningless divertissements. Greenwald told her interviewer that "people are willing to look again at the ugliness, and at the sadness, and at the tragedies of life, and not to brush them under the carpet. Part of that is to be willing to look at characters who are evil, who are cruel, who are violent, and let their stories be told."[92] Greenwald's reading of Thompson as a corrective to the hollowness and superficiality of much contemporary culture was echoed elsewhere.[93] In a 1987 commentary on 1950s pulp fiction, V. Vale and Andrea Juno noted that

> America is rediscovering, on a massive scale, the cynical, hard-boiled novels (Jim Thompson, David Goodis, Charles Willeford, and others) that were a product of the fifties/early sixties—the last transitional decade before television saturated language. . . . In contrast to the bland, homogenized speech and entertainment purveyed by today's mass media, this fiction was strong and colorful, etching vivid pictures in the reader's mind. The power of this language yet survives to speak to new generations of readers dissatisfied with the superficial, predictable quality of experience commonly accepted as adult entertainment.[94]

References to literate "ordinary folk," and the attack on homogenized entertainment, by Vale and Juno suggested that the work of Thompson and his peers should be read, against its actual existence as mass-market fiction, as "authentic."

In the 1997 expanded edition of *Hardboiled America* Geoffrey O'Brien reflected on the change of fortune accorded to Thompson's estate since the publication of the first edition in 1981: "What would once have been inconceivable was that Jim Thompson should seem, if not exactly a voice of reason, then at least a reassuring voice from down home, a both-feet-on-the-ground messenger from a time and place where things looked just as cheap as they were. In the faux Roman atriums of the mega-malls, amid the shrink wrapped luxuries of microchip art, any reminder of the drab and sullen world of Thompson's bellhops and roughnecks carried the pungent force of real blood, real oil stains."[95] The "real" that Thompson represented was seized on in the media buzz around the 1990 adaptations. The critic Lizzie Francke wrote, "Part of the resurgence of the Film Noir tradition," *The Kill Off* is "down beat and down right depressing, it sweeps the dirt right back from under the carpet of sanitised America."[96]

The temporal distance from Thompson's original publishing and consumption context is sufficiently far enough in the past to obscure a counterclaim of their inescapable status as products of a consumer culture, which must ultimately discount avowals of authenticity. Such historical amnesia is also registered in the fact that 1990s access to Thompson's "pulp authentic" is significantly eased by the lack in his stories of what we would commonly recognize as the dominant signifiers of the 1950s: rock 'n' roll, tail fins, the cold war, conspicuous consumption, juvenile delinquents, and so on. For the adapter of Thompson's work it is precisely the indeterminacy of any temporal signposts in his stories that makes them particularly useful in the construction of an imaginary, yet authentic, American pulp storyscape.

The conceptual link between authenticity and pulp fiction is always relative to that which is deemed inauthentic—the character types that populate soap operas, romantic comedies, action-adventure blockbusters, and so on. Rather than the formulaic character types and cartoon plotting of prime-time television and mainstream cinema, the Thompson adaptations offered a more individuated view of character, setting, and story, suggesting that they exist in a recognizable world of work, sex, and dirt: "*After Dark, My Sweet* segues from a thriller to a profound psychosexual tragedy."[97] "I don't think anybody will be thinking this [*The Hot Spot*] is a typical Hollywood film," Hopper says. "I hope it's a commercial film, and I hope it will have all the gloss and look of one, but it's not going to be your run-of-the-mill Hollywood movie. That's because of the locations, because of the characters."[98] Pulp fiction of the 1950s offered the 1990s a tawdry *déclassé* world that could be matched by relatively low film production budgets: "It was a cheap novel," said Stephen Frears, the director of *The Grifters*. "You have to humor the spirit of the cheapness; the idea of making a vast production out of it didn't seem right. To spend $20 million turning it into something polished . . . seemed vulgar somehow."[99] Of the American adaptations discussed here, however, only *The Kill Off* has truly limited production values, and it is the better for it.

The film is set in a rundown out-of-season seaside resort held together by gossip, plotting, small-time dope deals, and a spiderweb of telephone wires. In the film's brilliant opening a bedridden tattletale holds forth on an incestuous relationship between a middle-aged brother and his pregnant sister. Refusal to curb her gossiping leads to the siblings' double suicide. The drug-dealing impotent doctor's son gets his girlfriend hooked on heroin in order to spite her father. The father, who had raped his daughter when she was twelve, now runs a bar and employs an alcoholic to serve drinks. The alcoholic had killed his own wife and kids in a car crash, while inebriated; he is not a man at ease with himself. Business at the bar is so slow that a stripper is used to attract customers, but only the tattletale's much younger husband is seduced by her charms. All this is known to the tattletale—the drug addiction, the dealing, the rape, the cause of the fatal car crash—and she uses this information to her advantage—until one of her victims blows the back of her head off.

The film's dour story is anchored in a world in which the interiors look as if they have been lit with forty-watt bulbs, exterior compositions are cramped, and an overwhelming sense of entrapment is furthered by the use of a bandoneon (a type of concertina used in tango orchestras) on Evan Lurie's soundtrack, the music wheezing and choking back in upon itself. It is tempting to think of

The Kill Off as a transatlantic second cousin to the Finnish melodramas of Aki Kaurismaki, but it lacks his dark humor, just as it misses the comic irony found in Thompson's original novel. Though the *Penthouse* review of the film called it a "Film Noir for the '90s," *The Kill Off* is much less concerned than the other films in the cycle with making a link with a history of noir.[100] The one car in the film is a Chevrolet Impala, which might suggest the 1970s to an automobile enthusiast, but it is best thought of as being utterly anonymous. Haircuts are long and lank on the two younger members of the cast, suggestive of a contemporary Seattle grunge-style, and completely nondescript on the others; likewise the costumes of all the players. Furnishings are as beat-up and worn down as the seaside resort itself, signifying nothing more than lack of wealth and wherewithal.

The other 1990 adaptations of Thompson's stories, as well as films such as *The Hot Spot*, explicitly aroused associations with films produced in the decade following the end of the Second World War but steered clear of unambiguously setting their stories either in the present or the past. This produced a set of temporal conjunctions where imagined fragments of the 1930s, 1940s, 1950s, and 1990s clash. The temporal ambivalence of the films' settings was noted by contemporary reviewers: "a story that seems to take place in a film noir echo chamber";[101] "a torrid film noir";[102] "like the best '40s B movies" and "Jason Patric has the John Garfield quirks for the part";[103] "James Foley has shifted Thompson's tale from the 1950s to the present. And, unlike most Thompson adaptors, he resisted the impulse to stylise the material."[104] The film critic for *The Nation* wrote, "Set in the contemporary Southwest, [*The Grifters* is] full of racetracks, motels, leased-by-the-week offices and people who feel at home in them. It's a movie about the virtue of having low aspirations"[105] The critic for *Film Quarterly* remarked that in *The Grifters* the "sets and clothing do not assert any particular time period, so that they could belong almost as easily to Thompson's 1950s as to the present."[106] All this echoes *Body Heat*, which, David A. Cook noted, "fluctuates somewhere between forties moderne and 'Miami Vice' contempo, and though the story takes place in the middle of a record-breaking heat wave, no one in the small Florida city it depicts has air conditioning—only ceiling fans."[107]

Maitland McDonagh noted that "Frears didn't want to do a period piece, and he didn't have to. *The Grifters* unfolds in a world in aspic: racetracks, down-at-the-heels hotels, gloomy bars, and low slung apartment complexes."[108] The film is rife with anachronism, most notably a scene on a train when Roy Dillon (John Cusack) plays dice with a group of U.S. Navy sailors—a scenario that would have been eminently plausible when Thompson wrote the novel but in 1990 looks forced and fabricated. In an age when public space is increasingly privatized, the shared space of a train carriage, with its mix of classes, no longer resonates with meaning beyond a vague recognition that the scenario belongs to films made in the 1940s or 1950s. While the filmmakers chose to leave in

34. Publicity photo for *The Grifters* (1990). Roy Dillon (John Cusack) grifts sailors on a train.

some of the less disturbing anachronisms, they left out the story of Roy's nurse, procured by his mother, who, after having sex with Roy, reveals she is a Holocaust survivor. The exploitation of a concentration camp victim (she had been sterilized in Dachau) would have distorted an understanding of the protagonist beyond what the filmmakers considered acceptable. On hearing her revelation, Roy Dillon, as Polito writes, is unable to censure himself and "releases a foul belch from deep inside his culture. 'Roy wanted to vomit. He wanted to shake her, to beat her . . . it was *her* own fault.'"[109]

Ambivalent temporal settings are a defining feature of neo-noir, depoliticizing both the past and the present. The anachronisms are compounded by the displacement of the iconographic spatial setting of the dark city of classical noir to the arid, sun-bleached settings of southwestern desert towns, the small cities of Southern California, or the isolated small town of Nowhere America. Though it can be argued that the settings echo a group of films that have only lately been admitted into the core canon of classic film noir—*The Devil Thumbs a Ride* (1947), *Road House* (1948), *The Hitch-Hiker* (1953), *Jeopardy* (1953)—this says more about the needs of 1980s and 1990s culture than about generic tradition.[110] The transient antiheroes of 1930s and 1940s fictions and films were economic exiles from the American dream of plenitude. Their "outsider" status is marked against a coercive cultural consensus formed around material acquisition, moral conformity, and political and sexual conservatism. As Polito suggests, Thompson's drifters are alienated from political structures, but their characterizations are

A DENNIS HOPPER FILM

THE HOT SPOT 18 ☺ RELEASED BY
RANK FILM DISTRIBUTORS

35. Publicity photo for *The Hot Spot* (1990). Dolly Harshaw (Virginia Madsen) as retro-glam.

nonetheless political: "Thompson's crime novels of the 1950s and 1960s, with their shadowy Depression settings and anachronistic anti-heroes (grifters, roughnecks, traveling salesmen), reanimate this 1930s marginal man, but without the typical 1930s suggestion that his terrible circumstances are remediable."[111] The drifters in neo-noirs, however, are cultural migrants fleeing a contemporary landscape defined by the 1990s negatives of post-1960s, postfeminist, postcolonial, postindustrial America. In this sense the neo-noir outsiders are appropriating the authenticity of the drifter figure, wresting it from the social, political, and sexual context that had made it a potent emblem of dissent.

Between the production and reception of the 1990–91 cycle of films, the authenticity that filmmakers had sought in the pulp novels of the 1950s had dissipated. As Mike Newirth has observed, Thompson's writing, like that of his pulp peers, was often overshadowed by the fetishization of the books' original jackets and covers: "Reproduced in glossy postcard books and endlessly rehashed in film and advertising and rock band imagery, it is these unambiguous images that have resonated most powerfully for American consumers of the Eighties and Nineties."[112] The fetishization of the surface imagery of pulp fiction is similarly displayed in the self-reflexive performances of the actors in neo-noir films, which Corliss sees as a distraction:

> What lingers about the high-polished *After Dark, My Sweet* and *The Grifters* is the spectacle, entertaining but way off the point, of actors acting. They come close to fusing with their characters; instead they keep busy by commenting on them, playing up their desperate tawdriness. I wouldn't cede a moment of my pleasure watching Rachel Ward in *After Dark* or Annette Benning in *The Grifters* (or Virginia Madsen in *The Hot Spot*, another softcore essay in the hardboiled genre)—they all execute their cartoon strokes with, say, Ronald Searle's acid finesse. But still. These actresses are straining to slum. The quotation marks of backdated irony hang from their performances like rummage-sale earrings worn for their new value as trash chic.[113]

As a relic of an authentic America brought into view via the mass media industries of publishing, film, and television, Thompson, like the book jackets and slumming actors, became just another momentary distraction in the loop of a once illegitimate culture reworked as "hip." As the cultural critic Thomas Frank noted, hip consumption depends on staying "one step ahead" of the crowd through fostering an image of illegitimacy, such as that which constitutes the apparently "endless cycles of rebellion and transgression that make up so much of our mass culture."[114] The reclamation of Thompson's work from the forgotten margins of America's publishing history gave it the necessary air of illegitimacy, but on his elevation to exploitable box-office commodity his outlaw status diminished—he has become mainstream, as has noir.

Discussing the relative success of *L.A. Confidential*—"a hit but no box office bonanza"—*Newsweek* reported on the continued fascination with noir: "in the blockbuster-hungry Hollywood of 1997, nostalgia-driven noir is a no-no. Teenagers aren't interested in the '40s and '50s. 'If *Chinatown* were pitched today, it would be turned down,' says one studio marketer. 'Everybody avoids the moniker of "film noir" because it's so hard to sell a period piece.'"[115]

Placed against the contemporary cycle of retro gangster movies that sought to exploit the success of *The Untouchables* (1987)—*Miller's Crossing* (1990), *Bugsy* (1990), *Havana* (1990), *Dick Tracy* (1990), *Billy Bathgate* (1991), and *Mobsters* (1991), among others—the 1990 neo-noirs were not period pieces.[116] The 1998 adaptation of Thompson's posthumously published novella *This World, Then the Fireworks* shows how the hold on the contemporary was at best tenuous. The only temporal signifier in the original story is a reference to the bomb, yet the adaptation is sunk in a world of cars with white-walled tires, fedoras, 1950s lingerie remodeled for a Victoria's Secret catalog, cigarettes, and nickel-plated pistols bathed in blue and red lighting for night scenes and yellow and brown for daytime.

To give the film an added dimension of retro-authenticity, the film's producers drew on the talent of Pete Rugolo to provide the soundtrack. Rugolo first achieved notice as a principal arranger for the Stan Kenton Orchestra, later working with Peggy Lee, Mel Torme, and Nat King Cole, among others. He also produced Miles Davis's seminal album, *Birth of the Cool.* The percussion-heavy music track incorporates two mid-1950s recordings by Chet Baker, which further the film's bid for hip credentials. The filmmakers, however, overplay their hand, and hip quickly becomes cliché. Better by far is the soundtrack to *The Hot Spot*, which makes the most of a unique teaming of bluesman John Lee Hooker with Miles Davis. Davis's trumpet plays counterpoint to Hooker's over-and-over rhythm guitar and his otherworldly moans and groans, producing a blues rich in ennui and a perfect foil to the mannerist postures and weary shenanigans of the film's protagonists.

In his notes that accompany the compact disc of the soundtrack for *The Grifters*, Elmer Bernstein writes, "On the surface it appears to be simply a piece of seamy Americana, a story about three hustlers whose lives interact in the back alleys of society." But the style of the film, he believed, is much "more complex; the story is told with an odd kind of mordant humor, a touch of reality and a brooding darkness which imbues the whole with a teasing, elusive quality." This is a good summation of Thompson's appeal, though it is less true of the film, which actually has little of Thompson's black comedy that the French adaptations caught so well and that Bernstein's soundtrack evokes with its tangos and two-steps. In contrast, the French composer Maurice Jarre produced a sterile electronic soundtrack for *After Dark, My Sweet*—a humorless exercise in style.[117]

In their quest for period verisimilitude *Firework*'s producers lose what no doubt drew them to the project in the first place: Thompson's pulp aesthetic—a raw, delirious, sexually overwrought, psychological landscape peopled by misfits and losers who cling to an uncertain ambition to succeed, even if success means only being able to kick in the teeth of those less fortunate than themselves. The filmmakers fail to deal with Thompson's nihilistic view of the human condition, but then failure to remain "true" to Thompson marks, in one way or another, all the American adaptations, particularly the inability to find a cinematic means to reveal the fragmentation of character subjectivity that is central to his best work.[118]

Peckinpah remains the best American interpreter of Thompson but not with *The Getaway*, or indeed with any adaptation of Thompson's fiction. His most Thompsonesque film is *Bring Me the Head of Alfredo Garcia* (1974), which Peckinpah described as "the story of a man caught up in the brutality of the world around him, who loses all sense of morality with one act of violence begetting another, until there is no return to respectability, only retribution. The lasting theme of the film is that such acts only end in disaster for those

36. Publicity photo for *Bring Me the Head of Alfredo Garcia* (1974). Bennie (Warren Oates), an American piano player living in Mexico, becomes embroiled in violence in his quest for the reward money offered for the head of Alfredo Garcia.

involved."[119] The reviewer for the *Wall Street Journal*, however, did not agree with Peckinpah's interpretation and argued, instead, that the film is "so grotesque in its basic conception, so sadistic in its imagery, so irrational in its plotting, so obscene in its effect, and so incompetent in its cinematic realization that the only kind of analysis it really invites is psychoanalysis."[120] This would make an equally apt description of Thompson's fictions (as it also would for *Kiss Me Deadly* or Fuller's films). The reviewer for *New York* magazine thought *Bring Me the Head of Alfredo Garcia* "a catastrophe so huge that those who once ranked Peckinpah with Hemingway may now invoke Mickey Spillane." In the context of Thompson's reclamation, *Kiss Me Deadly*'s canonization, and Fuller's lionization, the reviewer's demotion of Peckinpah, from sharing the heights with Hemmingway to occupying the lows with Spillane, can be readily inverted.[121]

Peckinpah had met Thompson some years before his tenure as director of *The Getaway*; indeed, the two had worked together on a script.[122] Recalling the relationship, Samuel Fuller said, "Peckinpah really loved old Jim, and he loved his books about the dispersed, the depraved, and the recalcitrant."[123] "The first time I saw him he was dead," says Bennie (Warren Oates) of Alfredo Garcia. In typical Thompson fashion, Benny is soon doubling for the corpse of Alfredo.

It is pretty certain that those proselytizers for the proletarian pleasures that could be found in pulp, punk, and underground films, Levin, Ferguson, Agee, and Farber, contemporaries of Thompson, would not have found much to cheer about in the early 1990s cycle of neo-noir. The circumstances that had appealed to cinephiliac sensibilities with finely honed powers of discrimination had changed. No longer can you discover films for yourself while they play anonymously in rundown urban cinemas; neo-noirs are presold and prepackaged for a niche audience. They flatter that audience's sense of its own powers of discrimination, confirming an educated taste with their nuanced suggestion of transgression, while reinforcing the idea that a knowledge of film history is knowledge worth having. "The bulk of the audience who enjoys film noir," said the head of marketing at Warner Bros. in 1997, "are directors, film students, critics and the most ardent, generally upscale film enthusiast."[124]

Polito called Thompson's work "savage art," a designation that recalls Manny Farber's classification of Samuel Fuller as an "art brutist." Farber celebrated the director's work against the critical consensus of the time (1960s) because it rejected the "realm of celebrity and affluence" and instead embraced—or rather "burrowed" like a "termite" into—the "nether world of privacy." Fuller's films lacked the pretension to great art, engaging, instead, in the horizontal, which is to say democratic, mobility of both "observing and being in the world."[125] Like Fuller, Thompson forsook the pretension that his work was anything other than an ephemeral entertainment, a condition that has allowed the work to be reclaimed as unbesmirched by corrupt middlebrow or highbrow values and, instead, celebrated as a cipher for an authentic American culture.

Discussing a similar process in the production of seemingly authentic American folkways, Cantwell writes, "diverse fragments of authentic cultures already fixed unawares in the imagination by half-forgotten popular arts—the movies, perhaps, or the magazine ads of a generation ago, always capable of arousing an association but never of articulating it—call out like impounded dogs to the bewildered consumer."[126] Locating these associations, and giving them meaning, occupies much contemporary critical energy. Critical acts of reclamation still the "progressive" flow of culture and rework the canonical distinctions of the past, elevating the lowbrow, calling the middlebrow into contention, and disturbing a complacent highbrow. Such critical interventions are important in their questioning of hierarchal structure and received knowledge. This process of cultural dissidence was behind the move Thompson's fiction made from being a lowbrow's entertainment to a highbrow's found object to, eventually, middlebrow art-house fare. The latter are exemplified by the adaptations of *The Grifters*, *After Dark, My Sweet*, and *This World, Then the Fireworks*, where whatever is radical in Thompson's fiction is tamed and presented as a form of gentrified authentic Americana or reduced to an adjective—"Thompsonesque"—and used as a handy marketing tag.

Postscript

While I was in the final stages of preparing the manuscript for publication in June 2010, Michael Winterbottom's *The Killer Inside Me* was released, and at least three other Thompson adaptations were rumored to be in preproduction, including *Lunatic at Large*, an unfilmed and unpublished screenplay Thompson had written for Stanley Kubrick.[127] Discussing the latter, the producer Edward R. Pressman noted that "post-Tarantino this kind of thing has become new in a way. Things go in cycles."[128] Indeed they do. *The Killer Inside Me* stars Casey Affleck as the psychotic deputy sheriff, Lou Ford, and Jessica Alba and Kate Hudson as the two women he loves and kills. The film elicited a whiff of controversy over its two violent murder scenes and reports of booing at festival screenings in Berlin and at Sundance.[129] Like the 1990s Thompson adaptations, the film was marketed as a neo-noir or as something more than noir: "savage, bleak, blacker than noir." In defense of the violence in the film the director spoke about his fidelity to the source novel, claiming the film was as "true" to Thompson's story as he could make it.

Stylistically the film shares little with earlier neo-noir productions, rejecting the campiness of *The Hot Spot*, the retro-fetishism of *This World, Then the Fireworks*, the ironic quotation marks of *The Grifters*, or the downbeat grind of *The Kill Off*. The retreat from generic convention is immediately announced by the film's title sequence, which uses pop art graphics over which Little Willie John's 1956 classic rendition of "Fever" is heard. Neither the song nor the graphics have any particular connection to noir's iconography.

While the screenplay is remarkably faithful to the novel, retaining a good deal of the dialogue, all of the core events, and the story's structure, it still struggles to find a filmic equivalent to the source's first-person narration. The formal strategy undertaken by Winterbottom is first-person voice-over, albeit quite sparsely used, and to have Lou Ford never offscreen except when showing his point of view: "Lou's telling the story and everybody else is a character in his story," said Winterbottom.[130] The violence carried out against the two women is brutal and, in the first murder, sustained in a manner that makes the viewer uncomfortable, but the length of the scene and the graphic depiction of the violence is made even more disturbing by its contrast with the tenderness shown in the face of the killer and in the soft words he speaks as he pummels his lover. The disjuncture between his actions and words of affection is hard to stomach.

A good deal of newsprint has been spent arguing whether the murder scene is exploitative, sensational, and, most worrying, deeply misogynistic or whether it is a justifiable representation of violence against women that presents the true horror of such acts. What needs to be added to this debate is Winterbottom's desire to be as faithful as possible to Thompson's novel and to not flinch, as others have before him, from what is truly ugly and disturbing: "In the

37. U.S. poster for *The Killer Inside Me* (2010).

38. Publicity photo for *Pickup on South Street* (1953). Skip McCoy (Richard Widmark) makes strange love to Candy (Jean Peters).

book, the victims are Joyce and Amy. So for me, that was a given. This is the material—and we are going to make it."[31] Winterbottom makes lovers of pulp look at what they may prefer not to see: the fact that women in these fictions are more often than not human punching bags for the male protagonist, who uses them as objects on which to take out his frustration and sate his bitter rage. This is certainly so of *Kiss Me Deadly*, both book and film, but there is also evidence of this in all of the other films and stories discussed in these pages; think back, for example, to the display of sadomasochism in Fuller's films, where the hero tenderly rubs and soothes the bruised face of a woman, particu-larly the scene in *Pickup on South Street* in which Widmark's character knocks out Candy (Jean Peters) and then makes strange love to her. Winterbottom has done no more, and still done a good deal at that, by putting into plain sight what lies behind those images of debased, battered, and murdered women.

　　Winterbottom's view of Thompson's work is, I think, similar to that offered by the punk/postpunk group Pere Ubu, who discuss the writer's influence on their 2006 album *Why I Hate Women*. The band's singer explains: "My goal was to create the Jim Thompson novel that Jim Thompson never wrote. That's obsessive, but the best rock music is brutally obsessive." The title is "a mantra associated with the album's central character," not the singer's own. "When the title occurred to me, I thought 'this is going to be a nightmare,'" he acknowl-edges. "But I did not necessarily want there to be a soft option. . . . Knowing

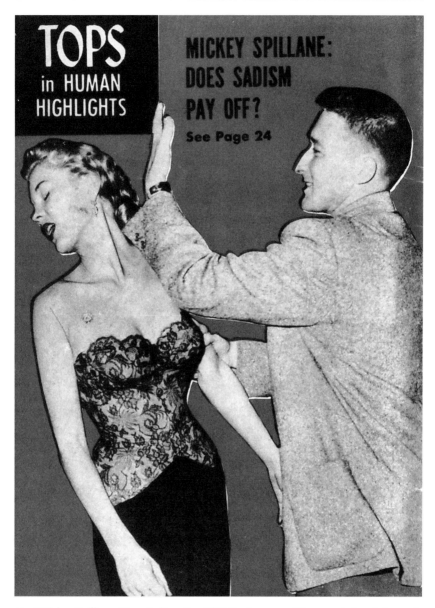

39. "Mickey Spillane: Does Sadism Pay Off?" (back cover of *Tops* magazine, July 1955).

what lay ahead, I was not happy. I searched in vain for an alternative. I was then determined to construct the album package in such a way that the consumer would have no easy outs, no pat answers. Pere Ubu does not dabble in irony. It is the last refuge of the weak-willed and cowardly. We are no cowards."[132] Winterbottom's *The Killer Inside Me* also refuses to dabble in irony.

As with *Kiss Me Deadly* the violence toward women is not the whole of the film. *The Killer Inside Me* also creates a dialogue between low culture and high, though here it is much more focused on music. Twice Lou Ford plays the piano in his parlor—a light blues figure when in the company of a man he will shortly kill, and a classical piece when he is on his own. While alone in the house, reading his father's books on psychiatry, he plays classical records. It is this private cultivated and erudite side of his personality that he hides from the world, playing up instead his good-ol'-boy persona. After he encounters the prostitute played by Jessica Alba, an encounter that climaxes with some rough sadomasochistic sex, Ford is shown in his police car returning to town, the radio blasting out Charlie Feathers's 1956 onanistic rockabilly rave up "One Hand Loose." The song is a perfect match with his character:

I'm a tip-top daddy and I'm gonna have my way
Keep away from the corners hear what I got to say . . .
Give me a free hand woman, let it swing by my side
A-give me one hand loose and I'll be satisfied
Turn loose!

It is a paean to the pleasure and curse of entrapment and release; the song clicks with Ford, who happily sings along for a bar or two. In contrast the classical music played at one stage by Lou, and over the end credits, is Richard Strauss's "Four Last Songs," which, as the British filmmaker Lawrence Jackson has noted, is "very much about death—apocalyptic imagery—and [is] famously sexual, Viennese, and Freudian. David Lynch used this same music in *Wild at Heart*, also a cocktail of repressed rage and sexual violence."[133]

There are no references to popular song in Thompson's novel, but the Feathers and Willie John songs are wholly apposite, working effortlessly alongside the visuals to support the film's theme and characterization. But it is the plethora of western swing performances that most forcefully leave their mark on the film. Behind the jaunty bonhomie, the fast times and high jinks that the songs seem to promise, there lurks a dark side, none more so than Spade Cooley and the Western Swing Gang's "Shame on You":

Shame, shame on you
Shame, shame on you
Took my heart as a token, When returned, it was broken
Hide your face, shame on you.

The song is given two airings: when Ford sings it with a fellow law officer before it segues into the Cooley recording, and then at the very end of the film over the images of Ford's burning home and the start of the credits. The song precedes the killing of Amy, its apparent jocularity at odds with the horror that follows. The disjunctive use of western swing catches something of Thompson's dark humor, which is much more subtly rendered in this film than in the two French adaptations. The filmmakers are keenly aware of the implications behind their choice of pop songs, even to the point of obscurity in their use of intertextuality, wherein the use of Spade Cooley's music takes on added significance. The bandleader holds a special place in the crime writer James Ellroy's cultural lexicon, and he is featured in the writer's story of his mother's murder, *My Dark Places*, which is as much an investigation of misogyny and male violence against women as it is an autobiography.[134] Beginning in 1944 with "Shame on You," there followed a string of top-ten hits for Cooley that ended three years later, though he continued to record and make a living on television and through live performances. His career came to an abrupt finale in 1961 when, in a pill- and alcohol-fueled rage, he beat and stomped his wife to death. A week after the murder, in a letter sent from jail, Cooley wrote to his friend and fellow musician Hank Penny. His parting words were, "What more can I say—you know I loved her."[135]

Conclusion

Hiding Out in Cinemas

The pulp writer and crime novelist Charles Willeford caught something of the tension that exists between the individuated artwork and the anonymous formulaic commercial product in a short story, originally called "The Sin of Integrity," published in *Gent* magazine, and retitled "Selected Incidents" in his short-story collection *The Machine in Ward Eleven* (1963). The story concerns the ruminations of a Hollywood film producer who is recounting his experience of working with a talented film director who recently committed suicide. The producer's audience is Charlie, a professional writer who has been engaged to ghostwrite his autobiography. The news that J. C. Blake has slashed his wrists causes a digression in the retelling of the producer's life story. The producer was responsible for bringing him to Hollywood after J. C. had achieved some notoriety as a theater director of avant-garde plays; he also made 16 mm films. Though a hard-nosed businessman, the producer is an aficionado of the avant-garde and has his own personal library of films: "The motion picture is an art form, Charles, all of us know that, and most of us keep private film libraries at home the way book publishers keep home libraries full of books."[1] The producer becomes J. C.'s patron and supports him in the writing of a screenplay based on the Pat Hobby stories of F. Scott Fitzgerald, stories Fitzgerald wrote for *Esquire* about an alcoholic screenwriter.

J. C. works on the script for two years and, in the producer's estimation, creates a masterpiece. The producer considers J. C.'s effort to be commensurate with the work James Joyce put into creating *Ulysses*. And both, when you boil them right down, are basically comedies, he thinks. But that is beside the point, because while you can take Joyce seriously, "Who, for God's sake, could ever take movies that seriously? Or any one movie?"[2] J. C. did. The producer has the script rewritten by contract screenwriters and turned into a thirteen-part television series. J. C. moves on to direct westerns and TV dramas. Good ones too, by all accounts. Why, then, ponders the producer, would someone with so much talent slice through their wrists?

Like his contemporary Jim Thompson, Willeford worked in the paperback pulp mill of the 1950s, producing ephemera for the fiction factory that sold sensational stories with lurid cover illustrations and racy titles: *Pick-Up*, *Wild Wives*, *Honey Gal*, *Lust Is a Woman*, and *Woman Chaser* are some of Willeford's early titles. Also like Thompson, Willeford's pulp legacy was discovered in the 1980s, but, unlike Thompson, Willeford had the good fortune to still be alive and to still be writing. Willeford gained considerable acclaim for his Hoke Moseley series of police thrillers, the first of which, *Miami Blues*, was adapted as a film in 1990.

"The Sin of Integrity" is a meditation on the cost to the artist of commercial compromise. J. C. resented the dictates of the marketplace on his art but depended on them in order to earn a living and as a means of financing his vision. J. C. may well be a stand-in for Willeford, or for any pulp author that aspired to produce serious work of lasting importance, but the story also tells us something about the relationship between art and commerce, whether litera-ture or film, that moves beyond recording the effect of the relationship on the artist. If the film producer in the story is a typical, albeit caricatured, example of those who control the means of production, his interest in the avant-garde is not just a personal foible, a means to shuck off accusations of being a philistine; it also has a commercial imperative.

The avant-garde's transgressive remit—its rejection of a complaisant moral-ity and capitulation to established social mores, and its boundary-breaking acts of unconventionality—has acted as a form of research and development for the cultural industries. The film producer is looking for ideas and talent to help pro-duce an expression of novelty in order to enhance the commercial appeal of his films to an audience jaded by standardized products. The innovations created by the avant-garde are open to exploitation by commercial agencies seeking to offer consumers products suggestive of the unconventional, the differentiated, and the individuated, and to sell this on a mass scale. In the context of this sce-nario the avant-garde is not anathema to the commercial industries but is one of the means at its disposal to refresh and reinvigorate, and even authenticate, its standardized products. This is the story that Willeford also tells; it is the story of the producer's secret stash of 16mm films.

On the other side of this coin of exchange, the story told in *Maximum Movies—Pulp Fictions*, is the idea that westerns, crime dramas, and other pulp tales—standardized products—have become the means of refreshing and rein-vigorating the avant-garde. This is the story that Greg Taylor tells so well in *Artists in the Audience*, his analysis of the film criticism of Manny Farber and Parker Tyler, and that Juan Suárez provides in *Pop Modernism*. I have expanded and broadened this story by exploring in some depth the genealogy of pulp: its shift from a lowbrow's distraction and entertainment to its transformation into the raw materials of a modernist's dramaturgy. My emphasis has been on pulp's transvaluation from "fiction for morons" to a form of masculine endeavor and respite—an authenticated response to effeminate cultures of consumption. With Lawrence Alloway as my guide, however, I have also returned to the examination of pulp as pulp, which considers the valuation of pulp not as a means of attacking the center, the middlebrow, such as the criticism practiced by Farber, but as a form worthy of study in and for itself as an industrialized art form.

The gendering of pulp has been a starting point upon which the debates around the contested values ascribed to the film version of *Kiss Me Deadly* and to the films of Samuel Fuller can be better evaluated. Gender does not subsume and efface the variety of voices and positions of interest, but it does provide a common underpinning beneath the struggles to give value to the various acts of consumption and discrimination. The recognition that gender provides something of a master narrative, helps to disabuse us of the notion that cultural objects, such as a particular movie, have intrinsic values undetermined by social forces, so that they might be conceived, like a great artwork, to transcend more materialistic considerations. As Michael Denning has written, no "popular cultural practice is necessarily subversive or incorporated; it takes place in a situation, becomes articulated with a 'party' in Gramsci's sense: an organized way of life, an alliance of class fractions, a conception of the universe, a historical bloc which creates the conditions for a political use or reading, the conditions for symbolizing class conflict."[3]

The chapters on *Kiss Me Deadly* and Fuller provide the groundwork for understanding how the film industry has exploited and made capital out of the vanguard critical work that validated the viewing and study of pulp fiction and films, producing the 1990s cycle of neo-noir. The neo-noirs demonstrate how a once illegitimate outré celebration of some of Hollywood's middling productions can, over time, acquire enough cultural capital to become the basis for a cycle of films that lay claim to an identity as something other than examples of Hollywood's middling productions.

While the romantic attraction of burrowing into an underground in order to secure one's sense of self as an authentic presence within a culture of conspicuous consumption (a process that underlies much of the academic activity concerned with the study of cult films) shows no sign of losing its grip on the imaginations of male scholars of popular culture, there is little mileage in pretending that the view from below can continue to produce insights on formulaic pulp movies as remarkable as those once provided by Farber, Ferguson, Sarris, and others. The unexplored riches of Alloway's film and art criticism, however, are suggestive of ways to continue the debate, to refresh and reinvigorate the study of Hollywood's maximum movies, to move beyond the reinscription of textual readings enforced by subservience to theoretical paradigms, such as those pertaining to film noir. Alloway's criticism provides us with the opportunity to see movies as an industrial art, not in order to efface the seeming contradiction between industry and art but rather to embrace that contradiction as a genuine antinomy, one that underlies our social reality.

By way of a concluding comment, let me return to what seems to be the enduring appeal of low-budget, lowbrow movies. Looking back from the viewpoint of the 1970s, Andrew Sarris wrote about the effects on film criticism of the continued fascination with the B movie:

> Nor is there today any genre lowly enough to be dismissed out of hand by the critical establishment. Kung-fu, porn (soft-core and hard-core), Damon and Pythias squad-car serenades, revisionist Westerns, regressive Disneys, black-power fantasies: all have their sociological and even stylistic rationales. The snobberies that afflicted supposedly serious film criticism in the 1930s, 1940s, and 1950s have now been superseded by an open-mindedness that errs on the side of credulity. . . . A disproportionate number of fondly remembered B pictures fall into the general category of the film noir. Somehow even mediocrity can become majestic when it is coupled with death, which is to say that if only good movies can teach us how to live, even bad movies can teach us how to die.[4]

Movies, or more literally, movie houses, are places of refuge, not least from the domestic sphere of influence but perhaps also from the more tangible reach of the long arm of the law (including the guardians of cultural values). A good number of film noirs feature protagonists "on the lam" and hiding out in cinemas. In *I Wake Up Screaming* (1942) the murder suspect Frankie Christopher (Victor Mature) tells Jill Lynn (Betty Grable) that he will show her "how to play hide and seek in the big city." They are standing outside the Rex Theatre—Open All Night—Adults Only—10¢—featuring the picture *Flames of Passion*. Versions of this scenario can be seen in numerous films, from *Crossfire*, via *The Third Man*, to *A bout de souffle*, *Bonnie and Clyde*, *Targets*, and *Mean Streets*. These figures on the run from authority have found a temporary sanctuary in the cinema. The theater provides shelter and conceals these fugitives from the law. The dark theater is both a public space and a space of intense isolation, not unlike another favored refuge for those being pursued, the public library, as in Douglas Sirk's *Shockproof* (1949). There is, of course, a neat correlation between these spaces of refuge given to film characters and those spaces occupied by film critics and scholars. Did the cinephile also see his or her reflection in the hunted outlaws who hide out in the picture houses and libraries located in cities' terminal zones?

NOTES

INTRODUCTION

1. Greil Marcus, "No Money Down: Pop Art, Pop Music, Pop Culture," in *POP*, ed. Mark Francis (London: Phaidon, 2005), 208–10, 209.

2. Pauline Kael, *Kiss Kiss Bang Bang* (Boston: Little, Brown, 1968), n.p.

3. For a fine book on the history of cinephilia see Christian Keathley, *Cinephilia and History, or, The Wind in the Trees* (Bloomington: Indiana University Press, 2006).

4. See Michael Kammen, *American Culture, American Tastes: Social Change and the 20th Century* (New York: Alfred A. Knopf, 1999); see also Lawrence W. Levine, *Highbrow/Lowbrow: The Emergence of Cultural Hierarchy in America* (Cambridge: Harvard University Press, 1988); Richard Ohmann, *Selling Culture: Magazines, Markets, and Class at the Turn of the Century* (London: Verso, 1996).

5. Quoted in Kammen, *American Culture, American Tastes*, 120.

6. Michael Denning, *Culture in the Age of Three Worlds* (London: Verso, 2004), 107–8.

7. Quoted in ibid.

8. Andrew Ross, "Containing Culture in the Cold War," in *No Respect: Intellectuals and Popular Culture* (New York: Routledge, 1989), 60–61.

9. Thomas Frank, *The Conquest of Cool: Business Culture, Counterculture, and the Rise of Hip Consumerism* (Chicago: University of Chicago Press, 1998), 31.

10. Quoted in David Robbins, ed., *The Independent Group: Postwar Britain and the Aesthetics of Plenty* (Cambridge: MIT Press, 1990), 185. Alloway's comments on his consumption of science fiction in the 1950s can be found on page 187.

11. See Jeffrey Sconce, ed., *Sleaze Artists: Cinema at the Margins of Taste, Style, and Politics* (Durham, NC: Duke University Press, 2007); Joan Hawkins, *Cutting Edge: Art-Horror and the Horrific Avant-Garde* (Minneapolis: University of Minnesota Press, 2000); Greg Taylor, *Artists in the Audience: Cults, Camp, and American Film Criticism* (Princeton, NJ: Princeton University Press, 1999). James Naremore's *More Than Night: Film Noir in Its Contexts* (Berkeley: University of California Press, 1998) was recently "updated and expanded" in its second edition (Berkeley: University of California Press, 2008).

CHAPTER 1   POSITION PAPERS

1. Mark Wigley, "Interstices 4," quoted in *Imagining the Present: Context, Content, and the Role of the Critic*, ed. Richard Kalina (New York: Routledge, 2006), 27n38.

2. Anne Massey, *The Independent Group: Modernism and Mass Culture in Britain, 1945–59* (Manchester: Manchester University Press, 1995). David Robbins, ed., *The Independent*

Group: Postwar Britain and the Aesthetics of Plenty (Cambridge: MIT Press, 1990). For an overview of Alloway's career as a museum and gallery curator see Alex Coles, "Curating: Then and Now," *Art Monthly*, April 2004, 1–4.

3. Robbins, *The Independent Group*, 94.

4. Quoted in ibid., 250.

5. Richard Hoggart, *Uses of Literacy* (Harmondsworth: Pelican, 1958), 251.

6. Graham Whitham, "Science Fiction," in Robbins, *The Independent Group*, 61–62.

7. Ibid.

8. Alloway comments on his consumption of science fiction in the 1950s in a retrospective statement on the IG published in Robbins, *The Independent Group*, 187.

9. Ibid., 43.

10. Lawrence Alloway, "The Long Front of Culture," *Cambridge Opinion* 17 (1959): 26; repr. in *POP*, ed. Mark Francis (London: Phaidon, 2005), 200–201; *Pop Art Redefined*, ed. Suzi Gablik and John Russell (London: Thames and Hudson, 1969); and *Modern Dreams: The Rise and Fall and the Rise of Pop*, ed. Brian Wallis et al. (Cambridge: MIT Press, 1988). Only *Cambridge Opinion* reproduces the cover of the issue of *Science Fiction Quarterly* discussed by the anonymous letter writer to illustrate Alloway's essay.

11. Barry Curtis, "From Ivory Tower to Control Tower," in Robbins, *The Independent Group*, 223.

12. Ibid., 33.

13. Lawrence Alloway, "Critics in the Dark," *Encounter*, Feb. 1964, 50–55.

14. See, e.g., "Monster Films," *Encounter*, Jan. 1960, 70–72; "Lawrence Alloway on the Iconography of the Movies," *Movie* 7 (Feb. 1963): 16–18; "Critics in the Dark," *Encounter*, Feb. 1964, 50–55; "Son of Public Enemy," *Arts Magazine*, Nov. 1966, 25–26; "Science Fiction and Artifacts," *Arts Magazine*, Dec. 1968, 39–41; "More Skin, More Everything in Movies," *Vogue*, Feb. 1, 1968, 186–87, 213.

15. Lawrence Alloway, *Violent America: The Movies, 1946–1964* (New York: MOMA, 1971), 9.

16. The complete screening program was as follows: *The Killers* (1946), *Desert Fury* (1947), *I Walk Alone* (1947), *Out of the Past* (1947), *Ramrod* (1947), *The Lady from Shanghai* (1948), *D.O.A.* (1949), *Sands of Iwo Jima* (1949), *White Heat* (1949), *In a Lonely Place* (1950), *The Steel Helmet* (1951), *The Big Heat* (1953), *Hondo* (1953), *The Naked Spur* (1953), *Pickup on South Street* (1953), *Suddenly* (1954), *House of Bamboo* (1955), *Kiss Me Deadly* (1955), *The Phenix City Story* (1955), *Attack!* (1956), *Backlash* (1956), *The Last Wagon* (1956), *Seven Men from Now* (1956), *Written on the Wind* (1956), *Man in the Shadow* (1957), *The Tall T* (1957), *The Tattered Dress* (1957), *The Case against Brooklyn* (1958), *The Left Handed Gun* (1958), *The Lineup* (1958), *Touch of Evil* (1958), *Warlock* (1959), *The Manchurian Candidate* (1962), *Johnny Cool* (1963), *The Killers* (1964).

17. Lawrence Alloway, "Pop Art: The Words," in *Topics in American Art Since 1945* (New York: Norton, 1975), 119–22.

18. Ibid., 119.

19. John McHale, "The Expendable Icon," *Architectural Design* 29, nos. 2 and 3 (Feb.–March 1959); repr. in Francis, *POP*, 201–2.

20. Alloway, "Pop Art," 119.

21. Repr. in Francis, *POP*, 198.

22. Alloway, "Pop Art," 121.

23. Ibid., 122.

24. Lawrence Alloway, "The Arts and Mass Media," *Architectural Design* 28, no. 2 (Feb. 1958): 84–85; repr. in Alloway, *Imagining the Present*, 55–59.

25. Alloway, *Violent America*, 58.

26. Ibid., 25.

27. Barbara Deming, *Running Away from Myself: A Dream Portrait of America Drawn from the Films of the Forties* (New York: Grossman, 1969), 6.

28. Alloway, *Violent America*, 19.

29. Quoted in Nigel Whiteley, "Toward a Throw-Away Culture: Consumerism, 'Style Obsolescence' and Cultural Theory in the 1950s and 1960s," *Oxford Art Journal* 10, no. 2 (1987): 3–27, 11.

30. See Massey, *The Independent Group*, 92–93; and Whiteley, "Toward a Throw-Away Culture."

31. Alloway, *Violent America*, 12.

32. Alloway, *Imagining the Present*, 26.

33. For more expansive investigation of Alloway's film criticism see Peter Stanfield, "Maximum Movies: Lawrence Alloway's Pop Art Film Criticism," *Screen* 49, no. 2 (summer 2008): 179–93.

34. Greg Taylor, *Artists in the Audience: Cults, Camp, and American Film Criticism* (Princeton, NJ: Princeton University Press, 1999), 44.

35. Manny Farber, "Nearer My Agee to Thee" (1958); repr. in Manny Farber, *Negative Space: Manny Farber on the Movies* (New York: Da Capo, 1998), 84–104, 87.

36. Farber, *Negative Space*, 114–16.

37. Manny Farber, "White Elephant Art vs. Termite Art," in Farber, *Negative Space*, 134–44, 137.

38. Quoted in Aaron Kahan, Douglas Nason, Al Quattrocchi, and Jeff Smith, eds., *The Art of Von Dutch* (Los Angeles: Tornado Design, 2006), 282.

39. Donald Phelps, *Covering Ground: Essays for Now* (New York: Croton Press, 1969), 120.

40. Farber, *Negative Space*, 14.

41. Manny Farber, "Underground Magic, Eccentric Vitality and Artful Direction Salvage Banal Stories," *New Leader*, April 20, 1959, 27–28.

42. Robert Warshow, *The Immediate Experience: Movies, Comics, Theatre and Other Aspects of Popular Culture* (Cambridge: Harvard University Press, 2001), 75, xli.

43. Phelps, *Covering Ground*, 119. Also in the same volume is Phelps's outstanding essay on Warshow, "Essays of a Man Watching" (213–29). Phelps's equally fascinating essay on a now forgotten film critic, William S. Poster, can be found in Donald Phelps et al., *The Word and Beyond: Four Literary Cosmologists* (New York: Smith, 1982), 295–300.

44. Warshow, *The Immediate Experience*, xli.

45. For two superb overviews of Manny Farber's criticism see Noel King, "Manny Farber," and Adrian Martin, "The Qualities I Like: Impressions of Manny Farber," both in *Framework* 40 (April 1999): 9–18, and 56–68.

46. Otis Ferguson, *The Film Criticism of Otis Ferguson*, ed. Robert Wilson (Philadelphia: Temple University Press, 1971), 412, 180.

47. Meyer Levin, "The Charge of the Light Brigade," originally published in *Esquire*; repr. in *Garbo and the Night Watchmen*, ed. Alistair Cooke (London: Secker and Warburg, 1971), 108–10.

48. James Agee, review of *Dillinger* (Monogram), *Time*, May 7, 1945; repr. in James Agee, *Agee on Film: Reviews and Comments* (New York: Library of America, 2005), 499.

49. Arthur L. Mayer, "An Exhibitor Begs for 'B's,'" *Hollywood Quarterly* 3, no. 2 (winter 1947–48); repr. in *Hollywood Quarterly: Film Culture in Postwar America, 1945–1957*, ed. Eric Smoodin and Ann Martin (Berkeley: University of California Press, 2002), 263–70.

50. The image of the "truant eye" comes from Roger Cardinal, "Pausing over Peripheral Detail," *Framework* 30/31 (1986): 112–30.

51. Manny Farber, "Crime without Passion," *New Republic*, June 3, 1946, 415–16; quoted in Taylor, *Artists in the Audience*, 45.

52. Farber, "Crime without Passion," 415.

53. Marc Eliot, *Down 42nd Street: Sex, Money, Culture, and Politics at the Crossroads of the World* (New York: Warner, 2001), 96–97. Another popular history of the locale is Anthony Bianco, *Ghosts of 42nd Street: A History of America's Most Infamous Block* (New York: William Morrow, 2004). See also Marshall Berman, *On the Town: One Hundred Years of Spectacle in Times Square* (London: Verso, 2009).

54. *The WPA Guide to New York City: The Federal Writers' Project Guide to 1930s New York* (New York: Pantheon, 1982), 29–30, 175. The guide has a short description of motion picture theaters in and around Times Square, noting those with stage shows, those that specialize in newsreels, and those that show foreign-language pictures (Yiddish, Russian, Chinese, etc.). There is a map of the theater district showing the location of the movie houses on pages 168–69.

55. Brooks McNamara, "The Entertainment District at the End of the 1930s," in *Inventing Times Square: Commerce and Culture at the Crossroads of the World*, ed. William R. Taylor (New York: Sage, 1991), 186.

56. Arthur Mayer, *Merely Colossal: The Story of the Movies from the Long Chase to the Chaise Longue* (New York: Simon and Schuster, 1953), 178–79.

57. *The WPA Guide to New York City*, 172.

58. Wilson, *The Film Criticism of Otis Ferguson*, 331–32.

59. Jonas Mekas, *Movie Journal: The Rise of a New American Cinema, 1959–71* (New York: Macmillan, 1971), 12.

60. Juan A. Suárez, *Bike Boys, Drag Queens, and Superstars: Avant-Garde, Mass Culture, and Gay Identities in the 1960s Underground Cinema* (Bloomington: Indiana University Press, 1996), 81.

61. This assumption is based on how the underground was discussed at the time in British film criticism; see, e.g., Tony Raynes, "The Underground Film," *Cinema* 1 (Dec. 1968).

62. David E. James, *To Free the Cinema: Jonas Mekas and the New York Underground* (Princeton, NJ: Princeton University Press, 1992), 95. For a more in-depth discussion of the overlaps between Farber's and Mekas's undergrounds see Peter Stanfield, "Going Underground with Manny Farber and Jonas Mekas," in *Explorations in New Cinema History: Approaches and Case Studies*, ed. Daniel Biltereyst, Richard Maltby, and Philippe Meers (Chichester, UK: Wiley-Blackwell, forthcoming [2011]).

63. Levin, "The Charge of the Light Brigade," 109.

64. Agee, *Agee on Film*, 105.

65. Phelps, *Covering Ground*, 37.

66. For a fictionalized and romanticized account of the milieu see Geoffrey O'Brien, *The Times Square Story* (New York: Norton, 1998).

67. Manny Farber, "Times Square Moviegoers," *The Nation*, July 4, 1953; repr. in *Cinema Nation: The Best Writing on Film from "The Nation," 1913–2000*, ed. Carl Bromley (New York: Thunder's Mouth Press, 2000), 405.

68. Ibid.

69. Mickey Spillane, *One Lonely Night* (New York: Signet, 1951), 24.

70. Manny Farber, "Blame the Audience" (1952); repr. in Farber, *Negative Space*, 55.

71. Mekas, *Movie Journal*, 75.

72. Pauline Kael, "Circles and Squares," *Film Quarterly* 16, no. 3 (spring 1963): 12–26, 20.

73. Pauline Kael, *Going Steady* (London: Temple Smith, 1970), 115, 129.

74. John Simon, *Movies into Film: Film Criticism, 1967–1970* (New York: Dial, 1971), 2.

75. Juan A. Suárez, *Pop Modernism: Noise and the Reinvention of the Everyday* (Urbana: University of Illinois Press, 2007), 64–65.

76. Raymond Durgnat, *Films and Feelings* (London: Faber and Faber, 1967), 145.

77. Laura Mulvey, *Fetishism and Curiosity* (London: BFI, 1996), 19–28, 20.

78. When UK students leave school at the age of sixteen (fifteen before 1972), they may choose to continue schooling at a "further education college" (FEC). If they prefer to stay on at school until they reach eighteen years of age, they can enroll in university (higher education). The liberal and general studies courses I refer to here were aimed at fifteen- to eighteen-year-olds who were employed but as part of their training (e.g., hairdressing, car mechanics, etc.) were expected to attend an FEC one day a week, hence "day release."

79. Jim Kitses, *Talking about the Cinema: Film Studies for Young People* (London: British Film Institute, 1974), 11.

80. For a comprehensive history of film and the British education system and its institutions, written by a key participant, see Terry Bolas, *Screen Education: From Film Appreciation to Media Studies* (Bristol: Intellect Press, 2009).

81. Reports from Wood, Dyer, and Wollen on their courses and experience of their new university posts are published in *Screen Education* 19 (summer 1976): 51–60.

82. Alan Lovell, *Don Siegel: American Cinema* (London: BFI, 1968), 41.

83. On these shifts see Philip Rosen, "Screen and 1970s Film Theory," in *Inventing Film Studies*, ed. Lee Grieveson and Haidee Wasson (Durham, NC: Duke University Press, 2008), 264–97; and Peter Stanfield, "Notes toward a History of the Edinburgh International Film Festival, 1969–77," *Film International* 2, no. 4 (summer 2008): 62–71. The politics and key figures at the BFI in the 1960s and 1970s are discussed in Colin McArthur, "Two Steps Forward, One Step Back: Cultural Struggle in the British Film Institute," *Journal of Popular British Cinema* 4 (2001): 112–27.

84. Stuart Hall and Paddy Whannel, *The Popular Arts* (London: Hutchinson Educational, 1964), 15. See also Paddy Whannel's obituary in *Screen Education* 35 (summer 1980): 3–4.

85. Alan Lovell, *Don Siegel: American Cinema*, rev. ed. (London: BFI, 1975), 4.

86. Ibid., 8–9. The effect of this on the discussion of action movies can be seen in the debates that swirled around *Dirty Harry*; see, e.g., Anthony Chase, "The Strange Romance of 'Dirty Harry' Callahan and Ann Mary Deacon," *Velvet Light Trap* 4 (1972): 2–7. To my knowledge it was not until 2002 that a journal article on the film ignored its social and political ramifications and focused exclusively on formal and stylistic questions; not surprisingly the article was written by Richard Combs, "Degrees of Separation," *Film Comment*, July/Aug. 2002, 50–53.

87. Colin McArthur, *Underworld USA* (London: Secker and Warburg, 1972), 150.

88. Ibid., 161.

89. Jim Kitses, *Horizons West* (London: Thames and Hudson, 1969), 8.

90. Ibid., 27.

91. Ed Buscombe, "Ideas of Authorship," *Screen* 14, no. 3 (autumn 1973); repr. in *Theories of Authorship*, ed. John Caughie (London: Routledge, 1981), 22–34, 32, 32–33 (page citations are to the reprint).

92. Steve Neale, *Genre* (London: BFI, 1980), 4–5.

93. For an analysis of the Cinema One and Studio Vista film series see Mark Betz, "Little Books," in Grieveson and Wasson, *Inventing Film Studies*, 319–49.

94. Jim Kitses, *Gun Crazy* (London: BFI, 1996).

95. Colin McArthur, *Dialectic! Left Film Journalism: A Selection of Articles from Tribune* (London: Key Texts, 1982). During the early 1980s McArthur was a regular contributor to the bit-part magazine *The Movie: The Illustrated History of the Cinema*; see, e.g., issue 54 (1981), in which he writes on gangster movies and Edward G. Robinson. He retired from the BFI in 1984. His publications on film and national identity include *Scotch Reels* (London: BFI, 1982); and *"Brigadoon," "Braveheart," and the Scots: Distortions of Scotland in Hollywood Cinema*, (London: I. B. Taurus, 2003).

96. Ed Buscombe, "The Idea of Genre in the American Cinema," *Screen* 11/12 (1970): 33–45.

97. Ian Cameron and Douglas Pye, eds., *The Movie Book of the Western* (London: Studio Vista, 1996), 11.

98. Laura Mulvey, "Visual Pleasure and Narrative Cinema," *Screen* 16, no. 3 (1975): 6–18; Laura Mulvey, "After Thoughts on 'Visual Pleasure and Narrative Cinema' inspired by *Duel in the Sun*," *Framework* 15/16/17 (summer 1981): 12–15.

99. Laura Mulvey and Peter Wollen (with Lee Grieveson), "From Cinephilia to Film Studies," in Grieveson and Wasson, *Inventing Film Studies*, 217–32.

CHAPTER 2   A GENEALOGY OF PULP

1. Michael Denning, *Mechanic Accents: Dime Novels and Working-Class Culture in America* (London: Verso, 1987).

2. Marcus Klein, *Easterns, Westerns, and Private Eyes: American Matters, 1870–1900* (Madison: University of Wisconsin Press, 1994).

3. John Locke writes: "Through the Thirties, the paper and the type of fiction printed thereupon merged in meaning" (John Locke, *Pulp Fictioneers: Adventures in the Story Telling Business* [Silver Spring, MD: Adventure House, 2004], 12).

4. Alvin Barclay, "Magazines for Morons," *New Republic*, Aug. 28, 1929, 41–44.

5. Locke, *Pulp Fictioneers*, 12. *Webster's Dictionary* does not provide a definition of *pulp* as a magazine or story type in its 1932 edition.

6. Richard Ohmann, *Selling Culture: Magazines, Markets, and Class at the Turn of the Century* (London: Verso, 1996).

7. Erin A. Smith, *Hard-Boiled: Working-Class Readers and Pulp Magazines* (Philadelphia: Temple University Press, 2000).

8. Sean McCann, *Gumshoe America: Hard-Boiled Crime Fiction and the Rise and Fall of New Deal Liberalism* (Durham, NC: Duke University Press, 2000), 50.

9. Arthur J. Burks, "Sweat Shop," *Writer's Digest*, July 1935; repr. in Locke, *Pulp Fictioneers*, 68–72, 70.

10. Bill Brown, ed., *Reading the West: An Anthology of Dime Westerns* (Boston: Bedford Editions, 1997), 27.

11. Robert Silverberg, "My Life as a Pornographer," in *Sin-A-Rama: Sleaze Sex Paperbacks of the 1960s*, ed. Brittany Daly et al. (Los Angeles: Feral House, 2005), 15.

12. Steven Heller, "Blood, Sweat, and Tits: A History of Men's Adventure Magazines," in *Men's Adventure Magazines* (New York: Taschen, 2008), 14. See also Adam Parfrey, *It's a Man's World: Men's Adventure Magazines, the Postwar Pulps* (Los Angeles: Feral House, 2003).

13. Letter republished in Locke, *Pulp Fictioneers*, 56.

14. Barclay, "Magazines for Morons," 42.

15. The *New Republic* article drew one defender of pulp out of the woodpile. In a letter published in a subsequent edition the correspondent argued that not all wood-pulps were of the poor quality ascribed by Barclay and that many had an authenticity in terms of detail and setting—"a tang of reality"—not found elsewhere. See the *New Republic*, Oct. 2, 1929, 177.

16. McCann, *Gumshoe America*, 52–53.

17. Ibid., 51.

18. Smith, *Hard-Boiled*, 32.

19. Ibid., 27.

20. Barclay, "Magazines for Morons," 42–43.

21. See, e.g., James Naremore, *Something More Than Night: Film Noir in Its Contexts* (Berkeley: University of California Press, 1998), 51. Naremore is particularly insightful on Hammett's and Chandler's shift from the pulps to writing for Knopf, and the movie adaptations that followed.

22. Raymond Chandler to Hardwick Moseley, April 23, 1949, in *Selected Letters of Raymond Chandler*, ed. Frank MacShane (London: Jonathan Cape, 1981), 172–74.

23. See William F. Nolan, *The Black Mask Boys: Masters in the Hard-Boiled School of Detective Fiction* (New York: William Morrow, 1985), 19–34.

24. Ibid., 267.

25. This is a composite of the adjective and nouns used on the paperback covers of his first seven novels. The sales figures for Spillane are notoriously difficult to authenticate; the figure of seventeen million is taken from Kenneth C. Davis, *Two-Bit Culture: The Paperbacking of America* (Boston: Houghton Mifflin, 1984), 180.

26. Ibid., 147.

27. For a history of the development of cultural elitism see Lawrence W. Levine, *Highbrow/Lowbrow: The Emergence of Cultural Hierarchy in America* (Cambridge: Harvard University Press, 1990).

28. Quoted in Davis, *Two-Bit Culture*, 232–33.

29. Ibid., 237.

30. Philip Wylie, "The Crime of Mickey Spillane," *Good Housekeeping*, Feb. 1955, 54–55, 207–9.

31. Ibid.

32. Albert E. Kahn, *The Game of Death: Effects of the Cold War on Our Children* (New York: Cameron and Kahn, 1953), 92.

33. Bernard Iddings Bell, *Crowd Culture: An Examination of the American Way of Life* (New York: Harper and Row, 1952), 31.

34. Ibid., 46. For a similar take on Spillane as symptom of moral malaise see Fredrick Lewis Allen, "Dames and Death," *Harper's*, May 1952, 99–101.

35. Christopher La Farge, "Mickey Spillane and His Bloody Hammer," *Saturday Review*, Nov. 6, 1954, 11–12, 54–59; repr. in *Mass Culture: The Popular Arts in America*, ed. Bernard Rosenberg and David Manning White (Glencoe, IL: Free Press, 1957), 176–85.

36. In response to a letter decrying Spillane's use of racist terminology Signet used the same defense as Spillane, claiming that the work of highbrow authors covered similar territory: "Your criticism of the phrases dinge-joints, jigs, high-yellow, reflect similar criticism we have had about such authors as Farrell, Caldwell, Faulkner and Thomas Wolfe. When appropriate to the character and his background we cannot forbid such terms to an author—unless he is speaking in his own person, or is intentionally offensive" (Letter from Donald Demarest [asst. editor], Jan. 10, 1949, General Correspondence, 1948–51, Box 68 1700, New American Library archives, Fales Collection, New York University; hereafter NAL archives).

37. Wylie, "The Crime of Mickey Spillane," 207.

38. Richard W. Johnston, "Death's Fair-Haired Boy: Sex and Fury Sell 13 Million Books for Mickey Spillane," *Life*, June 23, 1952, 79, 82, 85–86, 89–90, 92, 95.

39. *Pageant*, July 1954, 140–45.

40. *Picture Scope*, Sept. 1954), 34–38.

41. Dwight Macdonald, "A Theory of Mass Culture," *Diogenes* 3 (summer 1953): 1–17; repr. in Rosenberg and White *Mass Culture*, 59–73, 62 (page citations refer to the reprint).

42. George Orwell, "Raffles and Miss Blandish," *Horizon*, Oct. 1944; repr. in Rosenberg and White, *Mass Culture*, 154–64, 154 (page citations refer to the reprint).

43. The essay is reprinted in Rosenberg and White, *Mass Culture*, 149–53; and in *Detective Fiction: A Collection of Critical Essays*, ed. Robin W. Winks (Englewood Cliffs, NJ: Prentice-Hall, 1980), 35–40.

44. One might also add to this list David Bazelon, "Dashiell Hammett's Private Eye," *Commentary* 7 (1949): 467–72; Malcolm Cowley, "Sex Murder Incorporated," *New Republic*, Feb. 11, 1952, 17–18; Victor Ferkiss, "Cops, Robbers, and Citizens," *Commonweal* 62 (1955): 251–53; W. H. Auden, "The Guilty Vicarage," *Harper's*, May 1948, 406–12; and Dorothy L. Sayers, "Aristotle on Detective Fiction," *English* (1936): 23–35. The Sayers and Auden pieces have been anthologized in Winks, *Detective Fiction*, which also contains Krutch's essay (mentioned by Wilson), "Only a Detective Story," first published in *The Nation* (1944), and a later essay by Jacques Barzun, "Detection and the Literary Arts" (1961). Chandler's essay "The Simple Art of Murder" was published in December 1944 in *Atlantic Monthly*. The Maugham essay is collected in *The Vagrant Mood: Six Essays* (New York: Vintage, 2001). I have not been able to locate the De Voto piece.

45. Wilson, "Who Cares Who Killed Roger Ackroyd?" 153.

46. Cowley, "Sex Murder Incorporated," 17–18.

47. Gershon Legman, *Love and Death: A Study in Censorship* (1949; repr., New York: Hacker Art Books, 1963), 94.

48. Donald Phelps, *Covering Ground: Essays for Now* (New York: Croton Press, 1969), 257.

49. Legman, *Love and Death*, 23.

50. Richard Hoggart, *Uses of Literacy* (Harmondsworth: Pelican, 1958), 246.

51. Ibid., 263.

52. BBFC examiner's notes on *I, the Jury*, Dec. 13, 1953. British Board of Film Classification archives, London.

53. *Picture Post*, Dec. 12, 1953.

54. MacShane, *Selected Letters of Raymond Chandler*, 310–11.

55. Correspondence between Arthur Baker and Signet, in General Correspondence, 1954–57, Box 68 1702, NAL archives.

56. "Product Digest," *Motion Picture Herald*, July 25, 1953, 1926.

57. James Ellroy, *My Dark Places: An L.A. Crime Memoir* (London: Arrow Books, 1997), 99.

58. Letter from Signet to E. P. Dutton discussing sale of Spillane to Hollywood, Aug. 22, 1951, General Correspondence, 1948–51, Box 68 1700, NAL archives.

59. David S. Reynolds, *Beneath the American Renaissance: The Subversive Imagination in the Age of Emerson and Melville* (Cambridge: Harvard University Press, 1988), 170.

60. Charles J. Rolo, "Simenon and Spillane: The Metaphysics of Murder for the Millions," in *New World Writing* 1 (1952): 234–45; repr. in Rosenberg and White, *Mass Culture*, 165–75.

61. Stuart Hall and Paddy Whannel, *The Popular Arts* (London: Hutchinson Educational, 1964), 159.

62. For another British scholar's insights into the world of Spillane see Jerry Palmer, "Mickey Spillane: A Reading," in *The Manufacture of News: Social Problems, Deviance, and the Mass Media*, ed. Stanley Cohen and Jock Young (London: Constable: 1973), 302–13.

63. Phelps, *Covering Ground*, 37.

64. Richard Roud, "The French Line," *Sight & Sound* 29, no. 4 (autumn 1960): 166–71.

65. Thomas Elsaesser, "Two Decades in Another Country: Hollywood and the Cinephiles," in *Superculture: American Popular Culture and Europe*, ed. C. W. E. Bigsby (Bowling Green, OH: Bowling Green University Popular Press, 1975), 199–216, 207.

66. Lawrence Alloway, "Notes on Abstract Art and the Mass Media," *Art News and Review*, Feb. 1960; repr. in *The Independent Group: Postwar Britain and the Aesthetics of Plenty*, ed. David Robbins (Cambridge: MIT Press, 1990), 168.

CHAPTER 3   A WORLD OF SMALL INSANITIES

1. Library of Congress, National Film Preservation Board, www.loc.gov/film/nfr2005.html.

2. Richard Maltby, "'The Problem of Interpretation . . .': Authorial and Institutional Intentions in and around *Kiss Me Deadly*," *Screening the Past*, July 2000, www.latrobe.edu.au/screeningthepast/firstrelease/fr0600/rmfr10e.htm.

3. *Variety Weekly*, April 20, 1955, 6.

4. *L.A. Examiner*, May 19, 1955.

5. *L.A. Times*, May 19, 1955.

6. *Hollywood Reporter*, May 20, 1955.

7. Richard Roud, *A Passion for Films: Henri Langlois and the Cinémathèque française* (London: Secker and Warburg, 1983), 99.

8. Jean Domarchi, "Knife in the Wound," *Cahiers du cinéma* 63 (Oct. 1956); repr. in *Cahiers du cinéma, the 1950s: Neo-Realism, Hollywood, New Wave*, ed. Jim Hillier (Cambridge: Harvard University Press, 1985), 235–47.

9. Claude Chabrol, "Evolution of the Thriller," *Cahiers du cinéma* 54 (Dec. 1955); repr. in Hillier, *Cahiers du cinéma, the 1950s*, 158–63.

10. François Truffaut, *The Films in My Life* (London: Allen Lane, 1980), 93–94.

11. Jacques Rivette, "Notes on a Revolution," *Cahiers du cinéma* 54 (Dec. 1955); repr. in Hillier, *Cahiers du cinema, the 1950s*, 94–97.

12. Roger Tailleur, "The Advent of Robert Aldrich," *Positif* 16 (May 1956); repr. in translation in *Positif: 50 Years: Selections from the French Journal*, ed. Michel Ciment and Laurence Kardish (New York: Museum of Modern Art, 2002), 31–42.

13. Writing in 1960, Raymond Durgnat thought that the film's "quadrangular Mondrian planes" were "bathed" in a de Chirico light (Raymond Durgnat, "The Apotheosis of Va-Va-Voom: Aldrich and *Kiss Me Deadly*," *Motion* [1960]: 30–34). Writing in 1977, Jack Shadoian also noted the film's surrealist tendency, its "carefully and fastidiously distorted" world. He also considered the film's "cold design" to be like "a modernist painting in black and white" (Jack Shadoian, *Dreams and Dead Ends: The American Gangster/Crime Film* [Cambridge: MIT Press, 1977], 268). Perhaps Shadoian had in mind a black-and-white abstract expressionist painting by Willem De Kooning or Jackson Pollack, or Franz Kline, or Robert Motherwell? The link would have been supported, I think, by the British art critic Lawrence Alloway, who wrote on both *Kiss Me Deadly* and abstract expressionism: "I felt that the painting I liked and the mass media product which I liked was coming from the United States rather than the accustomed source in Europe. So that linked—it was natural, therefore—to like Hollywood and Jackson Pollock" (quoted in Anne Massey, *The Independent Group: Modernism and Mass Culture in Britain, 1945–59* [Manchester: Manchester University Press, 1995], 77).

14. James Naremore, "Authorship and the Cultural Politics of Film Criticism," *Film Quarterly* 44, no. 1 (autumn 1990): 14–23.

15. Louis Seguin, "Kiss Me Mike," *Bizarre* 2 (Oct. 1955), 68–71. Part of this review is translated into English in Garrett White's foreword to A. I. Bezzerides, *Thieves' Market* (Berkeley: University of California Press, 1997), xii–xiii. White's foreword is the best introduction to Bezzerides's work in fiction and film.

16. Robin Walz, *Pulp Surrealism: Insolent Popular Culture in Early Twentieth-Century Paris* (Berkeley: University of California Press, 2000), 3.

17. Morris Gilbert, "Parisian Cinema Chatter," *New York Times*, Feb. 9, 1930.

18. When *L'Age d'or* opened at Studio 28 in October, it also played on a mixed bill, this time with a Disney or Fleischer cartoon, a Soviet comedy, and Abric and Gorel's "Paris Bestiaux" (Paul Hammond, *L'Age d'or* [London: BFI, 1997]). Michel Gorel was a key film critic for *Cinémonde* and coined the term *poetic realism*. He wrote reviews of Studio 28 screenings for the mainstream press and was passionate about documentary.

19. G[avin] L[ambert], review of *Kiss Me Deadly*, *Monthly Film Bulletin* 22 (June–July 1955): 120.

20. See Steve Neale, *Genre and Hollywood* (London: Routledge, 2000), 151–78.

21. The quote comes from J. H. Matthews, *Surrealism and Film* (Ann Arbor: University of Michigan Press, 1971); cited in Walz, *Pulp Surrealism*, 10.

22. *Real*, Aug. 1955, n.p.

23. Lambert, review of *Kiss Me Deadly*, 120.

24. BBFC examiner's report on *I, the Jury*, Category "X" shown at the Eros Cinema, Catford, Lewisham, April 1, 1954. British Board of Film Classification archives, London.

25. BBFC examiner's notes on *I, the Jury*, Dec. 13, 1953. British Board of Film Classification archives, London.

26. Mickey Spillane, *Kiss Me, Deadly* (London: Corgi, 1961), 82.

27. Mark Murphy, "Sex, Sadism and Scripture," *True: The Men's Magazine*, July 1952, 17–19, 81–83.

28. Quoted in Lee Server, "The Thieves' Market: A. I. Bezzerides in Hollywood," in *The Big Book of Noir*, ed. Ed Gorman, Lee Server, and Martin H. Greenberg (New York: Carroll and Graf, 1998), 115–22, 121.

29. *Lowdown*, Aug. 1955, 24–25, 42.

30. Victor Weybright, Signet editor, to Peggy Waller at publishers E. P. Dutton, Jan. 30, 1950, General Correspondence, 1948–51, Box 68 1700, New American Library archives, Fales Collection, New York University; hereafter NAL archives.

31. Letter dated March 1, 1951, General Correspondence, 1948–51, Box 68 1700, NAL archives.

32. Charles J. Rolo, "Simenon and Spillane: The Metaphysics of Murder for the Millions," in *Mass Culture: The Popular Arts in America*, ed. Bernard Rosenberg and David Manning White (Glencoe, IL: Free Press, 1957), 168.

33. Weybright to Dutton, Sept. 12, 1949, *My Gun Is Quick* file, Box 68 1709, NAL archives.

34. Victor Weybright to Mickey Spillane, July 31, 1953, General Correspondence, 1948–51, Box 68 1700, NAL archives.

35. Ibid.

36. Quoted in Lawrence Alloway, *Violent America: The Movies, 1946–1964* (New York: Museum of Modern Art, 1971), 61.

37. John Landau, "Elizabethan Art in a Mickey Spillane Setting," *Theatre Arts* 39, no. 8 (Aug. 1955): 25, 87.

38. Michael Denning, *Mechanic Accents: Dime Novels and Working-Class Culture in America* (London: Verso, 1987), 200.

39. Victor Weybright to Alfred Knopf, Nov. 23, 1951, General Correspondence, 1948–51, Box 68 1700, NAL archives.

40. Letter dated Dec. 17, 1951, General Correspondence, 1948–51, Box 68 1700, NAL archives.

41. Letter dated Dec. 19, 1951, General Correspondence, 1948–51, Box 68 1700, NAL archives.

42. Tailleur "The Advent of Robert Aldrich."

43. Other than the "screen test," compressed (and extended) versions of Spillane's work are found in the newspaper comic strip, *From the Files of . . . Mike Hammer* (Phoenix Features Syndicate, 1953–54); repr. in Catherine Yronwode and Max Allan Collins, *Mickey Spillane's Mike Hammer: The Comic Strip* (Park Forest, IL: Ken Pierce, 1982); the radio show, *The Mickey Spillane Mystery: That Hammer Guy* (Mutual Radio Network, 1953), with Larry Haines and Ted De Corsia; the television series *Mickey Spillane's Mike Hammer* (1958–59), which ran for seventy-eight episodes and starred Darren McGavin; and a long-playing phonographic album that Spillane had a hand in producing.

44. Richard W. Johnston, "Death's Fair-Haired Boy: Sex and Fury Sell 13 Million Books for Mickey Spillane," *Life*, June 23, 1952, 79, 82, 85–86, 89–90, 92, 95.

45. Mickey Spillane, "The Screen Test of Mike Hammer," *MALE*, July 1953, 11–15.

46. Dan Nadel, *Art in Time: Unknown Comic Book Adventures* (New York: Abrams ComicArts, 2010), 150.

47. The strip ran from 1953 to 1954.

48. Raymond Borde and Etienne Chaumeton, *A Panorama of American Film Noir, 1941–1953*, trans. Paul Hammond (San Francisco: City Lights, 2002), 110–11.

49. Ian and Elisabeth Cameron, *The Heavies* (London: Studio Vista, 1967).

50. Blaise Cendrars, *Panorama de la pègre* (1935); quoted in and translated by Walz, *Pulp Surrealism*, 153.

51. The Bradbury Building was also used as a location in Joseph Losey's *M* (1951) and in Douglas Sirk's *Shockproof* (1949); much later it was used again in Ridley Scott's *Blade Runner* (1982).

52. Will Straw to the author, email correspondence, Nov. 2005.

53. *I, the Jury* screenplay, by Harry Essex, dated March 7, 1953, revised pages March 17, 1953, New York Public Library.

54. Max Allan Collins, "Mickey Spillane in Hollywood," *Psychotronic Video*, no. 28 (1998): 34–42.

55. Kevin Heffernan, *Ghouls, Gimmicks, and Gold: Horror Films and the American Movie Business, 1953–1968* (Durham, NC: Duke University Press, 2004), 37–38.

56. Victor Saville, "Shadows on the Screen" (Nov. 1974), unpublished manuscript, p. 229, British Film Institute National Library; unless otherwise noted, subsequent quotations attributed to Saville are from this manuscript.

57. In a press release from the public relations company Rogers and Cowan acting on behalf of Saville, it was noted he had bought the five-year exclusive picture rights to all of Spillane's novels, the $250,000 deal was announced on Friday, Dec. 19, 1952; see General Correspondence, 1948–51, Box 68 1700, NAL archives. Once Spillane realized the amount of money the films were making and how little he would profit from them, he sought to change the contract he had with Saville. Beyond his voicing of discontent with the deal to his editors at NAL there is no indication in the archives of how the matter was or was not resolved. It does appear, however, that Saville kept the film rights to the four novels he adapted as he was still the owner when *I, the Jury* was remade in 1982.

58. "Films the plot of which hinges upon various forms of aberrant behavior, especially amnesia, have become run of the mine" (Franklin Fearing, "Psychology and the Films," *Hollywood Quarterly* 2, no.2 [Jan. 1947]: 118).

59. *Picture Post*, Dec. 12, 1953, 48.

60. J. P. Telotte, "The Fantastic Realism of Film Noir: *Kiss Me Deadly*," *Wide Angle* 14, no. 1 (Jan. 1992): 4–18.

61. *Kiss Me Deadly* screenplay, 4. There are two undated versions of the screenplay held by the New York Public Library: a white paper version (130 pages) and a blue paper version (128 pages). They have been bound into the same volume. Unless otherwise noted all references are to the earlier white version.

62. It is useful to think about the opening of the film in the context of the various title sequence innovations that were taking place during the 1950s. See Will Straw, "Ornament, Entrance and the Theme Song," in *Cinesonic: The World of Sound in Film*, ed. Philip Brophy (North Ryde, NSW: Australian Film Television and Radio School, 1999), 213–28.

63. Mickey Spillane, *Kiss Me, Deadly* (New York: Signet, 1953), 8.

64. For contemporary accounts of misogyny and Spillane see Fredrick Lewis Allen, "Dames and Death," *Harper's*, May 1952, 99–101; see also Malcolm Cowley, "Sex Murder Incorporated," *New Republic*, Feb. 11, 1952, 17–18.

65. *Kiss Me Deadly* screenplay, 11–12.

66. *Kiss Me Deadly* screenplay, blue paper version, 12.

67. Mickey Spillane, *The Big Kill* (New York: Signet, 1951), 7.

68. *Kiss Me Deadly* screenplay, 89.

69. Ibid., 22.

70. Ibid., 32–34.

71. Quoted in Dan Glaister, "Girl Magnet, Bunny Magnate: The Movie," *Guardian*, June 26, 2007, 19.

72. "Mickey and His Mayhem Molls," *Real: The Exciting Magazine for Men* (Aug. 1955), n.p.

73. Sean McCann, "Dark Passages: Jazz and Civil Liberty in the Postwar Crime Film," in *"Un-American" Hollywood: Politics and Film in the Blacklist Era*, ed. Frank Krutnik, Brian Neve, Steve Neale, and Peter Stanfield (New Brunswick, NJ: Rutgers University Press, 2007), 113–29, 116–17.

74. Ibid., 117.

75. Durgnat, "The Apotheosis of Va-Va-Voom," 33: "A Chirico light bathes quadrangular Mondrian planes. Staircases become tunnels, galleries. The film's spiritual ancestry is not far to seek. Where have we previously seen the quiet yet terse rectangularities of Mike Hammer's well-appointed apartment?—of course, in Fritz Lang's *Siegfried*, only there it was flagstones of a medieval palace. And *Kiss Me Deadly* is the best crime fantasy since *The Testament of Dr. Mabuse*. The plot mechanics are less outrageous, the mood less realistic, more formal, chilly and archaic, but the characters seem more dehumanised."

76. An Italian exchange student in one of my classes on *Kiss Me Deadly* in the spring of 2007 pointed out that the pictures hanging in William Mist's gallery are not a studio artist's rudimentary attempt to replicate a modern art idiom but are in fact reproductions of the work of some of the leading contemporary Italian painters: Giorgio Morandi, Carlo Carra, and Massimo Campigli. These painters were part of the Metafisca artistic movement and Realismo Magico. I thank Enzo Lauria for this insight. Another student, whose name is now lost to me, pointed out that Soberin quotes Jesus to his disciples before the crucifixion: "Where I am going, it is not possible for you to go," which is from John 13:36. James Naremore notes the film also used snatches of music composed by Pyotr Ilich Tchaikovsky and Friedrich Flotow (see Naremore, *More Than Night*, 153).

77. Saville, "Shadows on the Screen," 129.

78. British Film Institute, ScreenOnLine, "Victor Saville," www.screenonline.org.uk/people/id/449163.

79. Saville, "Shadows on the Screen," 230.

80. Ibid.

81. Paul Johnson, "Sex, Snobbery and Sadism," *New Statesman*, April 5, 1958, 430, 432. See also Colin McArthur, *Underworld USA* (London: Secker and Warburg, 1972), 51; and Jerry Palmer's analysis of Spillane and Fleming in "Thrillers: The Deviant behind the Consensus," in *Politics and Deviance*, ed. Ian Taylor and Laurie Taylor (Harmondsworth: Pelican, 1973), 136–56.

CHAPTER 4   AMERICAN PRIMITIVE

1. Samuel Fuller, *144 Piccadilly* (London: New English Library, 1973), 8.

2. The novel had been first published in Britain a year earlier in a NEL hardback edition. Its first U.S. publication was in 1971 by Richard W. Baron, New York.

3. See Samuel Fuller, *A Third Face: My Writing, Fighting, and Filmmaking* (New York: Alfred A. Knopf, 2002). This autobiography lists eleven novels published in his lifetime but misses *The Rifle*, published in Dutch translation as *Het Geweer* (Antwerp: Soethoudt, 1981).

4. Fuller, *144 Piccadilly*, n.p.

5. Ibid., 10.

6. Phil Cohen, "144," *Oz* 45 (Nov. 1972): 10, 41.

7. Frank Mallen, *Sauce for the Gander: The Amazing Story of a Fabulous Newspaper* (White Plains, NY: Baldwin Books, 1954), 173.

8. For a gallery of composites that accompanied the more salacious and scandalous stories see the illustrated section in Mallen, *Sauce for the Gander*.

9. Samuel Fuller, *The Dark Page* (1944; New York: Avon Books, 1983), 146.

10. David Cochran, *America Noir: Underground Writers and Filmmakers of the Postwar Era* (Washington: Smithsonian Institution Press, 2000), 136.

11. *Variety*, July 1, 1963; *Hollywood Reporter*, July 1, 1963; *Los Angeles Times*, Sept. 10, 1963; *Cue*, Sept. 14, 1963; *Film Quarterly* 17, no. 2 (winter 1963–64); *Cinema* (Aug. 1963); *Herald Tribune*, quoted in J. Hoberman, "Crazy for You," *Village Voice*, Feb. 17, 1998. Unless otherwise noted all reviews are culled from the *Shock Corridor* cutting file, Margaret Herrick Library, Academy of Motion Picture Arts and Sciences (hereafter MHL-AMPAS).

12. Robert G. Dickson, review of *Shock Corridor*, *Film Quarterly* 17, no. 2 (winter 1963–64): 62.

13. "Soap Opera Prostitution," *Cosmopolitan*, June 1964, clipping, Fuller file, MHL-AMPAS.

14. Handwritten note appended to letter from BBFC addressed to Allied Artists, Dec. 30, 1965, BBFC *Shock Corridor* file, MHL-AMPAS.

15. BBFC to Warner Pathe Film Dist. Ltd., Nov. 11, 1963, BBFC *Shock Corridor* file, MHL-AMPAS.

16. Ibid.

17. Examiner's report on *Shock Corridor*, Oct. 2, 1963, BBFC *Shock Corridor* file, MHL-AMPAS.

18. Bertrand Tavernier, "Quelques notes sur un visionnaire," *L'Avant-scène* 54 (Dec. 1965): 6–7. Translated by Ronald Sonnet, with thanks.

19. Ronnie Scheib, "Tough Nuts to Crack: Fuller's *Shock Corridor*," *Framework* 19 (1982): 36.

20. Luc Moullet, "Sam Fuller: In Marlowe's Footsteps," *Cahiers du cinéma* 93 (March 1959); repr. in translation in *Cahiers du cinéma, the 1950s: Neo-Realism, Hollywood, New Wave*, ed. Jim Hillier (Cambridge: Harvard University Press, 1985), 145–55, 154 (all page citations are to the reprint).

21. Andrew Sarris, *The American Cinema: Directors and Directions, 1929–1968* (New York: Dutton, 1968), 93.

22. Ibid., 94.

23. George Lipsitz, *Time Passages: Collective Memory and American Popular Culture* (Minneapolis: University of Minnesota Press, 1990), 181.

24. Jack Flam with Miriam Deutch, eds., *Primitivism and Twentieth-Century Art: A Documentary History* (Berkeley: University of California Press, 2003), xiii.

25. Marybeth Hamilton, *In Search of the Blues* (London: Jonathan Cape, 2007).

26. David Will, "Classic American Cinema: Sam Fuller," *Framework* 19 (1982): 20.

27. Key French publications include a special issue dedicated to Fuller of *Présence du cinéma* 19 (Dec. 1963–Jan. 1964); a dossier on Fuller in *Cahiers du cinéma* 193 (Sept. 1967); the screenplay to *Shock Corridor*, *L'Avant-scène* 54 (Dec. 1965). There have been two books in French dedicated to Fuller: Olivier Amiel, *Samuel Fuller* (Paris: Henri Veyrier, 1985); and Jean Narboni and Noël Simsolo, *Il était une fois—Samuel Fuller: Histoires d'Amérique* (Paris: Cahiers du cinéma, 1986).

28. See Peter Wollen, writing under the pseudonym Lee Russell, *New Left Review* 1, no. 23 (Jan.–Feb. 1964): 86–89.

29. Quoted in Don Ranvaud, "An Interview with Sam Fuller," *Framework* 19 (1982): 26.

30. Will, "Classic American Cinema," 20.

31. See Peter Stanfield, "Notes toward a History of the Edinburgh International Film Festival, 1969–77," *Film International* 6, no. 4 (summer 2008): 62–71.

32. Lee Russell, "Howard Hawks," *New Left Review* 24 (March–April 1964); repr. in Jim Hillier and Peter Wollen, eds., *Howard Hawks: American Artist* (London: BFI, 1996): 83–86.

33. Edinburgh International Film Festival program (1969), 36.

34. David Will and Peter Wollen, eds., *Samuel Fuller* (Edinburgh: Edinburgh Film Festival, 1969).

35. Kingsley Canham, "Samuel Fuller's Action Films," and Colin McArthur, "Samuel Fuller's Gangster Films," *Screen* 10, no. 6 (Nov./Dec. 1969): 80–101. This issue also includes a review of the EIFF book (104). See also Colin McArthur, *Underworld USA* (London: Secker and Warburg, 1972).

36. See Peter Wollen, "Notes towards a Structural Analysis of the Films of Samuel Fuller," *Cinema* 1 (Dec. 1968): 26–29; "Samuel Fuller: A Cinema Interview," *Cinema* 5 (Feb. 1970): 6–8, and Paul Joannides, review of *Samuel Fuller*, ed. David Will and Peter Wollen, *Cinema* 5 (Feb. 1970): 9.

37. Kingsley Canham, "The World of Samuel Fuller," *Film*, no.55 (summer 1969): 4–10; *Brighton Film Review* (Sam Fuller Special!) 16 (Jan. 1970); Phil Hardy, *Samuel Fuller* (London: Studio Vista, 1970).

38. Nicholas Garnham, *Samuel Fuller* (London: Secker and Warburg, 1971).

39. In an online essay marking the death of Ian Cameron, the publisher of *Movie*, Perkins notes that Cameron was responsible for writing the first appreciations of Fuller in the journal *Oxford Opinion*; see V. F. Perkins, "Ian Cameron: A Tribute," *Movie: A Journal of Film Criticism*, no. 1, www2.warwick.ac.uk/fac/arts/film/movie/ (accessed Aug. 2010).

40. V. F. Perkins, "Merrill's Marauders," *Movie*, no. 2 (32). Issue 3 of the journal carried a small photo-spread on *Underworld USA* (8–9). *Movie*, no. 17 carried two interviews with Fuller, conducted by Stig Bjorkman and Mark Shivas (25–31).

41. See, e.g., Will and Wollen, *Samuel Fuller*.

42. V. F. Perkins, "UnAmerican Activities," *Movie*, no. 5 (3–6).

43. Peter Wollen, writing under the pseudonym Lee Russell, *New Left Review* 1, no. 23 (Jan.–Feb. 1964): 86–89.

44. Raymond Durgnat, "China Gate," in Will and Wollen, *Samuel Fuller*, 54.

45. Will and Wollen, *Samuel Fuller*, 10.

46. *Men Only*, June 1973, 34–38.

47. *L.A. Times*, May 30, 1953.

48. Greil Marcus, "Corrupting the Absolute" (1985), in *Ranters and Crowd Pleasers: Punk in Pop Music, 1977–92* (New York: Doubleday, 1993), 275–79.

49. Will and Wollen, *Samuel Fuller*, 35.

50. Joannides, "A Book Review," 9.

51. Gérard Gozlan, "The Delights of Ambiguity—In Praise of André Bazin," *Positif* 46 and 47 (June and July 1962); repr. in translation in Peter Graham, ed., *The French New Wave: Critical Landmarks* (London: BFI/Palgrave-Macmillan, 2009), 91–129.

52. J. Hoberman, "Three American Abstract Sensationalists," in *Vulgar Modernism: Writing on Movies and Other Media* (Philadelphia: Temple University Press, 1991), 23.

53. Ibid.

54. Michael Rogin, "Kiss Me Deadly: Communism, Motherhood, and Cold War Movies," *Representations* 6 (spring 1984): 1–36, 31.

55. Paul Willemen, "Edinburgh Debate," *Framework* 19 (1982): 48–50.

56. Will Straw, *Cyanide and Sin: Visualizing Crime in 1950s America* (New York: PPP Editions, 2006), 7.

57. See Jean-Louis Noames, "Entretien avec Samuel Fuller," *Présence du Cinéma* 19 (Dec. 1963–Jan. 1964): 1–19 (English translation published in Will and Wollen, *Samuel Fuller*, 91–125); Kingsley Canham, "I Shot Jesse James," in Will and Wollen, *Samuel Fuller*, 16; Sarris, *The American Cinema*, 93.

58. Quoted in Will and Wollen, *Samuel Fuller*, 94–95.

59. These stories are all reprinted in *The EC Archives: Two-Fisted Tales* (Timonium, MD: Gemstone, 2007).

60. For an account of the shifts in the address made to audiences by the World War II combat film see Jeanine Basinger, *The World War II Combat Film: Anatomy of a Genre* (Middletown, CT: Wesleyan University Press, 2003).

61. Dialogue is taken from the published screenplay in *Scenario Magazine* 4, no. 3 (fall 1998): 103.

62. Luc Sante, introduction to *New York Noir: Crime Photos from the Daily News Archive*, ed. William Hannigan (New York: Rizzoli, 1999), 8.

63. Hoberman, "Three American Abstract Sensationalists," 23.

64. Joannides, "A Book Review," 9.

65. Garnham, *Samuel Fuller*, 12.

66. Adam Parfrey, *It's a Man's World: Men's Adventure Magazines, the Postwar Pulps* (Los Angeles: Feral House, 2003), 215.

67. Ibid., 30.

68. Angela Carter discusses with Spillane the use of prostitutes in his fiction in *Men Only*, June 1973, 34–38.

69. See Michael Denning, *Mechanic Accents: Dime Novels and Working-Class Culture in America* (London: Verso, 1985), 200.

70. Samuel Fuller, "Les six commandments du film de guerre," *Présence du cinéma* 19 (Dec. 1963–Jan. 1964): 26; English translation in Will and Wollen, *Samuel Fuller*, 27.

71. Nicholas J. Cull, "Samuel Fuller on Lewis Milestone's *A Walk in the Sun* (1946): The Legacy of *All Quiet on the Western Front* (1930)," *Historical Journal of Film, Radio and Television* 20, no.1 (2000), 79–87.

72. Samuel Fuller, "Headlines to Headshots" (1974), repr. in *The Press: Observed and Projected*, ed. Philip French and Deac Rossell (London: BFI, 1991), 39–46. Coincidently, or not, the image of hoboes washing their feet in milk is used in William A. Wellman's *Wild Boys of the Road* (1933).

73. Parfrey, *It's a Man's World*, 28.

74. Alvin Barclay "Magazines for Morons," *New Republic*, Aug. 28, 1929, 43.

75. Letters page, *Two-Fisted Tales*, no. 24, Nov.–Dec. 1951; repr. in *The EC Archives: Two-Fisted Tales*, 2:28. Kurtzman's obsession with detail in his EC stories is documented in

David Hajdu, *The Ten-Cent Plague: The Great Comic Book Scare and How It Changed America* (New York: Farrar, Straus and Giroux, 2008), 197.

76. See, e.g., the interview by Max Allan Collins, "Mickey Spillane in Hollywood," *Psychotronic Video*, no. 28 (1998): 34–42.

77. "Producer Sam Fuller Divorced," *Hollywood Citizen News*, Oct. 8, 1959, clippings file, MHL-AMPAS.

78. *Hollywood Reporter*, Jan. 18, 1957, 2.

79. *Hollywood Reporter*, Feb. 6, 1957, 3.

80. *Hollywood Reporter*, Feb. 21, 1957, 1.

81. *Hollywood Reporter*, March 19, 1957, 3.

82. *Hollywood Reporter*, Feb. 28, 1957, 3.

83. *Hollywood Reporter*, March 8, 1957, 2.

84. *Hollywood Reporter*, March 15, 1957, 1.

85. *Hollywood Reporter*, March 27, 1957, 3.

86. Samuel Fuller to Andrew Sarris, *Film Culture*, no. 32 (spring 1964); Samuel Fuller, "What Is a Film?" *Cinema* 2, no. 2 (July 1964).

CHAPTER 5   AUTHENTICATING PULP

1. Jim Thompson, *A Hell of a Woman* (Berkeley: Black Lizard Books, 1983), 93.

2. Richard Corliss, "By the Book," *Film Comment*, March/April 1991, 42.

3. Maitland McDonagh, "Straight to Hell," *Film Comment*, Nov./Dec. 1990, 31.

4. *L.A. Times* quoted in Michael J. McCauley, *Jim Thompson: Sleep with the Devil* (New York: Mysterious Press, 1991), 302; William Stevenson, "Jim Thompson Mania," *Variety*, Aug. 22, 1990, 91.

5. Corliss, "By the Book," 42.

6. "For better or worse, a scholarly industry, including incomprehensible structural analysis of Cain's work and the movies derived from it, was one of *Double Indemnity*'s unintended consequences. For better or worse, we are now required to take Jim Thompson—and Elmore Leonard—more seriously than we probably should in part because of the train of events Wilder set in motion in 1943. And that says nothing about enduring the *film noir* pastiches a couple of generations of impressionable film school graduates insist on turning out for us now" (Richard Schickel, *Double Indemnity* [London: BFI, 1992], 21).

7. Those not cited elsewhere in the text are Terry Curtis Fox et al., "City Knights," *Film Comment*, Oct./Nov. 1984, 30–49; Luc Sante, "The Gentrification of Crime," *New York Review of Books*, March 28, 1985, 18–20; Peter Prescott, "The Cirrhosis of the Soul," *Newsweek*, Nov. 17, 1986, 90; Malcolm Jones Jr., "Furtive Pleasures from a Pulp Master," *Time*, Feb. 4, 1991, 71; David Thomson, "The Whole Hell Catalog—Reconsideration: Jim Thompson," *New Republic*, April 15, 1985, 37.

8. Taken from King's foreword to the 1989 Blood & Guts edition of *The Killer Inside Me*.

9. R. V. Cassell, "The Killer Inside Me: Fear, Purgation, and the Sophoclean Light," in *Tough Guy Writers of the Thirties*, ed. David Madden (Carbondale: Southern Illinois University Press, 1968), 230–38.

10. Robert Polito, *Savage Art: A Biography of Jim Thompson* (New York: Alfred A. Knopf, 1996), 338–39.

11. Geoffrey O'Brien, *Hardboiled America: The Lurid Years of Paperbacks* (New York: Van Nostrand Reinhold, 1981). Other works that mine a similar vein include the contemporaneous publication by Piet Schreuder, *The Book of Paperbacks* (London: Virgin, 1981); and Lee Server, *Over My Dead Body: The Sensational Age of the American Paperback, 1945–1955* (San Francisco: Chronicle, 1994).

12. Other than those discussed in the text, important reissue series of hard-boiled writers included Ballantine reprints of Cornell Woolrich, edited by Francis M. Nevins Jr. (eleven volumes, 1982–84); the Blue Murder series, which focused on source novels of noir and crime films, initially published by Simon and Schuster (thirteen volumes, 1988–89) and subsequently by Xanadu Books (eleven volumes, 1990), edited by Maxim Jakubowski; Jakubowski was also responsible for the Zomba Black Box Thrillers series (nine volumes, 1983–84), and No Exit Press Vintage Crime, which republished crime writers of the 1920s and 1930s (eleven volumes, 1987–88).

13. O'Brien, *Hardboiled America*, 121.

14. Quoted in Polito, *Savage Art*, 339.

15. Lawrence Block, "A Tale of Pulp and Passion: The Jim Thompson Revival," *New York Times Book Review*, Oct. 14, 1990, 37–38.

16. Quoted in Polito, *Savage Art*, 365.

17. Luc Sante, review of *Savage Art: A Biography of Jim Thompson*, by Robert Polito, *New Republic*, Dec. 25, 1995, 34.

18. Roy Hoopes, *The Biography of James M. Cain* (Carbondale: Southern Illinois University Press, 1982), 246. As if revealing some kind of meaningful continuity between American crime writers, James Ellroy has similarly been likened to the Russian novelist: *Time Out* describes him as a "Tinseltown Dostoyevsky." Promotional blurb in James Ellroy, *L.A. Confidential* (London: Arrow, 1994).

19. Cassell, "The Killer Inside Me," 233.

20. James Naremore, *More Than Night: Film Noir in Its Contexts* (Berkeley: University of California Press, 1998), 220. Dennis Hopper described *The Hot Spot* in similar terms: "It's more like *Last Tango in Taylor* than *Gigi Goes to the Beach*" (quoted in R. J. Smith, "Star Complex," *Film Comment*, Jan./Feb. 1990, 4–6, 6).

21. See, e.g., Paula Rabinowitz, *Black and White and Noir: America's Pulp Modernism* (New York: Columbia University Press, 2002).

22. See, e.g., Juan A. Suárez, *Pop Modernism: Noise and the Reinvention of the Everyday* (Urbana: University of Illinois Press, 2007).

23. See, e.g., David Cochran, *America Noir: Underground Writers and Filmmakers of the Postwar Era* (Washington: Smithsonian Institution Press, 2000).

24. Jim Thompson, *Savage Night* (London: Corgi, 1988), 153.

25. Jim Thompson, *The Killer Inside Me* (Greenwich, CT: Gold Medal, 1965), 130.

26. Jim Thompson, *Nothing More Than Murder* (New York: Vintage Books, 1991), 26.

27. Sean McCann, *Gumshoe America: Hard-Boiled Crime Fiction and the Rise and Fall of New Deal Liberalism* (Durham, NC: Duke University Press, 2000), 212–13.

28. McCann, *Gumshoe America*, 218.

29. Jim Thompson, *The Killer Inside Me* (New York: Quill, 1983), 93.

30. For a discussion of Thompson and proletarian fiction see Mike Newirth, "The Prole Inside Me," *Baffler* 12 (1999): 90–96.

31. Polito, *Savage Art*, 9–10.

32. In particular, I'm thinking of Nick Cave, who was an early champion of Thompson in the British music press and who posed for publicity pictures alongside copies of Thompson reprints; but there is also Green on Red, who named their 1987 album after *The Killer Inside Me* and dedicated it to the memory of Thompson, and bands that have named themselves after Thompson's stories, such as Memphis's The Grifters and the psychedelic pop of This World, Then the Fireworks. Furthermore, see Greil Marcus's linking of Thompson with Dadaist cutups in the context of his history of punk, *Lipstick Traces: A Secret History of the Twentieth Century* (London: Secker and Warburg, 1989), 206. Discussing the influence of noir on the postpunk New York No Wave scene, the filmmaker Jim Jarmusch recalled, "When I met one of my oldest friends, Luc Santé, the writer, we met at Columbia as students, and we were both devouring Richard Stark, devouring Charles Willeford, all this stuff, before other people were. But that was a little before that downtown scene, or before our connection to it" (quoted in Alan Licht, "Invisible Jukebox," *Wire*, Nov. 2009, 22).

33. From the unfinished novel *The Horse in the Baby's Bathtub*, cited in Polito, *Savage Art*, 295.

34. Michael Herr, *Kubrick* (London: Picador, 2000), 41.

35. O'Brien, *Hard-Boiled America*, 123.

36. See Karen Angel, "Independent-Bookstore Presses Keep Alternative Voices Alive," *Publishers Weekly*, April 21, 1997, 24.

37. Raymond Borde and Etienne Chaumeton, *Panorama du film noir américain, 1941–1953* (Paris: Minuit, 1955); translated by Paul Hammond as *A Panorama of American Film Noir, 1941–1953* (San Francisco: City Lights, 2002), 15.

38. Marcel Duhamel, preface to Borde and Chaumeton, *A Panorama of American Film Noir, 1943–1951*, xxiii–xxv, xxv.

39. A bibliography of Thompson's French translations is found in *Polar: Le Magazine du policier*, May 1979, 28–31.

40. Smith, "Star Complex," 4.

41. Marc Vernet, "*Film Noir* on the Edge of Doom," in *Shades of Noir: A Reader*, ed. Joan Copjec (London: Verso, 1993), 1–31, 2 (my emphasis).

42. Ibid., 26. Vernet refers here to *Film Noir: An Encyclopedic Reference to the American Style*, edited by Alain Silver and Elizabeth Ward (Woodstock, NY: Overlook Press, 1979).

43. Vernet, "*Film Noir* on the Edge of Doom," 1.

44. Nicholas Christopher, *Somewhere in the Night: Film Noir and the American City* (New York: Owl Books, 1998), xii.

45. Naremore, *More Than Night*, 4.

46. Vernet, "*Film Noir* on the Edge of Doom," 26.

47. Paul Duncan, *Film Noir: Films of Trust and Betrayal* (Harpenden: Pocket Essentials, 2000), 41. As a domestic appliance the videotape recorder was first marketed in large numbers during the early 1980s, paralleling the popular recognition of film noir as a category of film and making it possible for consumers to amass large private collections of film noirs.

48. As well as the programming of repertory cinema or television seasons, or in the recording and cataloging of private videotape libraries.

49. Steve Neale, *Genre and Hollywood* (London: Routledge, 2000), 156.

50. Robert Cantwell, *Ethnomimesis: Folklife and the Representation of Culture* (Chapel Hill: University of North Carolina Press, 1993), 79.

51. O'Brien, *Hard-Boiled America*, 4.

52. Vernet, "*Film Noir* on the Edge of Doom," 2.

53. Alain Silver, introduction to *Film Noir Reader*, ed. Alain Silver and James Ursini (New York: Limelight, 1996), 3–15, 6.

54. Vernet, "*Film Noir* on the Edge of Doom," 1–2.

55. Neale, *Genre and Hollywood*, 173.

56. Christopher, *Somewhere in the Night*, 232.

57. Leighton Grist, "Moving Targets and Black Widows: Film Noir in Modern Hollywood," in *The Movie Book of Film Noir*, ed. Ian Cameron (London: Studio Vista, 1992), 267.

58. Edward Gallafent, "*Echo Park* Film Noir in the 'Seventies," in Cameron, *The Movie Book of Film Noir*, 254–85, 254.

59. Foster Hirsch, *Detours and Lost Highways: A Map of Neo-Noir* (New York: Limelight, 1999), 15.

60. Neale, *Genre and Hollywood*, 165.

61. Naremore, *More Than Night*, 2, 10.

62. See note 45 above.

63. Rick Altman, *Film/Genre* (London: BFI, 1999), 61.

64. For a brief discussion of the 1970s noir/detective parodies see David A. Cook, *Lost Illusions: American Cinema in the Shadow of Watergate and Vietnam, 1970–1979* (New York: Charles Scribner's Sons, 2000), 207.

65. Lawrence Alloway, *Violent America: The Movies, 1946–1964* (New York: Museum of Modern Art, 1971), 44.

66. Robert B. Ray, *A Certain Tendency of the Hollywood Cinema, 1930–1980* (Princeton, NJ: Princeton University Press, 1985), 37.

67. Fredric Jameson, "Postmodernism and Consumer Society," in *Postmodernism and Its Discontents: Theories, Practices*, ed. E. Ann Kaplan (London: Verso, 1988), 13–29, 20.

68. That these films formed part of a cycle was noted in contemporary reviews and in the programming of film festivals; see, e.g., Brian D. Johnson, "The Reel Thing: Toronto's Film Festival Unwraps a Party Pack of Big Stars and a Treasure Trove of Good Movies," *Maclean's*, Sept. 24, 1990, 56; and Corliss, "By the Book," 41–44. Duncan, *Film Noir*, 86–88, lists thirty neo-noir titles for 1990, sixteen for 1989 and twenty-one for 1992.

69. See, e.g., William Luhr, *Raymond Chandler and Film* (New York: Ungar, 1982); Edward Thorpe, *Chandlertown: The Los Angeles of Philip Marlowe* (London: Vermillion, 1983).

70. Frank Krutnik, "Desire, Transgression and James M. Cain," *Screen* 23, no. 1 (May–June 1982): 31–44, 33.

71. Joyce Carol Oates, "Man under Sentence of Death: The Novels of James M. Cain," in Madden, *Tough Guy Writers of the Thirties*, 110–28, 111, 127–28.

72. Steve Dougherty, "With a New Wife, Son and Movie . . . ," *People Weekly*, Nov. 19, 1990, 119.

73. This is a line of inquiry that Linda Ruth Williams has so eloquently followed in *The Erotic Thriller in Contemporary Cinema* (Edinburgh: Edinburgh University Press, 2005).

74. David Bellos, *Georges Perec: A Life in Words* (London: Harvill, 1993), 652–53. Perec discusses the problems involved in the adaptation of Thompson's novel from page to screen and from America to France in Jean-Paul Gratias, "Entretien avec Georges Perec," *Polar: Le Magazine du policier*, May 1979, 20–21.

75. The film was originally to have been named after this tune. See Bellos, *Georges Perec*, 653.

76. Luc Sante, "An American Abroad," *New York Review of Books*, Jan. 16, 1992, 8–12. Maggie Greenwald, the director and screenwriter of *The Kill Off*, aligned herself in the tradition of the American exile in an interview to promote her film: "'I like my situation now, being in New York with one hand reaching out to England and the other across America to Hollywood. Yes,' she muses, 'I kind of like that'" (quoted in Lizzie Francke, "The Pay Off," *Producer* 10 [winter 1989], 10).

77. Polito, *Savage Art*, 497.

78. Ibid., 498.

79. Ibid., 417–18.

80. Ibid., 422.

81. "Playboy Interview: Sam Peckinpah," *Playboy*, Aug. 1972, 65–74, 192.

82. Virginia Wright Wexman, *Creating the Couple: Love, Marriage, and Hollywood Performance* (Princeton, NJ: Princeton University Press, 1993).

83. Final revised shooting script (Feb. 23, 1972).

84. For notes on the film's production see David Weddle, *"If They Move ... Kill 'Em": The Life and Times of Sam Peckinpah* (New York: Grove, 1994), 434–44.

85. In his liner notes to the compact disc release of the rejected Jerry Fielding score for *The Getaway*, Nick Redman notes that another ending was considered, which had the Greyhound bus that Doc and Carol were traveling on attacked by Mexican bandits who take the money and kill the couple (see liner notes, *Music for "The Getaway": Jerry Fielding's Original Score*, Film Score Monthly, 2005, compact disc).

86. "Viva Vega!" *Playboy*, July 1974, 80–83.

87. "Film Directors' Erotic Fantasies," *Playboy*, Jan. 1978, 106–19.

88. Milton Caniff's extraordinary achievement, *Terry and the Pirates*, has been republished in six volumes by the Library of American Comics (San Diego: IDW, 2008–9).

89. Jim Thompson, *The Getaway* (New York: Bantam, 1973), cover blurb.

90. Polito, *Savage Art*, 497.

91. For more on this cycle see Cook, *Lost Illusions*, 196.

92. Interview, "Jim Thompson," *Media Show*, channel 4, Feb. 11, 1990.

93. Since his death, a monetary indicator of the value placed on Thompson's work can be found in the records of auction houses; one sold a copy of his first novel in 1998 for $6,325 (see *Biblio*, May 1998, 62).

94. V. Vale and Andrea Juno, eds., afterword to Charles Willeford, *Wild Wives/High Priest of California* (1956 and1953; San Francisco: Re/Search Publications, 1987).

95. Geoffrey O'Brien, *Hardboiled America: Lurid Paperbacks and the Masters of Noir*, exp. edn. (New York: Da Capo, 1997), 173–74. The new subtitle reflects noir's rising market value in book publishing.

96. Francke, "The Pay Off," 10.

97. Robert Seidenberg, *"After Dark, My Sweet*: James Foley Translates Jim Thompson's Cynicism to Cinema," *American Film*, July 1990, 48–49.

98. Smith, "Star Complex," 6.

99. McDonagh, "Straight to Hell," 30–31.

100. The quote is reproduced on the packaging of the 1996 Xenon video release.

101. Stanley Kauffmann, "The Grifters," *New Republic*, Dec. 17, 1990, 26.

102. Dougherty, "With a New Wife, Son and Movie . . .," 119.

103. Ralph Novak, "After Dark, My Sweet," *People Weekly*, Sept. 24, 1990, 11.

104. Brian D. Johnson, "After Dark, My Sweet," *Maclean's*, Oct. 8, 1990, 73.

105. Stuart Klawans, "The Grifters," *The Nation*, Jan. 7, 1991, 23–24.

106. William Johnson, "The Grifters," *Film Quarterly* 45, no. 1 (fall 1991): 33–37.

107. Cook, *Lost Illusions*, 297.

108. McDonagh, "Straight to Hell," 30–31.

109. Polito, *Savage Art*, 448.

110. As an example see Barry Gifford's collection of plot summaries, *The Devil Thumbs a Ride and Other Unforgettable Films* (1988), republished in an expanded edition as *Out of the Past: Adventures in Film Noir* (Jackson: University Press of Mississippi, 2001). See also Greil Marcus's linking of *Detour* and *The Lost Highway* in *The Shape of Things to Come: Prophecy and the American Voice* (New York: Farrar, Straus and Giroux, 2006), 130–36.

111. Polito, *Savage Art*, 270. In his 1954 novel *The Blonde on the Street Corner*, David Goodis similarly "reanimates" the "1930s marginal man" and equally disavows any remedies. But Goodis unambiguously locates his story in "the year of Our Lord, 1936." Though the date is not given until the end of chapter 4, it has the effect of anchoring the characters within a set of historically positioned socioeconomic markers, which are rarely, if ever, present in Thompson's tales.

112. Newirth, "The Prole Inside Me," 90.

113. Corliss, "By the Book," 41–44.

114. Thomas Frank, *The Conquest of Cool: Business Culture, Counterculture, and the Rise of Hip Consumerism* (Chicago: University of Chicago Press, 1997), 31.

115. David Ansen, "The Neo-Noir '90s: *L.A. Confidential* Is One Sign That This Is a Decade of Danger, at Least in Our Fantasies. It's Stylish to Be Sultry and Shady," *Newsweek*, Oct. 27, 1997, 68. The "studio marketer" quoted by Ansen was Chris Pula, "the man in charge of marketing 'L.A. Confidential'" at Warner Bros.

116. For a discussion of this cycle of gangster movies see Esther Sonnet and Peter Stanfield, "'Good Evening, Gentleman, Can I Check Your Hats Please?' Masculinity, Dress, and the Retro Gangster Cycles of the 1990s," in *Mob Culture: Hidden Histories of the American Gangster Film*, ed. Lee Grieveson, Esther Sonnet, and Peter Stanfield (New Brunswick, NJ: Rutgers University Press, 2005), 163–84.

117. Elmer Bernstein, liner notes, *The Grifters: Original Motion Picture Soundtrack*, Varése Sarabande, 1990, compact disc; Maurice Jarre, *After Dark My Sweet: Original Motion Picture Soundtrack*, Varése Sarabande, 1990, compact disc.

118. Apart from those mentioned in the text, other Thompson adaptations are Roger Donaldson's 1994 remake of Walter Hill's script for Peckinpah's *The Getaway*; and Steven Shainberg's terminally dull *Hit Me* (1996), based on the 1954 novel *A Swell-Looking Babe*. Thompson's short story "The Frightening Frammis," directed by Tom Cruise, was part of the Showtime television series *Fallen Angels: Six Noir Tales for Television* (1993), which was reprinted alongside the other stories and their screenplays in an anthology with a preface by James Ellroy (New York: Grove, 1993). A further eight episodes were subsequently commissioned.

119. Quoted in Stephen Prince, *Savage Cinema: Sam Peckinpah and the Rise of Ultraviolent Movies* (London: Athlone, 1998), 145.

120. Quoted in Garner Simmons, *Peckinpah: A Portrait in Montage* (Austin: University of Texas Press, 1982), 207.

121. See Michael Sragow, "Sam's Last Stand," *New York*, Aug. 12, 1974, 57 (also quoted in Simmons, *Peckinpah*, 207). The romantic view of the artist that Peckinpah's army of hagiographers hold has tended to cast Peckinpah as an American visionary, on a par with such giants of literature as Herman Melville and Ernest Hemingway or the film-makers John Ford and John Huston. Though some of his more whimsical forays such as *Ride the High Country* (1962), *The Ballad of Cable Hogue* (1970), and *Junior Bonner* (1972), alongside his western masterpieces, share a common sentimentality through a fixation on the wounded individual and male camaraderie with Hemingway, Peckinpah is better understood as belonging to the less esteemed tradition of postwar pulp stylists. Like Philip K. Dick in his science fiction musings, Luke Short in his western writings, and Jim Thompson in his crime stories, Peckinpah understood and respected generic convention. For all the truth that the stories of the artist at odds with the system hold, it should also be remembered that Peckinpah made films that had real clout at the box office: *The Getaway* (1972), *The Killer Elite* (1975), *Cross of Iron* (1977), *Convoy* (1978). These are genre films that align him with his mentor Don Siegel and with other cinematic art brut stylists like Samuel Fuller, Robert Aldrich, and Anthony Mann. Sam Peckinpah was an extraordinary filmmaker who understood how to tell his stories visually, highlighting the filmic nature of his materials (the infamous slow-motion sequences are only the most obvious examples) while telling stories about heroes who have a severely restricted understanding of their inconsequential role within a fragmented and alienating modern world.

122. See Polito, *Savage Art*, 462, 489; and Simmons, *Peckinpah*, 156.

123. Polito, *Savage Art*, 462.

124. Quoted in Ansen, "The Neo-Noir '90s," 68.

125. Manny Farber, *Negative Space: Manny Farber on the Movies* (New York: Da Capo, 1998), 3–11.

126. Cantwell, *Ethnomimesis*, 44.

127. David Hayles, "A Blowtorch to the Psyche," *Times* (London), review sec., April 24, 2010, 8. Background to rediscovery of the "lost" Thompson screenplay was reported by Charles McGrath, "After Death, My Sweet: From an Idea by Kubrick, a New Film May Be Born," *New York Times*, Oct. 31, 2006, online version, www.nytimes.com/2006/10/31/movies/31scri.html (accessed June 6, 2010). IMDb.com also listed *Recoil* and *Nothing More Than Murder* as "in development" (accessed June 6, 2010).

128. Quoted in McGrath, "After Death, My Sweet."

129. The film has generated a great deal of publicity; see, e.g., the *Guardian*, Feb. 20, 2010, 9; *Film Comment*, May/June 2010, 35–37; the *Observer*, "The New Review," May 23, 2010, 20–22; and *Sight & Sound* 20, no. 6 (June 2010): 40–46, 79. Hadley Freeman pens a particularly robust defense of the film in the *Guardian* (sec. G2, June 9, 2010, 5). The *Observer* published a spread featuring contributions to the debate from film critics, an actor, and a crime novelist, and a short survey of other responses to the film; see the *Observer* "The New Review," June 13, 2010, 14–15.

130. Rob Greig, "Winterbottom: 'I'm Not a Misogynist,'" *Time Out*, June 3–9, 2010, 71.

131. Ibid.

132. The press release, from which the quotes by David Thomas, the singer, are taken, can be found on the Pere Ubu website: http://ubuprojex.net/press/ububio2006.html/ (accessed Nov. 6, 2010).

133. Lawrence Jackson to the author, email correspondence, June 10, 2010.

134. James Ellroy, *My Dark Places: An L.A. Crime Memoir* (London: Arrow Books, 1997). Cooley is mentioned on pages 28, 109, 128, and 270. Cooley is also name checked in some of Ellroy's novels, including *L.A. Confidential* and *American Tabloid*.

135. Nick Tosches, *Country: The Biggest Music in America* (New York: Stein and Day, 1977), 165.

CONCLUSION

1. Charles Willeford, *The Machine in Ward Eleven* (Harpenden: No Exit Press, 2001), 41.

2. Ibid., 49.

3. Michael Denning, *Culture in the Age of Three Worlds* (London: Verso, 2004), 111.

4. Andrew Sarris, "Beatitudes of B Pictures," in *Kings of the Bs: Working within the Hollywood Studio System—An Anthology of Film History and Criticism*, ed. Todd McCarthy and Charles Flynn (New York: E. P. Dutton, 1975), 48–53.

INDEX

ABOUT THE AUTHOR

PETER STANFIELD is a Reader in Film Studies at the University of Kent. He is the author of two studies of the western—*Horse Opera: The Strange History of the 1930s Singing Cowboy* (2002) and *Hollywood, Westerns and the 1930s: The Lost Trail* (2001)—and a singular study of America's gutter songs and the movies, *Body and Soul: Jazz and Blues in American Film* (2004). He is also coeditor of *Mob Culture: Hidden Histories of the American Gangster Film* (2005) and *"Un-American" Hollywood: Politics and Film in the Blacklist Era* (2007), both published by Rutgers University Press.